Wilhelm Raabe

NOVELS

The German Library : Volume 45

Volkmar Sander, General Editor

Wilhelm Raabe

NOVELS

Edited by Volkmar Sander

Foreword by Joel Agee

CONTINUUM · NEW YORK

1983
The Continuum Publishing Company
575 Lexington Avenue, New York, NY 10022

Copyright © 1983 by The Continuum Publishing Company

Foreword © 1983 by Joel Agee
Introduction © 1983 by Volkmar Sander

Printed in the United States of America

Library of Congress Cataloging in Publication Data
Raabe, Wilhelm Karl, 1831–1910.
Novels.

(The German library; v.45)
Contents: Horacker / translated by John E. Woods—
Tubby Schaumann / translated by Barker Fairley and
revised by John E. Woods.
I. Sander, Volkmar. II. Title. III. Series.
PT2451.A2   1983   833'.8   82-22097
ISBN 0-8264-0280-1
ISBN 0-8264-0281-X (pbk.)

Contents

Foreword: Joel Agee   vii

Introduction: Volkmar Sander   xi

HORACKER   1
Translated by John E. Woods

TUBBY SCHAUMANN   155
A Tale of Murder and the High Seas
*Translated by Barker Fairley
and revised by John E. Woods*

Translator's Notes to *Horacker*   312

Translator's Notes to *Tubby Schaumann*   317

Foreword

At the beginning of *Horacker,* having proposed to tell a "pleasant story" about the last School Vice Principal (who, like the last Keewee, "should be stuffed and revered as a species that one shall never again encounter"), Wilhelm Raabe takes his readers to the sunlit top of the highest mountain of the region where the story will take place, and proceeds, from this modest elevation of 1,800 feet above sea level, to point out this river and that forest, these fields and those steeples, among them one with a gold weathercock which helps the Vice Principal, an amateur weather forecaster, to foresee one of the most perfectly tempered midsummer afternoons in the history of literature. Then, after a page or so of leisurely looking about, Raabe begins to walk downhill, followed by his readers (for whose sake he lifts an obstructing branch), and explains, still descending, that the whole purpose of climbing up in the first place was to come back down in a mood imbued with "cozy delight in every earthly thing."

Such a circumlocutious beginning is clearly not designed to whet the appetite of that brutish fellow E. M. Forster deplored in *Aspects of the Novel* (deplored, I should add, with a wan smile of unwilling acceptance)—I mean the fellow who crouches in the cave of every reader's mind asking "What happened next?" Raabe is much less sympathetic to him than Forster, and one of the pleasures of reading Raabe is watching him bristle and skip off sideways the moment that heavy jaw begins to drop to ask the eternal question. More often than not, he will simply set one of his more loquacious characters chattering away as if whatever happened next mattered less, far less, than just about any procrastinating device

Wilhelm Raabe has to offer up in the moment. And the marvelous thing is that he is right, and that, moreover, what happens next happens exactly as and when it is supposed to: everything falls into place not only with precisely dove-tailing accuracy (just the technical feat of manoeuvering some fifteen characters in as short a novel as *Horacker* without the attentive reader's losing track of or interest in any of them is a remarkable achievement) but with an economy that is all the more surprising and beautiful after so many apparently irrelevant detours.

In *Tubby Schaumann*, Raabe dispenses with all diversionary tactics and launches his formidable title character into a head-on attack on the reader's expectation of dramatic plot development. Woe to the reader of this novel who cannot silence or at least muffle the "What happened next?" fellow within himself: he will end up slamming the book shut and depriving himself of as perversely ingenious an entertainment as he is likely to encounter in a lifetime of reading.

A hideous crime has been committed, no one knows by whom; no one, that is, except Tubby Schaumann, the mammoth-sized, sloth-like, time- and patience-devouring master of the *Rote Schanze*, local historian and amateur paleontologist, connoisseur of the Seven Year War and excavator of his own prehistoric counterpart (a giant sloth). This uninterruptible monologist, of all people, has solved the crime, knows the killer's identity, and sets about telling his exasperated interlocuters Who, What, Where, When, How, and Why—the whole story, in short—but at length, and with such exceeding gradualness and perpetual (though engaging and witty) digression that there are moments when you want to scream, along with his fictional listeners: "Monster, I've had enough of it. What do you want to say to us?" Not until the end of the book, or, more likely, until an at least partial re-reading, will it become apparent that the real subject is not the criminological puzzle but Schaumann's (and, by implication, Raabe's) triumph over the philistine man of action who narrates the story (spicing it with comments about drunk, unruly, or otherwise contemptible "Kaffirs and niggers" he had to contend with on his South African sojourn), and over the townspeople who have always mistaken Schaumann's thorough, slow-grinding, omnivorous intelligence for feeble-mindedness and his lifelong self-containment at the *Rote Schanze* for lack of ambition and imagination. There is more than a touch of self-portraiture in this, and much of the reader's enjoyment will be found in ferreting out the inner correspondences between Tubby Schaumann and his beanpole-thin but equally expansive and slyly contemplative creator.

It is little wonder that such an unconventional author was barred from what would have been the best-seller lists of his day, had such lists been kept; and it seems unreasonable of him to have complained of that fact. But neither would it be fair to consign him to some high, obscure shelf among the annals of European letters, as if he were merely a writer's writer, or a literary historian's. No author could, in fact, be more solicitously attentive to the reader of his choice: the branch lifted at the beginning of *Horacker* is emblematic of Raabe's attitude throughout. This ideal reader is, above all, independent, skeptical, critical, fond of reflection—intelligent, in short: not a "highbrow," but someone who would agree with Laurence Sterne (one of Raabe's literary progenitors) that "people should think as well as read"; or, even more ideally, a reader with a novelist's imagination, like the "one among thousands" Raabe describes in *Horacker,* who, seeing a new house being built where some day soon nine hundred and ninety-nine people will live, asks himself: "What all do you suppose will happen in that new house?"

JOEL AGEE

Introduction

Wilhelm Raabe is one of the major German novelists of the nineteenth century, yet he and his work are little known to readers outside the German-speaking countries. In this he shares the fate of his German-speaking contemporaries Theodor Storm, Gottfried Keller, and Theodor Fontane, extraordinarily gifted writers all in an age of giants, who, unlike their immediate predecessors Goethe, Schiller, E.T.A. Hoffman, and the Romantics, were not translated during their lifetime and had little or no influence outside their native country. But in Germany, Austria, and Switzerland their novels and tales were popular and became classic texts that were widely read in schools and exerted a powerful influence lasting to this day.

During the nineteenth century German literature took a different turn from that of England and France. One reason was that, as in Italy and in contrast to its other neighbors, there was no nation. There was also no undisputed capital like London, Paris, St. Petersburg, where national energies could focus to produce a society and in its wake a social literature and a reading public to sustain it. This same lack of political cohesion, this splintering into a multitude of small semi-autonomous, and, by necessity, provincial states was all to the good for the development of music. The competition of the cities and principalities with each other produced a great variety of composers and high performance standards. Not so in literature, not even in Austria. Political disarray was also responsible for a delay in social change. The Industrial Revolution had long since fundamentally altered the social fabric in England and France when Germany, the "belated nation," came into existence after the Prussian wars with Denmark (1864), Austria (1866), and France (1870/1). With the emergence of the nation-state and the growing preeminence of Berlin, came also the delayed change in literature: with Rilke, Thomas Mann, Kafka, and Hesse German writing again joined the mainstream of literary fashion.

But to say that German political and social conditions were different during the second half of the nineteenth century is not to say that the literature of that period was any less profound. Rather, its focus was narrower. Instead of being concerned with society, it concentrated on the individual; instead of describing the interaction between man and his swiftly changing social environment, it reflected upon the slow and painful development of the inner-directed self.

In most of the great German novels of the nineteenth century—Adalbert Stifter's *Indian Summer,* Gottfried Keller's *Green Henry,* all of Raabe's major works—plot is reduced to as near nothing as possible, and we are offered instead the gradual realization that external "reality" is shaped by consciousness. The narration itself, more often than not, is therefore also not presented in linear fashion but mediated in thoughtful reminiscence. This often does not make for very exciting reading, just as Kafka, Thomas Mann, or Joyce, whom these novels foreshadow, are not "exciting" but bring about new different kinds of insights.

When Wilhelm Raabe was born in 1831, Goethe was still alive and Queen Victoria, who would become the longest reigning English monarch and was to lend her name to that age, was only twelve years old. Raabe was twelve years younger than Walt Whitman, ten years younger than Dostoevski and Flaubert, three years younger than Tolstoi, and about the same age as Mark Twain and Brahms. When he died in 1910, the same year as Edward VII of England, Queen Victoria's son, the aeroplane had been invented, the first moving pictures had been made, and Rutherford had built the first model of the atom. Between these dates, the death of Goethe and the beginning of the atomic age, Raabe spent his life outwardly calm but inwardly torn to the point of self-destruction and involved in the upheavals of his time.

Raabe was born in Escherhausen, a small town in northern Germany, in the duchy of Brunswick. His father, a jurist in the civil service, was transferred often, so the family had to move frequently. That also meant attending different schools for the young boy who, although an avid reader, consequently developed a hearty dislike for formal education. His father died when he was 14 years old. A few years later young Raabe quit school and moved to the city of Magdeburg where he became an apprentice in a bookstore, but it soon became apparent that he was not suited for the profession. In 1854, he went to Berlin to enroll as a non-matriculated student at the university, attending lectures in philosophy, history, and literature. That same year, he started writing *Die Chronik der Sperlingsgasse* [The Chronicle of Sparrow-Lane], which was published in 1856 and received some favorable reviews. Buoyed by that success, the proud author, now aged 25, decided to make writing his sole career, a rather extraordinary decision considering the fact that there was as yet no universal copyright law and hence no provision for regular royalties. All he could hope for was to sell each manuscript once. Few writers in Germany had tried this before him, and none successfully. Most of his contemporary fellow writers held down more traditional jobs, such as minister (Mörike), school superintendent (Stifter), editor-journalist (Fontane), or judge (Storm). Consequently, Raabe, like Dickens twenty years before him, had to keep writing profusely and at a steady pace. During the next fifty years he wrote thirty novels and more than forty tales and novellas.

This enormous output is usually grouped into three periods, according to the three residences where Raabe lived. From his short stay in Berlin, he returned to Wolfenbüttel, where during the next six years he wrote twenty stories and novels, most of which first appeared in *Westermanns Monatshefte,* a popular and influential magazine with large circulation, thereby firmly establishing his reputation. Among them were historical novellas like *Unseres Herrgotts Kanzlei* ["Our Lord's Chancery"], describing the siege of Magdeburg in 1550, and *Die schwarze Galeere* ["The Black Galley"], about the capture of the Spanish ship "Andrea Dorea" by the Dutch in the harbor of Antwerp in 1599, probably Raabe's best known, although by no means best, work.

In 1862 he married and moved to Stuttgart, then the capital of the Kingdom of Württemberg in southern Germany and a lively center of literary activities where he remained until 1870. Among the equally prolific outpouring of narratives during this second period is the so-called Stuttgart trilogy. These three novels, *Der Hungerpastor* [1863, The Hunger-Pastor], *Abu Telfan* [1867, A. T., or the Homecoming from the Mountains of the Moon], and *Der Schüdderump* [1869, The Plague Wheelbarrow], are not really interconnected. The first is the rather sentimental rags-to-riches story of how a poor shoemaker's son eventually becomes a parson and a "respected" member of society. Unfortunately, this simplistic novel became very popular and is one of the only two novels of Raabe's (the other being *Abu Telfan*) ever translated into English until the present volume. *Abu Telfan* is a far more sophisticated attempt at criticizing contemporary society. The protagonist Leonhard Hagebucher (as an in-joke Edward's ship in *Tubby Schaumann* bears the same name) has just returned from Africa. This allows him to experience bourgeois society from a distance—to see it with fresh eyes—and the result is a critical alienation. After dealing with the lower and the middle class, the third novel then deals with nobility whose moral standards are found wanting.

Shorter and, on the whole, better narratives of this period are historical novellas like *Holunderblüte* [1863, "Elder-Blossom"], about the fate of a Jewish girl in Prague; *Else von der Tanne* [1863], the story of a child accused of witchcraft during the Thirty Years War; and *Des Reiches Krone* [1870, "The Imperial Crown"], a love story set in medieval Nuremberg.

In 1870, Raabe moved to Brunswick, back to his native northern Germany, where he remained without interruption for the last forty years of his life. This period saw the emergence of major works such as *Horacker* (1876), *Alte Nester* [1879, Old Nests], *Pfisters Mühle* [1884, Pfister's Mill], *Unruhige Gäste* [1885, Unruly Guests], *Das Odfeld* [1888, Odin's Field], *Stopfkuchen* [1881, Stuff-cake or Tubby Schaumann], *Die Akten des Vogelsangs* [1896, The Chronicle of the Vogelsang], and *Hastenbeck* (1899). It is mainly on those works of his Brunswick period that Raabe's modern reputation rests.

Of these, two are included in this volume, but others might have been chosen as well. *Pfister's Mill* is probably the first novel in

German letters dealing with industrial pollution and the problems that arise from allowing too many chemicals to destroy a river. *Odin's Field* describes a day during the Seven Years War, an insignificant skirmish in a sideshow of the great war, at an insignificant place, and filtered through the ramblings of a retired old schoolmaster. Yet with Raabe, things are rarely what they first appear to be, and the reader ultimately realizes that *Odin's Field* is not so much about the making of history as it is about the sense of history and historical consciousness. In an age obsessed with history, the book's refusal to glorify the past represents a sharp break with the tradition of the historical novel. This extraordinary story was not only far ahead of its contemporaries, the historical novels of Sir Walter Scott, Stendhal, C. F. Meyer, even Flaubert and Fontane, but remains unique to this day.

As great as these and other novels of Raabe's late period are, a choice had to be made, and *Horacker* and *Stopfkuchen* will have to do. Raabe himself thought *Stopfkuchen* was his best work and has on the whole been seconded by literary criticism. In both works we find Raabe at the height of his powers. The former shows him in the tradition of Jean Paul, the earlier German writer of poetic tales, the latter is without precedent, apart perhaps from Sterne's *Tristram Shandy,* which Raabe greatly admired. In *Horacker* there is a "midsummer magic that is seldom captured outside Shakespeare," as Barker Fairley aptly put it. The setting of *Tubby Schaumann,* too, is idyllic, the novel's subtitle notwithstanding, yet in both narratives there is an underlying current of malevolence. Instead of experiencing the moral satisfaction that usually follows the apprehension of a criminal in a detective story, the reader and with him society, stands, himself, accused. This irritating disillusion of the reader's expectation is brought about through Raabe's narrative technique, which, a challenge today, was even more so during the nineteenth century. For the expectation of that period was that a novel would be linear, horizontal rather than vertical, that it would tell a straight tale with a beginning, a middle, and an end. We get little of this in *Tubby Schaumann;* obviously Raabe's mind is on something else. A better title, Barker Fairley suggests, might have been "Schaumann, or how he talked the others down."

The main purpose of *Tubby Schaumann* is not to tell a tale but, on the contrary, to destroy our interest in plot or any kind of "action" and to focus our attention on something else. A good example is Raabe's use of the various layers of time. The present is comprised of thirty days at sea during which Edward, the narrator, writes down his story. What motivates him to do this are the last day and a half of a visit to his home town and the conversations with Schaumann. A third layer of time is formed by the reminiscences of the two boyhood friends, spanning the last twenty-five years. Finally, in Schaumann's incessant reflections there is yet another stretching of time, back to the siege of the town during the eighteenth century and, through his paleontologic hobby, further to prehistoric periods. All these different layers of time are skillfully mixed and interwoven. In the end we realize that all the digressions, interpolations, and interruptions are meant to shift our attention from events of the plot to events occurring in the mind. In the midst of a literary period often referred to as the age of Realism, an age full of positivist optimism, Raabe's narrators doubt whether reality can be represented "objectively." The orderly and comprehensible world of their novels is destroyed and replaced by the mirror image of a reflecting mind. Action, and hence reality, thus can no longer be simply told, or brought into a single strand of narrative, but is portrayed as it appears to a thinking consciousness—broken, distorted, iridescent. All the difficulties incurred in writing the story, the diversions, digressions, intrusions, doubts, become an important part of conveying the message, at least as important as the action itself. The resulting impression is that all reality is relative because its appearance always depends on subjective consciousness—on how, by whom, and when it is perceived.

If by "modern" in literature we understand an attitude according to which the description of conscious and subconscious events take precedence over action, where subjective nuances of expression and feeling are more important than communication of "objective" facts, where reality is filtered through the medium of consciousness, through the impression it leaves on an individual, then there is no doubt that Raabe is more truly modern than most writers of his time. Heinrich Schaumann is not only a close relative of Tristram Shandy but an intuitive predecessor of many protagonists of twentieth-century fiction as well. Lawrence Sterne, for all his fame, really had no successors in the experimental daring of his style. Raabe's narrative technique in many ways bridges the gap between this eighteenth-century innovator and the final shattering of tradition in the twentieth century.

Up to now, Raabe has been practically inaccessible to English-speaking readers. Of all his works, only two novels (*Abu Telfan,* 1881, *The Hunger-Pastor,* 1885, 1913), and two short stories (*The Black Galley,* 1937, *Else von der Tanne,* 1972) have ever been translated, and none of these are still in print. Furthermore, all four are among Raabe's lesser works in scope, if not in quality. The present volume, therefore, can serve as an introduction of the "real" Raabe to the English-speaking public. The two novels on the following pages were translated especially for this volume: *Horacker* by John E. Woods, *Stopfkuchen* by Barker Fairley and John E. Woods.

Only two books on Raabe have been published in English, but both of them are excellent and can be recommended highly for further reading. They are: Barker Fairley, *Wilhelm Raabe. An Introduction to his Novels,* London & N.Y.: Oxford University Press, 1961; and Horst S. Daemmrich, *Wilhelm Raabe,* Boston: Twayne Publishers, 1981.

V. S.

HORACKER

Chapter 1

Once it was a common sight in the fields and forests of New Zealand, but now it is no more. The last one to be captured was stuffed and is considered a great rarity. And like the kiwi—the last kiwi—so, too, the last school vice-principal should be stuffed and revered as a species that one shall never again encounter. For our part, we would gladly lend a willing hand; perhaps others can then provide the straw, wire, and camphor—the latter to prevent moths; but as for maggots, we should like to reserve the extermination of that particular creature for ourselves. Our aim is to write an amusing story, and if there is anyone for whom we feel an obligation to do so, then that old gentleman, the *last vice-principal,* is our man. He always disapproved of lies presented to him amid tears and sobs; but he loved to fashion a tall tale himself and make it devilishly believable. Naturally, he kept no record of the times he had himself been taken in; other people, however, are said to have been malicious and disrespectful enough to have done so now and again—his colleagues, for example, not just his pupils.

If now we climb the highest mountain in the region [1]—rising little more than eighteen hundred feet above sea level—the view comprised by the panorama is rimmed not only by the horizon but also by the borderline beyond which he, Eckerbusch, never ventured, with the exception of three years spent at the university. It is a region one may take substantial pleasure at having been born in, a quite lovely region in the true sense of the word.

A river, one that has also found a spot in Schiller's *Xenias,* winds its way there with many a bend. Hills and meadows and fields and

3

woods pass in charming variation. A forest, as famous as it is large, advances for a rather long stretch very close to the river and extends on to the west far beyond our purview. Many a parish steeple can be seen—beneath which suitably parochial politics are practiced. We, however, are attracted to one particular steeple, its slated spire thrusting pointedly toward heaven; we are attracted to the shiny gold weathercock that turns atop it and up toward which Vice-Principal Eckerbusch turns his gaze from the window of the fifth form whenever he wants to know which way the wind is blowing. The old gentleman has also been keeping a record of the wind for more than thirty years now and is respected in the community as an authority on matters of weather. Worried housewives who need sunshine to dry their wash are in the habit of sending to him and asking, "My compliments to Herr Vice-Principal Eckerbusch, and does he think it likely that it will rain tomorrow?"

And the old man always has an answer at the ready, and if it turns out that he has been mistaken, then it is most assuredly never his fault, but rather always that of "the cursed fellow in Haparanda, Hernösand,[2] or Constantinople who is in arrears with his meteorological observations." Things must come to a pretty pass before science lays the blame for such mistakes on the weather itself.

But now, as we stand here atop the aforesaid mountain and gaze about us, sunshine lies upon the land. When now and then a cloud formation of curious shape and color glides across the blue and throws a shadow on the green, why that can only enhance the charm of a fine day. We come down the mountain, bringing with us a cozy delight in every earthly thing; and that was, of course, the sole reason why we raised ourselves so high—all eighteen hundred feet high!—above the heads and roofs of our fellow men. We descend and pass first through a thick tangle of hazel bushes. We must carefully bend the branches to one side to prevent their whipping us in the face; oh, and we clearly recall the days when Vice-Principal Eckerbusch sat here in the brush and made more than just hay. For by no means did he upon retirement receive his full salary as a pension!—Our path leads through high timber, across neat and pretty mountain meadows, through rather dirty villages; until at last a narrow overgrown track, one that adds considerable difficulties to our descent, brings us out at the edge of a precipitous slope. Below, the river rushes by, swift and energetic, and the only slow thing about it is the barge that slowly, dolefully crawls toward the mountain, drawn by short-winded nags trudging along the stony tow path. The track now dives off to the right and zigzags down the hill; it merges into a country lane and leads us to another village nestled beside the river.

There we find our ferry and ferryman and float out across the water. Two youthful personages, both having just outgrown boyhood and, in what would seem to be the overnight fashion of asparagus, their shirts and trousers—fourth- or perhaps fifth-form lads—cross with us, and one of them addresses the other.

"Say, Karl, I know somebody who's going to be surprised four weeks from today."

"And who's that?"

"Why, my old man, *naturellement*! Despite all my cramming and swotting, there hasn't been a day in the last three months when he didn't swear I'm so lazy I stink. Pooh. Well, just let him get a whiff of me after the holidays four weeks from now! If he doesn't have to hold his nose then, it'll only be because he's got one whopping case of the sniffles."

The second ideal of a mother's tender heart, having sprawled himself out as far as possible on one of the ferry's benches, does not answer at all, filled as he is with an infinite delight in human existence. He registers approval only with a grunting groan and the delight written on his face.

The holidays—the dog-day holidays have begun; these two winsome lads with their botanizing flasks and hatchets are returning home now to their paternal roofs at the end of their first excursion out into the wide and countless splendors of nature. And oh, what wouldn't one give to be in the shoes and to share the feelings of one of these two scamps! Or better still, the shoes and feelings of them both; for who can ever have enough of life's bliss when it is served up to him by heaping spoonfuls?!

Let us as quickly as possible make the acquaintance of the last vice-principal, Dr. Werner Eckerbusch! All good opportunities rush by and seldom return; the good days of life on this earth all go their way. And at the moment, as we lay a hand on old Ecker-busch's shoulder, the dog-day holidays are already drawing to a close once more, and the mood of the boys on the boat is most certainly no longer what it was—just four weeks ago.

Chapter 2

Now our readers are imagining all sorts of things other than those that will be found here, in a story in which the author was a most conscious participant.

Across the way a house goes up, right before the windows of a thousand people. All thousand of them will follow the construction with interest, from the excavation of the cellar to the installation of the last windowpane; but nine hundred and ninety-nine of that thousand will merely remark, "A handsome house!"—or, "I can't say I approve of the place!"—or at any rate, "Those would make fine lodgings for me. I could put my sofa there—and my books—and the cupboards, and the view is quite nice, too!" But, among those thousand people, there is one who will be given to quiet and somewhat melancholy meditation, who will ask of himself and fate: "What all do you suppose will happen in that new house?"

From within his own tight, trim four walls, this one person gazes through those empty windowpanes, watching the carpenters and masons at their work across the way; he lays his brow to the windowpane, that thin wall of glass separating him from what lies beyond, and thinks of birth, life, and death, of the cradle and the coffin. And it is for this one person that we write, have always written—though we hope to have a multitude of readers.

We are now six months into the year of '67, the North German Confederation[3] has been established, and the last vice-principal is in complete agreement with his having been incorporated into it by this turn of universal history. Two of his former pupils fell at Königgrätz[4] serving the Prussians, one at Langensalza[5] serving the

7

Hanoverians and one—"a dreadful rascal, but otherwise a fine lad"—was declared missing following the attack of the Hungarian hussars in the battle of Custozza.[6]

"That poor devil was such a beast, he often sent me practically through the roof, and many's the time I informed him that he'd be a nail in my coffin, and—now this has happened to him! . . . Good heavens, that's really the only thing that I cannot forgive him in the end, because now I'm forced to deal with him even in my dreams every so often," old Eckerbusch would say.

"At least I've managed that much," said his colleague, or better, semicolleague Windwebel. "Up to this point I've made *them* keep their distance in my dreams."

"That's because you have a young wife, my friend!" replied the old vice-principal.

It was a remarkable month, that month of July in the year 1867! It was amazing what all was happening in the world, each event making obtrusive demands that an already quite confused humanity pay attention and give it due consideration. In Paris the World Exposition was in progress, and Louis Napoleon, the third of that name, was still pretending to be in a frightfully good mood, absolutely jubilant, although Max of Mexico[7] had just been executed at Querétaro by wicked Juárez. Gregarinae were discovered crawling in ladies' chignons, and Santa Anna, erstwhile president of Mexico, also died during the month.[8] Gathered to his fathers was Heinrich the Sixty-seventh, reigning prince of the Principality of Reuss, the younger line.[9] Gera mourned. King Otto of Greece[10] passed away; but it is not certain whether Athens mourned. In any case, no one went into mourning in Germany when Thurn and Taxis yielded up its four-hundred-year-old postal license.[11] Many books, brochures, etc., continued to appear concerning the War of '66; but the greatest wonder was to take place toward the end of the month: *The Turks were at the Rhine!* Sultan Abdul Aziz[12] was to visit King Wilhelm in Koblenz.

Now one would think that all these items and many others we have not enumerated would have amply supplied ample food for thought for the region we just surveyed from atop the mountain; but—quite the contrary!

The region was not in the least concerned about the Parisian

World Exposition, Emperor Napoleon the Third, the Emperor of Mexico, the Prince of Reuss-Schleiz, President Santa Anna, and King Otto of Greece. The region was concerned about just one thing—Horacker.

Horacker was rampant in the land.

But between two and three o'clock on a Thursday afternoon, the twenty-fifth of July (i.e., on the day after the Turkish invasion), Vice-Principal Eckerbusch was walking up and down in his garden with Assistant Master Dr. Neubauer. We are in the thick of things—in the middle, midway—in short, *in mediis rebus*,[13] as the Latinists say, and we have Latinists to deal with here. And oh, our poor rusty scholarship! We, who eat our literary bread in the sweat of our face, know what it means to have known something once!

Chapter 3

The young philologist looked a bit drowsy and not a little out of sorts while the older was very bright-eyed and cheerful as the two of them strode back and forth beside an ivy-covered wall on the shady side of the garden.

"And for this the old fogey had me roused from the sweetest of holiday siestas?" muttered the young man to himself.

"I find five minutes of meditation after a meal quite sufficient, my friend," said the old man, "after which I am once again ready to take on most anything. And so you will walk with me to Gansewinckel,[14] won't you? It may well be the last excursion of our days of liberty. You know the misery and drudgery begins anew soon enough, and there could be rain tomorrow."

"Of course I know," grumbled the assistant master, "which is all the more reason . . ."

He did not finish his sentence; but the good-humored old man knew already what he intended to say and took wry, malicious pleasure in letting him chew a while longer on the ivy leaf he had ripped off, before coaxing him on by saying, "Our colleague Windwebel is coming along, and I expect him to appear directly."

"Now that, I grant, makes it all most tempting!" groaned the assistant master, coming to a halt with a lurch and spitting out the bitter stem of *Hedera helix*.[15] "No, I must tender my most dutiful thanks, but some other time please! . . . I definitely have other matters to attend to during these last days of vacation."

"Of course you do, tremendously useful matters!" grumbled the vice-principal and added to himself, "O thou freshest shaft of light in Wisdom's Temple! Since She hath sent thee us from on high, we have indeed first remarked how great was that gloom in which we sat e'er this!"

The elegant younger man, however, seemed to sense the gist of the compliment the older one was mulling over in his bosom.

"God, what fellows!" he then muttered to himself, and the faculty *in corpore* [16] had a large portion of self-confidence, only recently transferred from the city to the province, to thank for this silent outburst.

And now it was old Eckerbusch who in turn sensed the gist of what it was Dr. Neubauer was muttering.

"Ah yes," he remarked with uncommon good cheer, "it is indeed a sort of Eleusinian mystery the way the world now and again appears to us to be much more trivial than it is in reality—"

"And here comes your colleague Windwebel!" said the assistant master. "Just between us, my friend, if there is one thing I do not understand, it is how you can be on such familiar terms, indeed to the point of daily intercourse and intimate friendship, with such a shallow, insignificant fellow. Whenever I've given the chap a rap of my knuckles, he's always sounded hollow to me."

"Really?" asked the old gentleman, feeling constrained once again to add a silent comment to his spoken word.

"Stuff . . . !" he began, "and raspberries!" he added, and then concluded with a deep intake of breath, "well, not everyone can view life through the eyes of a pedantic bookbinder."

He took a sharp pull on his pipe and, puckering his lips to a fine point, blew the smoke out into the twenty-fifth of July. "Well, what would this world be with nary an itch nor a scratch! Welcome, my dear Windwebel. It has been a long time since I've awaited your arrival as eagerly as at this moment!"

The assistant master ripped another leaf from the ivied wall, and their colleague, Herr Windwebel, approached, smiling and ready for their walk.

And, we hope, he will approach us now as well; there he came, here he comes with genuine laughter in his face, wading through the gooseberry bushes of his old friend and of our story.

He stepped quickly toward them, lifting his light straw hat from his brow and calling out, "Here I am, gentlemen, and I do hope I haven't kept you waiting. Actually it was my Hedwig, you see, who kept you waiting. You know, of course, that when a man takes a young wife he soon learns what it means to be given useful instructions for his journey. Please, for my sake, don't stumble! And don't drink cold water if you get overheated! . . . And please, just for me, keep your nose wiped! And are you really going to leave without a kiss, Victor? . . . And listen to me, don't do any foolhardy climbing! My only solace is that Vice-Principal Eckerbusch will have you under his eye."

Vice-Principal Eckerbusch laughed heartily; but Dr. Neubauer seemed to think it his duty to remain that much more serious.

"Most amusing!" he said, apparently desiring to heighten the mirth of the moment further still.

"Dr. Neubauer will not be accompanying us, Windwebel; we have disturbed his afternoon slumbers in vain. All nine muses have him in their clutches, and we two simply don't know how good we have it with just our two females—you with your young Hedwig and I with my good old Ida. Come along, Windwebel, and we'll have another cup of coffee before setting out. Will you join us, Dr. Neubauer?"

"I really must decline, thank you," said the assistant master in a tone of voice and with a wave of the hand as if in reality he were none other than wise Cicero upon the receipt of a jocular invitation to drop in for a moment extended by that sprightly cutthroat Marcus Antonius.[17] With that, he departed, saluting *formaliter*,[18] and the old man watched him go, at first a bit bewildered and cross, but then an even sunnier grin followed.

"Well, Windwebel, why don't we just let him lie there in peace on his sofa. And we'll go up to my dear old wife!"

"With pleasure, my friend," replied the drawing-master of the gymnasium as he took the vice-principal's arm. Doctor Neubauer did not, however, depart with the intent of lying upon his sofa once more; rather, he sat himself down stiffly at his desk, seeking his own peculiar sort of consolation by setting several aphorisms to paper. We do not wish to withhold these from our wise public, for it is indeed possible that they may serve as consolation to one or other of our readers, and that would delight us greatly.

The assistant master wrote as follows:

A. Who leaves the strongest impression? The man who calmly goes his own way.

B. When the beast rears its head, the real man can only wait with infinite patience.

C. Truly, no man understands the tragedy in the life of another.

D. Yesterday I read in Aulus Gellius [19] concerning the oaths of the Romans, male and female.—Only the men swore by Hercules, by Castor only the women; but by Pollux both sexes.—*Aedepol!* [20] Amid what beasts of both sexes must one vegetate here! . . .

E. Is there no nation where to remain unknown or to be forgotten by the citizenry is accounted an honor?

In the hope that we have done our part to prevent this young man, Herr Assistant Master Dr. Neubauer, from being forgotten by *his* nation, we shall leave him for now to the awful gravity of his character and views on life and join the vice-principal and drawing-master as they climb the stairs to the chambers of Frau Eckerbusch, whose kindly old face certainly did not grow gloomy when she caught sight of Herr Windwebel.

Looking up cheerfully from her knitting and shoving her horn-rimmed spectacles up onto her forehead, the old woman cried, "*Mehercle,* [21] so you're trying to lure my old husband away from me again, are you?"

"*Mecastor* [22] is the correct form!" said the vice-principal. "But once again it is I who am doing the luring. Lord, Ida, what a mother of the Gracchi [23] you would have been had heaven seen fit to grant us children. But now, Windwebel, have another quick cup of coffee and we shall be on our way. We'll put a bottle of Château Bilberry in the pouch; and Winckler will take care of any subsequent potables when we've arrived in Gansewinckel."

"Eckerbusch! Eckerbusch!" cried the matron as she put down the coffeepot. "Windwebel, I most solemnly charge him to your conscience, to your very soul. He only becomes aware that he has a reputation to uphold when someone else makes him aware of the fact, and then he only wants to kick the traces all the more. I beg you, Windwebel, look after him for me—"

"You can depend on me completely, Frau Eckerbusch."

"I shall indeed. You and Hedwig aren't the ones who have to iron the rheumatic aches out of his back with a flatiron whenever, as is his custom, he has tracked down the dampest spot in the entire forest to sit down in. So please think of me and for my sake mind that he doesn't do it this time. Sometimes he purposely picks out an ant hill to sit down on; and you know how little regard he normally pays to his position when he meets up with a pack of his pupils! . . . So do look after him for me—and in return I'll probably pay your little wife a visit and see that she comes to no harm." Then with a laugh she added, "And, my lord, oh Horacker! Be on your guard for Horacker as well! All at once I find yet another worry lodged in my throat so that I can't swallow! . . . Horacker! It's all stuff and nonsense, but if I had thought of him earlier, neither of you would have been given permission to walk to Gansewinckel today!"

"Did you slip the Château into the pouch, my friend? . . . Fine. Now let us apply ourselves to getting out of the house; this is far past remedy! You, my dear Windwebel, have the good luck not to have to concern yourself with metrics and so live in blissful ignorance of what a proceleusmatic[24] is and of how pleasant it rings in one's ears when such a woman breaks out in pure proceleusmatics, becoming, so to speak, a monster of *rhythmus domesticus*.[25] Oh Horacker, rheumatic aches, reputation and no end of it! *Vale*,[26] old woman, have you no message for me to give the pastor or his wife Billa?"

"Give them my regards, Eckerbusch. And then you two can notify them that Frau Hedwig and I will soon be coming by for some of their sour milk. Will you do that, dear Windwebel?"

And dear Windwebel said that of course he would; and the town saw the vice-principal and the drawing-master of their illustrious gymnasium making good use of yet another holiday; that is to say, many of the folks living in the neighborhood watched them depart, remarking, "There they both go again." And beneath such words lay the hidden wish: "Wouldn't I love to join *those* two myself. Sure as anything old Eckerbusch will have another adventure today."

Dr. Neubauer likewise stepped to his window, pen in hand, and watched his colleagues making for the town gate; and since once again there was no one else to do it, so he did the deed himself and praised himself exceedingly for it—he gave them a yawn of almost alarming proportions.

Afterwards he allowed the world to continue in its delusion that today, at this very moment, he was pursuing his great literary, poetical, philological mission in life—while he stretched out once more on his sofa with the *Journal of Literary Divertisements.*[27]

Chapter 4

Gansewinckel, with its gardens, meadows, and fields, was tucked in the forest like a sequestered nest; and the church, naturally, had arrived to perfect this idyllic scene by setting a parish there for a nest egg—and we hope next year's Easter Bunny will reward us for the charming image. Ah, if only duck eggs were not constantly being shoved under that worthy old hen Ecclesia for her to hatch! But whatever sort of eggs the citizens of Gansewinckel may have pecked their way out of, at the moment the whole lot of them had waddled off from their pastor and were merrily and mockingly swimming, splashing, and diving in the swamp of human depravity, and there on the shore Pastor Winckler stood, or rather ran back and forth, fuming and fretting more than a bit—with his feathers all ruffled, which is to say, he was ready to take quill in hand and write a report for the consistory.

That the farmers of Gansewinckel were more than a little given to poaching, that now and again they stole from one another, that their love of quarreling provided an honest living for several lawyers—all that was their own business, and old Pastor Winckler knew well enough how to deal with it. He had both the body and the spirit for the task. He considered—in the middle of the nineteenth century!—Christian Fürchtegott Gellert to be the author of classics [28] and reserved a place of honor for a dog-eared edition of that gentleman's fables both upon his desk and in his head, making daily use of it in both locations. He understood how to provide apt citations from his Fürchtegott at opportune moments; he had even tried that method today when countering the chairman and elders of the vestry, but this time had met with defeat. At the

16

moment, when—to all his other vexations—we thrust ourselves upon him, he is sitting at his desk growling to himself, with a furrowed brow and a pipe that has gone out. His right hand lies balled in a fist atop his concordance, his left hand limp and open in his lap. His lambs departed with sneers of derision on their faces; the farmers of Gansewinckel think they have a good tight hold on him this time. At the very least they have dumbfounded him beyond all measure, and his wife Billa, too. Out by the garden hedge, beneath the shade of the nut trees, where you can watch the path that leads to the near side of the forest, stands the afternoon coffee—cold for over an hour now. And there is only the warm July day to thank that it has not grown colder than it is.

" 'fternoon, Frau Winckler. We've just let the pastor know how things stand," Chairman Neddermeier had said, grinning at that clerical lady as he led the farmers in single file past the parsonage kitchen door. The fattest fellow in the delegation, and in the village, the freeholder Heinrich Degering, had even laughed out loud without bothering to hide his "bumpkin's mug" behind his hat. And now—Frau Billa Winckler sat opposite her disheartened husband in his study, and both her hands lay limp in her lap.

"Oh, Krischan!"[29]

And the pastor, after first searching for his handkerchief with his left hand in order to wipe away the sweat, once again let his fist fall heavily on his concordance to the Bible.

"Oh, wouldn't I just love to . . ."

We are acquainted with the most reverend consistory, and so in the best interests of the spiritual shepherd of Gansewinckel, we shall deny ourselves and our readers the pleasure of appending the words represented by those dots. What Krischan Winckler truly wanted and desired at this moment, however, wanted with all his heart, wanted with abandon, could in no way be fully expressed by the words he refused to swallow. Of that we can be sure.

"There they go in triumph at having finally gotten you by the collar, my dear," groaned Frau Billa. "Oh, how I'd love to wade into them now at the tavern. There they sit with their thick heads together, laughing at you, and oh! how they're going to enjoy your sermon this coming Sunday. And oh! how I'm going to enjoy it, even if I don't know yet whether I'll survive till then! I don't so much as want to show my bonnet over the fence until this whole business is settled! Winckler, do you intend to go into town today yet and speak with the authorities?"

"First I have to collect my own thoughts again," moaned the pastor. "How can I talk to anyone about it until I know myself whether I'm standing on my feet or on my head? . . . That's what I get for being so good-hearted!"

"And what do I get?" asked his spouse. "Just look at this floor! Not one of those half-dozen louts left without having spat on my clean floor. Has the schoolmaster shown himself yet? I must say I can't wait to see the look on his face when he hears these revelations. Oh, Krischan, Krischan, you'll offer felicitations and Böxendal will sing, and I know the consistory only too well. They'll let him sing and you felicitate. But I'll say this, you'll go to His Majesty himself about this business before I'll let it come to that either for you or for me, and that's my mind in the matter and—there—there comes the schoolmaster through the garden! Didn't I tell you? Dear Lord, the way the man is running and the face he's making! I wouldn't want to be one of *their* sons in his classroom right now."

"But I would!" grumbled the "excellent vicar of Grünau."[30] "It would be more pleasant than being pastor of Gansewinckel."

At this juncture the schoolmaster of Gansewinckel flung open the door to the study.

"Herr Pastor—excuse me, Frau Winckler. Herr Pastor, I ask you—is it possible?"

"Even now I still consider it impossible, dear Böxendal. But sad to say, the old parchments read to that effect. You are to pipe for your quarter-money,[31] and I am to dance for mine. For those four pennies every four months we are both to make a personal appearance each New Year's Day before every paterfamilias in the parish."

"And I'm supposed to sing a verse from the hymnbook for every farmer?! Oh, Lord God Almighty!"

"And I'm required to address each of them with a few well-chosen words wishing them all things good and lovely. Böxendal, they have it in writing, and we should have been cleverer than ever to have submitted a petition to abolish this miserable quarter-money in the first place."

"But it's been buried and forgotten for more than a century now at least. Why, Herr Pastor, not one of my predecessors in the office since the Seven Years' War—"

"Which is why it's called a time-honored tradition!" the pastor broke in upon the schoolmaster with a groan. "And we stirred up the whole thing again ourselves; and I know my Gansewincklers— oh, Böxendal, Böxendal, you need only ask my wife about my views in the matter—"

"Frau Winckler, you should see and hear what my wife has to say to this affair!" the schoolmaster of Gansewinckel said, turning to that broken matron.

"I shall simply die," moaned the dear old soul. "Böxendal, if the consistory refuses to be reasonable, I shall not survive the first of January, 1868. As far as I'm concerned, this surpasses even Horacker!"

"Listen, my dear friend," said the pastor suddenly to his schoolmaster, "the whole affair is indeed a vexation. But I would give anything to hear you sing just once for the vestry chairman and for freeholder Degering."

And with a smile he shoved his black velvet cap back and forth over his worthy pate.

"That's just like you, Winckler," said his wife with grave indignation. "Sure, go right on and felicitate—but for my part, I only hope Horacker sets a torch to every one of their barns first. I wish no man evil, but in this case human kindness has come to an end. Just let someone from the village ever come to this parsonage again asking for my drops for the cramps or my cure for diarrhea!"

"Dear Böxendal, both our better halves will calm themselves down again in due time," the pastor remarked, turning to his schoolmaster. "Let us then give reasonable and deliberate consideration to what we are to do in order to provide this unfortunate business with a turn to the better for all concerned. And above all, let us not allow Horacker and all other such un-Christian notions to get mixed up in these things!"

But as for us in our role as author, it is our duty, our Christian obligation at precisely this moment to bring on Horacker and see to it that he does get mixed up in these things.

Chapter 5

It is a wonder that the cuckoo did not fill the woods that summer with the call of Horacker! Horacker! and kept instead to his old standby of cuckoo! cuckoo! Apparently he thought it superfluous to join in the general cry, and he was without doubt correct. Village and town, hill and dale echoed quite enough already with the curious word and name: "Horacker! Horacker! Cord Horacker!"

Seldom has the population of a region been gripped by a more comical panic than this, ever since the day Horacker of Gansewinckel set up shop in the great forest as a bold highwayman and bloodthirsty murderer—that is, since about fourteen days or three weeks ago. In vain had the public prosecutor written to the local newspaper declaring on his honor, so to speak, that there was little, or better, no truth at all to these dreadful rumors; in vain did he personally assure anyone who would listen that although Horacker himself was no phantom, *Horacker the Highwayman* must unquestionably be interpreted as a myth. Not a soul, not one farmer, and still less one farmer's wife, believed either his written or oral assurances, and even with the townsfolk, male and female alike, he had no end of trouble.

Oh, the public prosecutor, sure, he could say and write things easy enough, sitting there in his office among his documents; sure, he could have his gendarmes escort him everywhere he went, even to the skittle grounds of an evening. Whereas they, the farmers out in the forest villages, could do no such thing. Behind every bush Horacker lurked, ready to leap out at them, at their wives and daughters; but butter, cheese, eggs, and chickens must get to town somehow, and nothing was safe from this new Bückler, Schinderhannes, Bavarian Hiesl, or Hundssattler.[32] To that extent, the farmers of the neighborhood had much more confidence in the highwayman than in public prosecutor Wedekind. The one was certainly very much alive, and the other—could say whatever he liked easy enough.

Not just in the villages, but in town as well people knew all about and talked of the manifold crimes of Horacker. We were present a short while ago as Frau Vice-Principal Eckerbusch warned her reckless husband and his colleague Windwebel about him. Even people who laughed at these tales of carnage took a heavier walking stick than usual when going for a walk and preferred the company of as many companions as possible when enjoying the pleasures of nature and the cool, shaded paths of the great forest, where until three weeks before all was harmless. And even then, when each could depend on the other, if there was a rustling in the underbrush, they would cast a somewhat nervous glance over their shoulders and take a firmer grip of their walking sticks.

The prosecutor had only the local newspaper, but Fama, as we know from mythology, has many thousands of tongues at her disposal. From day to day the accounts of Horacker took on ever bolder, ever more garish colors and forms. The conversations in both tavern and gentleman's club centered around the deeds of Horacker; Horacker was debated in the kitchen and in the parlor; it was with tales of Horacker that the wife amused her husband, the child his parents, the grandmother her grandchildren, the grandchildren their grandfather. When, after some cross-country journey, the head of the house was restored home to his loved ones safe and sound, bones unbroken and money pouch still in his pocket, he was greeted by wife and children not with the customary question, "What did you bring us?" but rather they encircled him and hung on him crying, "Didn't you meet up with Horacker?" And seldom did anyone arrive home who had not met up with Horacker, if not personally, then by way of the scandalmongers. Seldom in such a short time as this had so many tales been warmed up all over again out of the pages of the *New Pitaval*[33] or from the offerings of Basses Publishing of Quedlinburg[34]—all of them taking their start from that day when, on the slopes of

Owl's Head Mountain, Horacker had jumped out into the path of an old butter-woman. At this point we are thrown into hot and cold terror at having left old Eckerbusch and Drawing-Master Windwebel to wander all alone till now in that wild forest, never once offering ourselves as an escort. And might it not all too easily come about that we ourselves should have to deal with the public prosecutor afterwards? What if some unpleasantness should have occurred as a result of our neglect and, for example, following only what dreadful things our noses might tell us, we should stumble upon their mutilated bodies lying beside some path in the wilderness?

Vivat, they are still alive! *Vivant in saecula saeculorum!*[35] Wending their way up from town and making the somewhat difficult march up along a narrow path that led between a rather deep ravine and broad, sunny fields, the two had now arrived at the edge of the forest, the old philologist's main purlieu of pleasure since earliest childhood. Following this same ravine and these same fields of rye and wheat, he had borne every care that had ever oppressed or inconvenienced him in life to three oak trees that stood at a corner of the forest and shaded some benches constructed of fieldstones piled atop one another. From beneath these trees he had gazed down at his home town not a hundred, but a thousand times, not just in summer, spring, or fall, but on the bitterest days and evenings of winter—and then and there resolved matters in his mind.

The vice-principal had many good friends and acquaintances in town and country, but among the best were these three oaks. And the friendship was a mutual one, definitely the best sort in such situations.

"Here he comes again!" the dryads called out to one another in delight, and the old trees put their merrily rustling heads together, and sometimes the question arose in the leafy crowns: "Whom is he bringing with him today?"

So it was this day; and—

"Μα 'Απολλωνα,[36] his colleague Windwebel!" cried the three classical maids of the wood, peeking with still greater delight from out of the rustling branches down onto the path.

Vice-Principal Eckerbusch likewise greeted his three favorite trees and sat down for a moment on one of the benches to catch his breath after the hot climb. His colleague stood there studying the light as it fell on the river and the mountains on the far side of the valley beyond the town.

"Here I sat as a third-form lad and did my Cornelius Nepos [37] lessons; and sometime you must ask Ida what all else I've done up here. Windwebel, you traveled much in the world before you came to us here. You, my friend, have known many a lovely spot in any case. But as for me, I have never discovered a lovelier one than this here in all the classics. Just imagine, there, where you are standing now, is where I also once stood, and here, where I am sitting, is where my proceleusmatica of these many long years once sat. *'Aura veni!'* [38] I called, for it was a very sultry summer evening and a cooling breeze would have been most welcome. But what said my Procris—no, I'd best call her my Ida? 'Oh, Lord, Instructor Eckerbusch—dear Werner, are you really and truly in earnest? Well then, I've nothing against it either!' . . . And so, Windwebel, as God would have it we tumbled right out of the *Metamorphoses* and into the middle of the *Ars amatorica* [39] and went back down to town to tell our parents. Good heavens, how time marches on! But now let us continue our journey as well. Winckler, who at that time was starving as the curate in town, joined us in wedlock. Now that he's in Gansewinckel you can no longer tell what a thin shadow he cast on the wall in those days. Yes, but his wife and farmers have filled him out right properly now."

The drawing-master looked down at himself, now at his right side, now at his left, and considered what his Hedwig might be able to make of him, given his salary and what he earned extra from private lessons.

"It's nice, of course, for an artist not to get too fat," he muttered, "but it's not absolutely essential for him to be quite as lean as I am now."

They departed, and the dryads in the dark crowns of the oaks giggled more merrily than before. They, too, had a keen recollection of that sweet summer evening when Instructor Eckerbusch had called out for a cooling breeze and Miss Ida Weniger had so totally misunderstood the classical quotation, and yet had understood it so perfectly well.

It had been a very long time ago to be sure, but a nymph of this sort, living in an ancient oak tree, has the very tenacious memory of an old maid; and so they could recall not just Eutropius[40] and Cornelius Nepos, but Publius Ovidius Naso[41] as well, particularly since the latter had sung their praises in such a delicious and charming fashion. For Herr Eckerbusch there could be no more pleasant comrade for a hike in the forest than his colleague Herr Windwebel, and the converse was equally true. What the one failed to see, smell, or hear, the other was sure to hear, smell, or see. They had at their disposal, or better yet, they stood under the spell of an imagination that, though it often enough served as a source of amusement for staider folk, likewise enormously enhanced their own amusement in the world and its show. They most assuredly were not to be counted among those worthy individuals who always look for a bridge whenever they find a playful woodland brook leaping directly across their path.

"One grows older," sighed the vice-principal. "It used to be that there wasn't a bird or a farmer in the bush whose whistle I could not imitate, but for that one needs teeth. And I've gradually come to suffer a lack of those. Everything reminds one of the grave, Windwebel, of man's unavoidable destiny."

"But—the master first proves himself under constraint,"[42] quoted the drawing-master. "Yours will always be the model imitation of a cat and a dog doing battle. Your achievements as the cat that's had its tail stepped on are downright overwhelming."

"Do you think so, dear friend?" the old gentleman asked, flattered. "Yes, but remember, precisely that cacophonous feat, which I personally believe I have brought to something like perfection, pleases my wife not at all, and there is not an evening when we invite company in for a bowl of punch but what I am first requested to refrain from such foolishness and not to make a laughing-stock of myself and of her, my Ida. Well, next time you shall do your farmer's wife trying to stuff a piglet into a sack; and your wife, your little Hedwig—"

"Has placed that under the strictest interdiction, and never helps me button on my cravat before we set out to follow an invitation without begging me with tears in her eyes to keep my promise."

"Bah, those are honeymoon prohibitions and honeymoon

promises. What all haven't I promised in that way! . . . Go right ahead and squeal; and I'll meow and spit as well. Do other people—does our colleague Dr. Neubauer hide his talents under a bushel? Doesn't he write poetry and then read the poems aloud? Just let him finish his Epos of '66, and then you're in for an experience. Though I'll grant you, I can't execute my Hinz[43] and the poodle in hexameters."

"Dear friend," the drawing-master whispered close to the vice-principal's ear while looking nervously about to all four quarters of the globe, "dear friend, here we are in the middle of the forest—our ladies are not present, nor our colleague Herr Neubauer—have you ever heard my asthmatic pug who has just done something not very nice upon my lady's sofa?"

"Never!" cried the old man, every limb twitching in anticipation. "Out with it! Out with it!"

They were in a snug green spot in the wilderness, surrounded by trunks of tall, slender beeches, vaulted over by shade. Two squirrels, who till now had been gaily chasing one another among the trees, sat right down and watched and listened like connoisseurs of the art; but the fact that neither Frau Ida Eckerbusch, nor little Frau Windwebel, nor Herr Assistant Master Dr. Neubauer were in the audience as Herr Windwebel came out with it was, of course, all to the good. What emerged was a pure, an ideal creation!

"If I had the necessary, Windwebel, I'd build you a theater all of your own!" crowed the vice-principal. "If I could trust these old bones I'd turn a cartwheel here on the spot. Encore, my best, my matchless friend! Not a thought, not an image but what it is perfectly expressed in that sound! It is a veritable melodramatic work of art, Windwebel! From now on, your future is assured after every second bowl of punch! I have merely viewed the art from Mt. Nebo.[44] *Vivat* the pug and my lady! Bring them on again!"

The two squirrels withdrew by hurried bounds; the two comrades of the road, of the arts, and of the soul advanced further into the wood, the vice-principal bearing the sandwiches and Drawing-Master Windwebel with the bottle of Bordeaux, the "Château Bilberry," in his back coat pocket. They traced their way along heavily overgrown, serpentine paths; and since each followed wherever his respective fancy took him—to enjoy displays of color, configurations of clouds, beetles, vegetation—and since both alike were good friends of button mushrooms, goatsbeard, and other edible fungi, they often wandered away from all beaten paths whatever. And when once again they found themselves stuck in the underbrush, old Eckerbusch in fact stuck rather fast to a thornbush that had tenderly set its hooks into him, Windwebel remarked, "My friend, this would be just the opportunity for him. Do you know what I wish?"

With a final tug that tore his coat free of the brambles, the old man replied, "You have a multitude of wishes, as do I. Well, Zeus probably knows best what would be expedient for two hardpressed schoolmasters on such an afternoon as this as we approach the end of the long holidays! What, for example, do you have for a wish this time around?"

"That we would run into him or he into us."

"Into whom? Into what?"

"Into Horacker, of course! Just imagine the triumph and wonder of it all, the recognition from higher up and perhaps a medal of honor from the very top, if we should manage to collar him and rid the neighborhood of him!"

"Windwebel?!" cried the vice-principal. "What an idea! You are absolutely right once again. Horacker! . . . Here we are ensnared in the wilderness, thinking of nothing in particular. And what a triumph it would indeed be, if we should return, leading him along—to our friend Wedekind out on the skittle grounds! Horacker, Horacker! Always assuming of course that he doesn't collar us and rid the neighborhood of us! . . . But it's all the same! I'd give the Château Bilberry for the chance! Go ahead and call out, Windwebel; if I only could give my dear old wife the pleasure . . . just call out big and bold! Loud as you can! In point of fact it's his legal duty to do us the favor; give him a bold, loud call!"

"Horacker! Horacker! Horacker!" shouted the drawing-master into the forest, and—

"Cuckoo! Cuckoo! Cuckoo!" came back the call.

"Now I ask you, Windwebel, do you hear that rogue, the *Cuculus*—the *Cuculus canorus*?[45] Does that not sound as if our Ida and Hedwig, my old wife and your young one, had sent him after us to remind us of our duties as husbands—and you of yours as a future father? I tell you, Windwebel, my good proceleusmatica does not trust either you or me to have the reason and understanding of our colleague Dr. Neubauer."

"He's sitting at home scanning verse."

"I don't begrudge him that in the least!" said Vice-Principal Eckerbusch in a soft, sepulchral voice. "And spending slaughter dreadful Steinmetz now storms Schweinschädel.[46] I can't say at the moment whether my hexameters or my historical facts are in order or not; I don't even want to know. Our most pressing task is to make sure that that bottle of red wine arrives in Ganse-winckel uncorked. Keep an eye out for a cozy spot as we move on, good Windwebel. I've carried our dry provisions in my coat pocket long enough, too."

The gymnasium's drawing-master also knew his Latin. *"Restauremos nos!"*[47] said he. And old Eckerbusch, who likewise had not left the entirety of his Latin behind with his fifth-formers, responded, "Winckler would never forgive us if we did not arrive with both hunger and thirst intact. *Restauremos nunc;*[48] which is to say, let us refresh ourselves here a bit for the present, that we may restore ourselves fully hereafter in Gansewinckel."

Chapter 6

It did not prove difficult to find a site in these woodland hills corresponding exactly to the laudable intent the two friends had declared to be theirs. Eckerbusch and Windwebel, however, understood better than most people—the one in his capacity as scholar and the other as an artist—to select the loveliest spot from among the classical works of nature. On this occasion they hardly needed to leaf through nature's volume at all.

The heather was in bloom! . . .

There on the soft rise of a glade, encircled by timber and a thick growth of underbrush, the vice-principal and the drawing-master found several tree stumps inviting them to take a cozy seat and—amid blooming heather—all sorts of signs (crumpled old newspapers and red-lacquered corks) indicating that others had already had the "sensible idea" to stop here.

"Do you recall the last time we sat here together?" asked the vice-principal, and his colleague did indeed recall it, since it had hardly been three weeks before. He already lay comfortably stretched out in the blooming heather, and since one greasy sheet of newspaper lay rather close at hand, he picked it up in his fingertips and read:

"Hirtenfeld's Austrian Military Almanac for 1867 has provided a final listing of the losses of the Austrian Army last year, according to which the number of dead, wounded, and missing for the Northern Army was 62,789, for the Southern Army 8,470, making a total of 71,259 casualties."

The vice-principal, seated on a tree stump, sighed and held the bottle of red wine between his knees. "There is nothing decent and reasonable to be had in this world without some corresponding misery. Let that rag be, Windwebel, and let us stick to the Frenchman we've got with us today! May dreadful Ares come to my aid, can I possibly have forgotten the corkscrew?"

Thank heavens this was not the case, though had it been, both gentlemen would have known what to do: they would have dealt with their Frenchmen "by simple force of nature," which is to say, they would have broken his neck.

"And here we have our Moltke!"[49] shouted the vice-principal, and the cork prudently yielded to superior strategic intelligence and—in this quite particular instance—the German schoolmaster.[50]

The drawing-master was already chewing on a ham sandwich.

"Proficiat, collega. Jovi Liberatori!"[51] said the vice-principal, regarding the sun through the red juice of the grape, and then at once he toasted his younger friend. "You have seen a great deal of the world, Windwebel. You were in England—"

"As the drawing-master at a Pedagogical Institute in Leeds. You, too, should have had the pleasure!"

"You were in Switzerland—"

"Three weeks with the sniffles, and without ever once having seen the Alps for all the rain and fog."

"Do you know anything better than in such weather as this ever and again to set yourself down in a spot like this one? You need only ask Dr. Neubauer! Now there's a fellow with circumnavigatorial notions and poetical wings, who knows how to express himself. He was in Rome and had more luck than you did in Switzerland. He actually saw the Pope; and can you guess what he told me recently?"

"I haven't the slightest," said Windwebel.

The old man grinned and put his best talents of imitation in tone and mime to work. With peevish pathos he said, "You're not mistaken there, Herr Eckerbusch! In centuries past, anyone who wished to be intellectually a part of his times had to go out and mix in with the world's tumult. Today it is otherwise. Today, gentlemen, one sits quietly, one ought to sit quietly, and let the great waves with all their wealth of ideas ebb and flow right over one's head! What does it mean nowadays for someone to measure the pyramids or stand in the thick of battle? Gentlemen, the discovery of the sources of the Nile, the searching out of the North Pole, or even personally firing a rifle in war means, I would maintain, but little anymore when compared to what the ruminative thinker accomplishes by quiet, meaningful sitting-still. When compared to the electric telegraph, all personal experience, all personal participation is curiously insignificant—"

"I'm still looking forward to the Epos of '66, though, most decidedly I am!" cried the drawing-master, doing his own gazing at the sky now through the wine; and avoiding all pathos, the vice-principal moved on to the provisions for the journey supplied by his proceleusmatica and laughed. "Is it possible that Horacker might get the notion—"

At precisely that moment something rustled behind him in the underbrush, and he wheeled about just as swiftly as his hiking companion sat up in his bed of heather.

Horacker!

They smiled at one another, but nonetheless each put his walking stick where it could be easily grabbed, and Windwebel took personal charge of the bottle of château—automatically, instinctively.

In point of fact someone was working his way through the thicket slowly and, so it seemed, very cautiously, and the steps whispered in the foliage as they approached the two friends. Eckerbusch put on his hat, and Windwebel got to his feet, standing there expectantly for some time, the bottle in his left hand, his stick held firmly in his right.

"Parturiunt montes,"[52] muttered the vice-principal, and—behold there was the little mouse! Out of a hazelnut thicket crept an old, old woman dressed in rags and holding by its handle an earthenware pot, her sole weapon of defense or offense. On the spot, the drawing-master declared her to be "an extraordinarily splendid background figure."

As she caught sight of the two men, her alarm was considerably greater than theirs. She stood there trembling, and not just with age, and stuttered, "O merciful savior!"

"Salve Silvana![53] Come along, come along, we only eat wicked schoolboys," old Eckerbusch called to her in a kindly voice. His

colleague Windwebel reached for the sketchbook in his breast pocket, examining with the enraptured eye of the practicing artist each rag and tag on the old woman's wretched body, while at the same time skimming through the hues and tints of his color box.

"Marvelous!" he murmured. "Venus Aphrodite could have glided out of that wood and it would have made no difference to me. But she is a truly enchanting fright. O Adriaen Brouwer,[54] O thrice holy Rembrandt van Rijn, here indeed is a most ghastly enchantment! Just stand right there for five minutes, good woman; and afterwards I'll give you two and a half silver pennies."

"And I a glass of Château Milon," said the vice-principal. But then adjusting his spectacles, he at once called out, "Just a moment, Windwebel. What's wrong with the old woman? She's trembling all over. Lord, she's fainting. Have we caused her such alarm?"

It appeared so—it was so. Speechless with fear, the old woman sat there now in the blooming heather as the two gentlemen drew closer.

"Give me the 'Souvenir of Pyrmont,' " cried Eckerbusch, and the drawing-master obliged by handing him the fancy glass embossed with said motto.

"Take heart, good woman!" said the old man, rousing her. "As for me, my worthy pupils play many more shenanigans on me than I on them; and the worst this fellow here will do is stuff you into his sketchbook. Here, take a swallow of red wine. Try it, Silvia, and tell me honestly whether you share my suspicion that I've been cheated, as usual. And here's a roll and a piece of ham for you, too. Well?!"

The old woman reached first for the bread and ham, but then for the "Souvenir of Pyrmont" as well. Then suddenly she broke out in loud, vehement sobs, in veritable wailings.

"It ain't no use . . . I can't go on . . . every bite, every swallow just churns away inside me . . . dear, good gentlemen, I thank you for your kindness . . . but I can't bear it no longer! . . . There he sits out there, and here I sit, miserable and afraid . . . oh, what a wretched, godforsaken life, if only I could say what it is I feel right now and what would really make me happy!"

"Confound it all!" shouted old Eckerbusch. "Who's sitting

where? At any rate we're sitting here and for all I care—we care—you may give vent to your feelings to whatever extent you like. I am Vice-Principal Eckerbusch, and that gentleman there is our gymnasium's drawing-master, Herr Windwebel. Take another drink of the ruby and please be kind enough to unbar the dungeon of your heart."

"O dear God, I'm Widow Horacker!" stammered the old lady, letting bright tears run down into the "Souvenir of Pyrmont"; the vice-principal, however, called out for the second time, "Confound it all!" and Windwebel dropped his sketchbook and with both hands grabbed hold of the tree stump that he had sat himself down upon—people have been known, after all, to fly off into the air when confronted with less interesting news than this.

But all the floodgates had burst for the old woman; the vice-principal, who had long ago brought his proceleusmatica in under cover, was reminded of many a steady rain and many a downpour of earlier, younger days, while Windwebel unabashedly recalled his Hedwig's bridal tears, but neither had ever seen or heard anything quite like this.

When the common folk weep, they do so in proper style. And Widow Horacker wailed as if she had been called upon to liquefy all the misery of this world.

"Oh, gentlemen, gentlemen, if only you gentlemen would take pity upon us! Oh, God, yes, I'm Widow Horacker, and my son is hiding out there in the woods, perishing before my eyes for hunger and want. And he can't bear it no longer, nor can I. How could I sit here and eat and drink? I had intended to bring him out a pot of soup; but in the village they watch my every step, my every move. I'd be so happy if only I could see him back in the reformatory again, I'd thank God for it every day and every night. But he is much too afraid, you see, and much too ashamed besides, and so I have to watch him turn into a savage, until someday they'll come and find him starved to death. Oh, gentlemen, gentlemen—it ain't no fault of mine—I'm his mother and he's my only child—shall *he come out of the woods now?* Will you, out of the goodness of your good hearts and for God and Jesus' merciful sake, give him a bite to eat and a swallow of this red wine here to drink? Can I bring him word of what you've said to me? Oh, if only you could see him, then you'd know why I, his mother, can't sit here and be cheerful and be taken good care of, eating and drinking."

The vice-principal blew his nose, wiped his spectacles, folded his hands between his knees, watched a caterpillar climb the tree stump between his legs, looked over at his colleague, and said, "Am I not right, Windwebel, in thinking you'd like to have your Hedwig here with you now? For my part, I'd love to have my Ida here."

And then turning to the old woman, he yelled as if in a rage, "And now may the deuce and all take it if you, you—you Widow Horacker—don't stop that tootling at once and drink up your glass."

"The rest of the bottle is for Horacker!" cried the drawing-master.

"The rest of the bottle is for Horacker!" said his colleague Eckerbusch. "Turnkey, lead in Horacker! By which I mean, old woman—mother, you strange old character, you—go fetch your boy! . . . Oh, Windwebel, at last an adventure while out on a holiday excursion! Well, just wait till I get home this time."

Meanwhile his colleague had been assisting the great highwayman's mother to get up out of the heather. It cost him some labor to set her back on her feet; but hardly was she standing again, when she began to hobble off with the greatest possible haste toward timber and underbrush and in a screeching voice, still half smothered in tears, clamored, "Cord, Cordchen, my boy! Come out!"

The vice-principal turned to his younger friend to remark, "If this is not a tale to tell, my friend, why—then paint me one! Oh, yes, if only we could have our wives take part in this affair! Oh, if only we had our skittle club here with us now!"

"And Assistant Master Neubauer," suggested Windwebel.

"Hm," said old Eckerbusch, "I don't know. Are you absolutely convinced, Windwebel, that he'd see the matter just as we do?"

"Hm," muttered his colleague, "perhaps at the moment his firmest conviction would be that Mother Horacker has disappeared into the woods with our 'Souvenir of Pyrmont.' "

In point of fact that is how matters seemed to stand. With the glass in one hand and the sandwich in the other, the old woman had crept back into the underbrush. True, one could still catch rustlings in the decaying leaves of the year past, but people other than Herr Dr. Neubauer would also probably have followed close on her heels, just by way of precaution.

And yet her trembling voice off in the woods spoke against all such mistrustful surmises, though, granted, ever fainter and more distant came the sound of: "Cord, Cordchen my boy, my boy!"

The vice-principal and the drawing-master remained calmly seated on their tree stumps, the first with his chin propped on the head of his walking stick, the second with a pencil between his teeth and his pocket sketchbook in his hand.

Suddenly it seemed to them that it had grown strangely silent in the forest. They no longer heard the woodpecker that had been hammering at a pine tree not far from them; they no longer even heard the cuckoo. Man has but two ears, and when he strains too hard to hear something, even those two very often forsake him.

"Hm," remarked the vice-principal, when only the shrill call of the crickets was still audible, that of Widow Horacker having fallen completely silent, "now she is having to plead with him and he will offer resistance—not trusting anyone anymore and not wanting to come out under any circumstances. Hm, hm, this affair is, as I've said before, most interesting, but it's growing a bit worrisome all the same. What do you say, Windwebel; you're the sort of person who inspires trust, the sort—well, you understand what I'm getting at! How would it be if you now were personally to go crawling about back there in those thickets?!"

"And come crawling back out dead?" shouted the drawing-master. "With pleasure, if it would be of any use. But as I read humanity, this murderous highwayman would at once flee by gigantic bounds into the wilderness. Quiet! Do you hear that? . . . Well now, the old lady has carried the day after all! She's bringing him and we've got him! Dearest friend, just picture that alfresco, what the world will say when you and I bring him back!"

"Hm, hm," muttered old Eckerbusch, "do you really consider that to be our duty? I must admit I have not regarded it from that angle until now. Hm, dear friend, how would it be, do you think, if we were to leave the rest of our provisions and what's left of the red wine here for this criminal and to withdraw before he appears? Why, only recently when we had to remove Brase—you know, the sixth-former, unfortunately one cannot say 'fine sixth-former'—from the gymnasium, what a nervous state that put me in; good Windwebel, do we really owe it to the state to turn Horacker over to them? Even if he should come along of his own free will, I would still find the whole matter highly unpleasant—and you, as I've come to know you, would feel the same way!"

"Frau Eckerbusch—" his colleague began in rebuttal, but got no further than the lady's name before the old man had already interrupted what he had to say.

"To be sure, to be sure! She called my attitude toward Brase—and I repeat, one cannot call him a 'fine lad'—a remarkable instance of weakness; but putting all that aside—what would you say to laying a thaler here beside the bottle before we hastily set out once again for Gansewinckel?!"

"Too late, my friend," said Windwebel, "here he is!"

Horacker, the highwayman, emerged from the thicket; or rather, with both cheeks still stuffed with Frau Eckerbusch's ham sandwich, he was dragged out of the dark forest by Widow Horacker, who held him by a flap of his jacket. And should the malefactor prove as bloodthirsty as he was ravenous with hunger, then the ladies among our readership can hope for an appalling scene in our next chapter.

"Good heavens!" stammered the vice-principal. The caterpillar mentioned previously, having continued its peaceful, circumspect climb, had now arrived at his vest; it lifted its head and made a face as if it were about to cross his cravat and disappear beneath it. Never again would it have such a favorable opportunity.

Chapter 7

O h, good heavens! we all cry and find ourselves perfectly justified in doing so. Here we are once again in the pitiless grip of necessity, of a mind or in the mood to feel great feelings, without the least notion of where we are to go with such lofty emotions! And such is the case each time the necessity arises for us to wallow in carnage and conflagration, conquered cities, surging seas, fire-spewing mountains, smashed skulls, spattered brains, and spilled entrails. The devil only knows why it is that whenever others get their way to vent their historical-tragical-romantical spleen just as they please, there is not a soul, not a dog, not a cat, and least of all not Clio herself, the muse of that patchwork kind of history so favored by our modern educated classes, who cares in the least about our soaring transports.

This results from one's having heard the year toll 1870 loud and clear, from having heard it not in a soundless vacuum, but in the echo of old and solemn bells. How many people are there who pay heed to those lingering tones and echoes at each clang that marks the present hour?—By the flap of that gray jacket, of the sort issued by the state reformatory to those committed to its care, the old woman held tight to her son. Following her haggard, trembling hand came Horacker the Highwayman, very weak in the knees himself—trembling, emaciated, ragged—a piece of humanity laid waste by hunger, cold, damp, and all the other privations associated with a prolonged, unsheltered stay in the open air! A tall sprout of a nineteen-year-old lad, still in the process of growing right out of those reformatory trousers! A figure of youth, the very sight of which was enough to make Windwebel-the-artist's mouth start to water all over again.

Strangely, however, that draftsman just let his arms fall limply to his sides and stared with gaping mouth at this Son of the Wilderness,[55] until at last he had composed himself sufficiently to call his colleague Eckerbusch's attention to the bandit.

> "Behold on rocky heights,
> The robber proud and wild and bold,"[56]

he stammered; and Eckerbusch, stammering with equal difficulty, stammered in turn:

> "In the forest's deepest chasms, hidden deep
>   in caves and brakes,
> Rests the robber bold and reckless, till by Rosa's
>   hand he wakes!"[57]

"Yes, I'm Widow Horacker," wailed the old woman, "and this here is him, and now you can see for yourselves, good, kind gentlemen, if he ain't a piteous sight! But you would have to be his mother to know what it means to have a heart and how it can ache inside you. He's been running around the woods like this, cursing the whole countryside, ever since he run off from the correctional house, even though they'd given him such a nice report and all and would've let him out in just six months come Christmas and he would've been 'prenticed to a tailor. If you only knew what it's like to be his mother and have the police in your house every day and have your every move spied on day and night by all Gansewinckel and all the other villages, too. You just try to bring him something to eat out here in the forest and keep him in clean clothes! . . . Oh, Cord, Cord, eternity can't be as long as those nights I've spent a'sitting on my straw mattress wide awake for worry over you!"

"Well, you certainly do appear to be a pretty ugly customer, Horacker," groaned the vice-principal and blew his nose in a remarkably loud fashion. And then he took hold of the widow by her arm and shouted, "Sit down, good woman; sit down there—it's where I've been sitting myself, that stump's the most comfortable one! . . . Windwebel, I wish we had our wives here!"

"Or our colleague, Dr. Neubauer," muttered the drawing-master.

The highwayman sobbed softly; the old woman sat holding her face in her hands.

"Give her a bit of red wine and give that scoundrel with the chattering teeth there a swallow, too, Windwebel!" growled old Eckerbusch; and the widow, who instinctively still clasped the "Souvenir of Pyrmont" in her lap, declined the wine for herself and pointed entreatingly to her son.

"Give him another swallow, good sir. And if you still have a mother yourself, then God bless her! He's got the fever, too, the lad does; and all he's ever taken from other folks by force was a crock of drippings that he took out of Frau Brinckmeier's dossier, her from Dickburen, when she fell asleep alongside the road, and for that the newspaper started in to call him a murderer and a ravager of maidens, and the chief investigator was to see me, and two troopers came and hauled me off to the chief magistrate. They've rung the alarm bell in all the villages in the forest three times now on his account; and now you see him and can tell me yourselves, good gentlemen, whether such a creature as him looks like he commits a murder once a day! They say he killed a gentleman from the court, too, and they almost beat me to death in Gansewinckel when I wouldn't vouch for their story that this poor bag of bones here was heading up a band of thirty men. Why, if you, sirs, was to put him in your pea patch, there's nary a sparrow that need take fright of him; and now, Cord—my unfortunate boy—now you tell the gentlemen yourself what's on your heart; I'm at the end of my miseries!"

"Wait, Widow Horacker," called out Herr Eckerbusch, who seemed unable to fill his eyes with the sight of this terrible captain of brigands, "whatever still remains of our stores should be stuffed into him first! Hold the bottle to his mouth, Windwebel! Oh, if only my Ida could see him like that now! . . . Let him have the whole bottle, Windwebel! Let him have all the ham, too . . . Lord, the very picture of misery, Horacker, is it really you? . . . Windwebel, I want you to do him in oils for me, too!—Our colleague Dr. Neubauer is lying there on his couch this very moment imagining he's having some great adventure! And is he ever! . . . Oh,

Horacker, Horacker! . . . Take your time, Horacker . . . It's all for you, down to the last crumb! Oh, if only I had my proceleusmatica here with me now!"

The great bandit gulped and swallowed the way only a truly famished person can, all the while whimpering and moaning very softly like a sick pup. For the present he was unable to speak, but from time to time he would use the torn sleeve of his jacket to wipe the tears from his haggard cheeks and swollen red eyes.

"You may sit down, too, Horacker, if that would be more comfortable," suggested the drawing-master. "There's a stump right behind you. Slowly. That's it! . . . Not so hasty, not so hasty—what great luck this fellow wasn't present for the feeding of the five thousand, he would have stood the whole miracle on its head! Five thousand loaves aren't enough for this one man, and I have nothing else with me except a little bag of peppermint cookies my wife stuffed into my pocket."

"Well, stuff them into him," shouted the vice-principal eagerly.

The great highwayman sat there on his tree stump, attended by the two schoolmasters, one to his right and one to his left, like a sick child with its nurses. The brigand's mother, however, sat across from him with folded hands, watching him eat and drink, swallow and gulp. She sobbed incessantly and heaped no end of blessings upon the two kind gentlemen. She could not find words to express her grief or her delight, her fear or her gratitude—and should it so happen that, deep in the Apennines, we should one day sleep the sleep of Rinaldo Rinaldini, we would at any rate much prefer to be awakened by her than by the hand of the loveliest of Rosas. One can always depend on Widow Horacker, even if all Gansewinckel is watching her every move; whereas one cannot be exactly sure under what conditions the fair Rosa might be willing to go over to the carabinieri and to be lifted up by the cavalry captain himself to ride behind him on his horse.

"Cordchen! Oh, Cordchen," murmured the old woman, "you see, you see—oh, if only you had come out of the woods before this!"

But Cord Horacker merely belched out a coarse, almost bestial sound and looked nervously over his shoulder. "Good God," the old woman cried. It was a deer perhaps that, despite her last words, forced this new cry of fear from her, as it rustled its way along somewhere off in the thicket. No murderer ever listened with greater terror to the wind in the treetops: unfortunately even the best of consciences is not equal to a situation so full of nervous upset. The widow went so far as to grab hold of the tail of Vice-Principal Eckerbusch's coat and only let go again when he bravely placed himself between her and Master Longears, who of course immediately took off in the opposite direction when he caught sight of the strange goings-on in the woodland glade.

"Don't be alarmed, madam," said old Eckerbusch. "There he goes hopping off to the third declension, *lepus, leporis, lepori*![58] Your perfect epicene! A grammatical term that embraces both genera, both you and me, Widow Horacker! . . . Yes, thank God it was only a rabbit; calm yourself, Windwebel! And you stay seated, Lips Tullian!"[59]

Now Lips Tullian was a character in that volume of Gellert treasured by Pastor Winckler of Gansewinckel, and it was at this moment that the vice-principal first got the notion of leading his highwayman off to Gansewinckel and Pastor Krischan Winckler. With considerable relief, he termed it "a fine idea"; and he was right, it was one.

"Hah, you gentlemen ought to have to spend just one day and one night leading the life I've had to put up with for three weeks, that would do you good," groaned Cord Horacker, speaking up now for the first time, if his hoarse wheezings can be called speech. "People has it too good in the workhouse. I got no more to say."

"Ah, Cordchen!" whimpered the widow.

"They'll add another two years to my sentence as soon as they nab me, and the old lady's no better off neither—"

"It was all on account of love, gentlemen, that he ran off like that!" sobbed Widow Horacker, interrupting; and the brigand captain laid his arms upon his knees and his head upon his arms. "But you'd best let Frau Winckler tell you about that, and Pastor Winckler; they arranged things very nicely, they did—"

"And here I sit!" howled Cord; Vice-Principal Eckerbusch, however, who had the feeling that things had taken a nasty turn for the worse, looked to the drawing-master and asked in a fash-

ion most typical of him, "Well, good colleague? Do you understand any of this, my friend?"

"Just a moment more, Herr Eckerbusch!" muttered Windwebel,
looking up from his sketchbook. "Just three strokes more, and I
have him. Do me a favor and raise up your head for a minute,
Horacker. Will the public prosecutor ever be glad to—"

The public prosecutor!

It would have been better had Herr Windwebel not spoken those
two words. Horacker the Highwayman did in fact raise up his
head, but only for the briefest moment, staring wide-eyed and with
mouth agape at the busy artist. In the next second he had already
leaped to his feet—and was gone—vanished—in three great
bounds: over the tree stump, through heather and broom, and
head over heels into the woods; and for his part all the drawing-
master could do was stare at the departure with mouth agape and
eyes wide.

So surprised was the vice-principal that he lost his balance where
he sat. And the old woman just stood there with arms upraised in
absolute terror, shrieking, "Cord! Cordchen! Be reasonable!"

But there now came mere rustlings from far and deep within the
forest, and Cord Horacker was not rèasonable.

"There, now you see," the widow lamented, "that's how he's
always been. And now all the world can run after him and not
catch him neither. He'll run on now for a good four weeks more,
and him and me'll be blamed for everything, and I mean everything that happens! That's the way he's always been, and I say he
gets it from his father, even if no one'll believe me. Oh, dear, dear,
dearest God, and I'm his mother and the one and only soul in all
this world that knows what a good heart he has!"

"What a beastly, what an unmitigated disaster!" shouted Vice-
Principal Eckerbusch, getting to his feet again with some difficulty.
"But that's the way you've always been, Windwebel! You know
what your nerves are like! Ah, if I could only—"

"What my nerves are like?" screamed Windwebel. "Ah ha! Well,
by thunder and confound it all anyway!" And shoving his little
sketchbook with the album page drawn for the public prosecutor
into his pocket, he grabbed his hawthorn walking stick and taking

a *single* bound through heather, broom, and underbrush, he was off after Horacker the Highwayman.

"And now more than ever do I wish we had had our colleague Dr. Neubauer here with us!" stammered old Eckerbusch, seating himself once more in exhaustion. "He would most assuredly have collared and arrested the rascal before ever giving him that château for a tonic. Hm, hm, it's more boring, true, but there are advantages to taking along such a terribly reasonable man when two fellows such as Windwebel and I are set free of our wives and let loose upon the bosom of nature."

Chapter 8

At the parsonage in Gansewinckel, the clerical lady is still sitting, her head in both hands, in the shade of her garden opposite the cold coffee, and the clergyman himself is sitting in his study with his head opposite a copy of the document that had aided his farmers in achieving that contemptible triumph over their shepherd described above. The idyllic scene was still the same, village and parsonage looked just as pretty as before; but neither Frau Billa's agitation nor good Krischan Winckler's stupor had moderated in the least. On the contrary, their moods had grown worse the more they thought things over, depicting to themselves the garish details of the situation now taking shape.

With each passing moment, the spiritual shepherdess foundered ever more helplessly amidst the ugly demands of the parish, and the more her emotions struggled against those demands, the more vividly her imagination worked at painting the farmers—and their wives—before her mind's eye. She, Rectoress Winckler, was wandering, so to speak, from door to door in the village in premature celebration of the New Year.

"Just try to find cause for rejoicing in that!" she groaned and for the twentieth time that day abandoned the attempt to pick up a lost stitch in the woolen stockings she was knitting for that husband of hers upstairs. "If the consistory refuses to be reasonable, I at least shall not live to see Christmas Day. Lord knows, I have never thought it beneath my dignity to poke about in sickrooms and sit beside childbeds; but a piece of wickedness is a piece of wickedness for ever and amen, and I know my Gansewinckel inside and out. Dressed in surplice and bands—with Böxendal right

43

behind! And they've got it in black and white—in black and white; and when a farmer gets something in black and white, then everyone knows what that means. You can bring on the Pope and the Sultan of Turkey, Frederick the Great and Emperor Napoleon; and unless they've got something blacker and whiter to show him, he'll not back down, and even then it's not so certain by a long way! I know my Gansewinckel. In that respect the village fools go right on learning from the bigger fools, and the biggest fools are the cleverest and stand firmest by their rights. Böxendal will sing, my husband will felicitate, I shall die, and the most worshipful consistory will even rejoice in the fact and speak of an intimate and salvatory relationship between pastor and parish. Oh, I know the gentlemen of the consistory, too, I do!"

"If only I didn't know the consistory so well," sighed Krischan Winckler in his study at exactly the same moment. He had just taken his reverend head from his hands and laid them, exhausted and downhearted, on the papers, parish registers, and other documents on his desk. He had surrounded himself with all the chronicles dealing with his parish and groped from one clerical precursor to the next, back into the mistiest past, and from his window he had a view of his church and along its wall of the gravestones of his predecessors in office, reaching back to the beginning of the seventeenth century.

"There they lie, and here I sit!" he cried. And then suddenly he banged his open hand down onto the yellowed pages so that the dust flew up about him as he shouted, "Had it been my own demon who whispered to me to stir up the mold of centuries because of those four paltry pennies, then I wouldn't say anything. Yes, indeed, if only I had got myself into this mess! . . . Now, of course, she is sitting down there in the shade and she'll deny that she ever first put the wretched notion to abolish the quarter-money into my head, and afterward, to top things off, Conventional Wisdom comes along and would have you believe that, though the whole world may abandon you and there is no solace anywhere, there is still comfort upon the bosom of your faithful wife. Comfort? Bosom? What fiddlefaddle! What nonsense! But I should love to have him here right now across from me, that fellow who brewed up this afternoon's mischief two and a half centuries ago, all for the sake of base Mammon. Poor devil! . . . Great God, what dreadful hunger the man must have had! . . . Well, I too know the revenues of the parish of Gansewinckel—he's probably lying down there along the wall as well, so may he rest in peace . . . In peace! How I'd like to rest—to live in peace myself; but is that ever possible in this vale of tears and altercations?"

He sighed heavily and shoved his black cap around a bit. But then his eye fell on his favorite source of comfort, on old Christian Fürchtegott, and so he recited:

> "By nature we are taught to fight,
> So quarrel, brother, 'tis your right;
> You see, the others wish to stun you;
> Yield not to them, be hard, be true
> And give your interest its due.
> Hold to the right or they've undone you." [60]

And once again his hand fell onto the documents, but this time his fist was balled.

"And worse luck! They're the ones who are right, absolutely right, right to every jot and tittle! I've got to take it; Böxendal has got to take it! Gansewinckel pipes and the schoolmaster sings, and I, I shall dance. And afterwards I'll have my peace here in Gansewinckel, I shall indeed, if not—down there along the church wall. Even the consistory president himself could not manage it in this life, no matter what sweet, mild, and pastorally wise winks he may give me the day after tomorrow. Ah, my dear brother of the clergy, you ought to thank the Almighty that He has opened for you this new ecclesiastical path to the hearts of your parishioners.—Pretty bunch of hearts! And my best thanks but no thanks for the new path. Viewed from my standpoint, he may say what he likes; viewed from his, of course, he is quite right—ah, if only come next January first, I could send him out to felicitate the farmers of Gansewinckel!"

This thought, this idea or fancy, to let the consistory president serve in his stead, to let him deliver the edifying *quid* for the *quo* of the Gansewinckler's quarter-money, to let him use his homeletical and rhetorical skills to maintain for future generations those traditional rights and privileges of the church that had been handed down to us by worthy and pious forefathers—this notion simply had to have an uncommonly cheering and gladdening effect on the pastor of Gansewinckel. He walked over to the window and with laughing eyes scanned the rows of gravestones along the church wall.

"Many of them would take great pleasure in rising to witness that scene," he murmured, and the refreshment he found along this byway of the imagination was so considerable that it allowed him to reach anew for his cold pipe and walk with it over to his tobacco box.

"Afterward we would, of course, have him here at our table in the parsonage," he rumbled on to himself, "and I know my Billa; I'd not begrudge her the enjoyment of having the good president at her table after he had made his felicitations."

"Oh, do come down and drink your coffee now, Krischan! It really can't get much colder," came the call of the apostrophized lady at just that moment from the garden.

And the pastor of Gansewinckel called back to her in a voice whose tone showed an almost fully regained composure, "In a minute, dearest! I'm just trying to decide whether I want to bring Voss's translation of Homer[61] or his *Luise*[62] down with me as the final assuagement to all vexation."

He was pressing the last three pinches of shag into the bowl of his pipe, when fate once more set him under its thumb, saying, "No, no, Christianus Winckler, old fellow, later perhaps, but not just yet! One must not always yearn to sit peacefully on soft cushions."

A great uproar was to be heard from the rooms below. This was followed by heavy steps in the hallway and then on the stairs; and amid all the thumping, angry rumblings of male voices came what sounded like the loud weeping of a young woman.

"Now I ask you—" stammered the pastor of Gansewinckel, but he had no time at all to make his wishes known. The door to his study was already flung open and once again he had the pleasure of seeing before him—the village elders, which is to say, the fattest and most prosperous of its inhabitants, which is to say, those whose weight, whose burden was heaviest in the parish and, now and then, upon his soul.

There they were again: Chairman Neddermeier and Degering

and Klatermann and Kumlehn, and all the other names inherited from their fathers along with the farmsteads. Once again they pushed and shoved their way into the tranquil study chambers of their good-hearted pastor. And the chairman, who was dragging a young, disheveled female of about eighteen years behind him by the wrist, shouted, "Herr Pastor, if ever we'll get a sure hold on Horacker, we've got one now! That's my opinion, Herr Pastor—not yet knowing what yours may be. We'll squeeze syrup out of a sawbuck now;—her here, this vagabond here, will lead us straight to the scoundrel. Show some respect, girl, make your curtsy, Lottchen Achterhang, and show the pastor how grateful you are for all the good manners you've been taught."

"Merciful father in heaven, Charlotte?! Lottchen?!" stammered the kindly old man, so shocked for the moment he could find neither support nor footing in any quarter. "Is that you? Is that really you? But just look at you! Where did you come from? And how did you get here?"

Looking helplessly all around, he stuttered out his wife's name, and that was the first indication he was recapturing his aplomb.

"Billa! Billa!" he then called out the window into the garden in his loudest voice, and that was the second indication.

"Yes, indeed," said the brawny village nabob insultingly, "go right ahead and call for the rectoress. We found her, I mean this vagabond here, crouching in the underbrush behind Haneburg's hedge, her apron full of carrots stole right out of Haneburg's garden, a right fine meal for such a perfect little miss, Herr Pastor. Sure, just take a look at her, this is how your perfect little miss comes back home, Herr Pastor, and since she won't give us nary an answer, we thought it best to bring her here p.d.q. to your study, Herr Pastor, since you probably still know how to deal with her and how to pry her jaws apart, and we'll be happy to invite your wife in as well, so that we can finally get to the bottom of this Horacker business; because where the girl is, you won't need look far for Horacker—that much has been clear, sad to say, since the beginning of creation, by which I mean to say since they both started scandalizing the village and the parish. If there's someone here who knows me to be wrong, let him speak his piece."

"Nope, he's right about that!" all the farmers in the circle grunted. Against that background, the voice of Frau Billa Winckler, the pastor's wife, sounded just that much clearer and more reasonable as at that moment it broke into the muffled hummings and grumblings of that gathering of true friends, neighbors, and parishioners.

She knew how to make her own way through the crush to the front, and there she now stood in her husband's study, fervently desirous of knowing what had happened this time. Naturally the central figure who would at once have provided an explanation for this new tumult had completely escaped her notice in the initial excitement, and it was a wordless gesture by Christian that first called her attention to that figure.

Frau Billa lifted her hands and gave a protracted cry of alarm.

"Lord Jesus—Lottchen! And in the same state as when we took you in ten years ago! Girl, girl, is it really possible that this time the village was in the right and I in the wrong? Is this the respectable person I made out of you? Girl, oh, my girl, where did you come from, and what are you doing here now in Gansewinckel dressed in such rags and in such a general state of shambles?"

From exhaustion, shame, and simply from her own overpowering misery, the unfortunate creature had slowly slipped down into the pastor's armchair. She laid her head on her arms and sobbed, and without once lifting her face went on sobbing as she said, "Pastor Nöleke read it aloud to us out of the newspaper, and—so I came on foot all the way from the other side of Berlin. Yes, I've done wrong by my employers and by Frau Winckler and by Pastor Winckler—but—I couldn't do anything else. I ran off like a thief in the night after the pastor read that to us out of the morning paper."

"Can you make any sense of this, Winckler?" asked Frau Billa, clapping her hands together.

"If the child came by foot from Berlin, then of course she can't be in full possession of her reason. Now, Lottchen, try to remember, get hold of yourself; be a good, sweet girl again. What did Pastor Nöleke read to you from the newspaper?"

With an almost savage motion, the poor thing raised her sunburned, haggard, not very clean, tearstained face from the bulging horsehair of the old stuffed chair and looked directly into the kindly old face of Krischan Winckler, as if seeking there the surest and best solace in life.

"That they're looking for Cord Horacker in the forest! That Cord has become a highwayman, that Cord's a murderer! And it spread from one newspaper to the next, and I left a letter in my room on my trunk asking them to forgive me for our Lord's sake, because I certainly and truly wouldn't want to disgrace anybody but myself. And I haven't slept in a bed for eight days and haven't had anything to eat except for what grows in the fields; but once a child did give me a bit of bread and out on the road a soldier gave me two pennies and after it got dark I went to a village and bought another loaf."

Frau Winckler laid her hands across her back, turned halfway around and mutely regarded the chairman of the Gansewinkel vestry for a moment. Then she spoke in a remarkably calm voice, whereas her spouse had completely lost his composure, and every farmer, to a man, had taken hold of his nose between fore and middle fingers and joined in a general sniffling as a token of his disbelief.

"Now I will tell you something, Neddermeier. You have brought Lottchen Achterhang here to my husband in his study, and for once you could not have done anything better. But do you know what the next best thing is that you could do?"

"Nope!" said all the farmers in chorus.

"Then I shall inform you of that as well; you will, in point of fact, do me the kindness to leave the girl here alone with the pastor and me for now."

"Yes, but what about Horacker, Frau Winckler—" the chairman tried to interrupt. "In my official capacity I—"

"And I in my official capacity am solely and exclusively responsible for Lottchen Achterhang now. Exclusively! Do you understand me, Neddermeier? I have not been without some use as the pastor's wife in this village, and I'll soon be marking my twenty-fifth anniversary in that capacity. So, you will now descend the stairs softly, Herr Chairman; and we two shall yet have another word about the New Year's felicitations. For today, we'll simply let all the rest of our dear friends in the village express their felicitations to one another. I shall, at any rate, appear next January first, and it won't be in vain that I shall go from house to house in the village. Oh, I've got my list of wants and wise sayings all prepared! No, no, I too am quite happy with the whole affair just as it stands; it is the *very* opportunity I've always felt was lacking! You can depend on it, neighbors; the parsonage won't be accepting any more gifts from the parishioners from here on out. You shall pay, and dear old Christian here and I will come and express our thanks. Oh, it's been ages since I've so looked forward to something as I do to next New Year's Day! But for now you can also do me a favor and go on home. Should I, Herr Chairman, have further need of you in this present matter, I shall send for you . . ."

Had it been the pastor of Gansewinckel, Herr Christian Winckler, who had delivered himself of all this and had he done so in a tone similar to that taken by his spouse, we would most politely have to decline the honor of providing any guarantee whatever for the success of his speech. We are indeed certain that the farmers of Gansewinckel would have offered numerous objections, interpreted many things in quite another light, and most assuredly would not have departed—not just yet.

But, upon hearing the speech of their shepherdess, they went—with much shoving and jamming themselves into a clump—stepping backwards out the door and down the stairs.

Only the chairman ventured to offer yet another word.

"We all know, Frau Winckler, that you know everything much better than us; and if Pastor Winckler shares your opinion, why then, so do we. I'm speaking now of both Lotte Achterhang and Cord Horacker. But as far as the quarter-money goes, we weren't the ones who brought that matter up in the first place, and old customs being old customs, we just accustomed ourselves to coming over here with what our forefathers put down in black and white, 'cause what's fair for one is fair for others, and there ain't nothing free in this world, something us farmers know better than anyone—meaning no offense. But Frau Winckler, you're always as welcome at my door as rain after a long drought, and if you'll offer me felicitations, I'll offer the same to you; and we've never been in arrears with our tithes and pledges and services and all our other obligations, for as long as there's been a Gansewinckel.

But what's right is right, until it's settled differently, and as vestry chairman I have to take my stand for what's best for all concerned, and that's just my confounded duty. Now wouldn't that be some vestry chairman, voted fair into office and confirmed by higher authorities, who would trot off ever so obligingly with his head tucked between his hands and knees, all in the name of the whole parish, whenever all of a sudden and at one fell swoop someone comes along and tries to convince him that they ought to just throw away a perfectly good claim on pastor and schoolmaster what nobody thought about for a thousand years."

"Fine, fine, Neddermeier!" puffed Frau Billa. "You can depend on it; I'll most certainly be there on January first should my dear husband here be prevented from doing so. And the Lord will most assuredly see to it that my wishes blossom and flourish. If need be, I'll even take Böxendal's duties on as well and sing you all a very nice verse from the hymnal. Dear Lord, I seem already to have a premonition of the exact number and verse—

> 'Oh how savage my desires,
> Unenlightened is my mind.
> 'Gainst Thy love my heart conspires,
> To my duties I am blind.' [63]

Though there are many fine hymns under the rubric of repentance and conversion. If you tell me about your duties, Neddermeier, then I must tell you about mine; no offense intended!"

"Whoo . . . hah!" said all the farmers standing outside Krischan Winckler's study, and for the first time there arose a foreboding that in resurrecting the old parchments and parish privileges they might very well have cut a supple switch to be used across their own backs. Remarkably crestfallen, they dispersed to their peaceful cottages, and, for the present, did indeed yield up Lottchen Achterhang to the pastor and his wife. No man must obey a must, says Lessing; [64] but the farmers of Gansewinckel found this must a must.

Chapter 9

Christian knew his Billa. In the long and pleasant years of their marriage, he had had ample opportunity to know her better and better. One would think that since all things have limits, that would be the case here as well; only it was not so. Krischan Winckler was forever surprised anew by his wife, the opportunities for which knew no end.

At the moment he sat with his body bent forward, his feet pulled in under his chair, and his hands on his knees, and stared at his wife, smiling, but with one wrinkle more on his honest, cheerful brow, admiring her and at the same time encumbered by the urge to shift his cap once more from one ear to the other.

And as the door closed behind his good friend, Vestry Chairman Neddermeier, he said, "Hm—I am forced to admit yet once again, Billa, you know how to handle things."

"That's my opinion as well, and I thoroughly enjoy myself while I'm at it, but that is not our main concern at this moment," replied his faithful spouse. "Now come here to me, Lotte! I forbid you to make any faces; just stand up and show the pastor the face the good Lord let grow there, and briefly tell us what you have to say, but with details this time, as is only proper when you're dealing with your Christian benefactors. If you start beating about the bush, you know me and you know that I know how to put a stop to that."

"O God, O God!" she sobbed when spoken to, pressing her face still more deeply—if that was possible—into the cushions of the chair belonging to the pastor of Gansewinckel.

Instead, it was Krischan Winckler who stood up, laying a soothing hand on his wife's arm, and saying very softly, "Dear, I think I know best how to handle this."

One is disgusted at the sight of spiders devouring each other, says Gotthold Ephraim Lessing, to whom we referred at the close of the previous chapter, in one of his "Letters of Antiquarian Content." [65] He does not add that no spider must obey a must. Ah, the world is indeed antiquarian, devoid of every regard for moral law or aesthetics, i.e., founded from its inception on the notion that spiders will eat each other!

There it is—so easily spoken, so quickly written, so fleeting to the ear, and so barely noticeable to the eye when printed—that little word: one!

Who is *one*? One does not relish watching spiders dine on each other;—one relishes oysters;—one establishes a business and one relishes the bitterest competition with everyone else. One has well-founded hopes of advancement at the office, for one has been told that the man whose position one would gladly occupy is lying dangerously ill with typhoid and is certain to meet his fate quite soon, leaving a large family behind him. One has the ineffable desire to be the one who hangs the finest painting in the art exhibition; one would love to overwhelm all rivals in the competition for the erection of a monument in honor of the nation's greatest statesman but recently deceased; one would like this; one would like that, and—one is perfectly within one's rights; for otherwise, one asks, why is one put on this earth at all?

But one has been put here—strangely enough! And now and then one bears the name of Cord Horacker or Lotte Achterhang, and even when one hears it said in the village every day that it would have been better had one never been born, one is a long way from believing it; but for all that one knows what grim hunger is and that everything one sees except for one's own hide belongs to someone else.

At the parsonage one may well say: "Billa, you must concern yourself once again with the Achterhang girl, and I've asked that young rapscallion, Cord Horacker, to come round again this afternoon. And do send the widow those old winter trousers of mine—that boy is running around again like an Indian without tattoos, and it can't go on! Just can't go on! One simply cannot sit by and watch."

But in the village, at that same hour, one says: "Last night they were into the cabbage and potatoes again. Oh, wouldn't one love to skin the scoundrels alive. One isn't permitted to use set-guns and one can't catch them like rabbits with snares." Oh, that terrible, that wonderful, that sublime little word:

one!

It is the darting, lustrous foam upon the waters; it is the stagnant black of the deep. But let *us* proceed—we who like the kings of this earth dare not, for the dread and shame of it, write the word "I"! . . . One is often accused of the most monstrous impudence, when one is only filled with a most delicate aversion to arrogance.

Years before, the parsonage had done a good turn by Lottchen, the last remnant of the poorest cottagers in the village. Christian Winckler and his wife Billa had taken the child out of dreadful filth and total intellectual and physical degradation and into their own home, employing her first in the fields and gardens, but later on in the kitchen, and had made of her what Frau Winckler called "a human being." Only under the instruction and discipline of a Frau Billa Winckler could such a pedagogical experiment have succeeded, and it did succeed, against all the expectations of Gansewinckel.

"We didn't think it would work, but she managed it after all—and what a nice young thing the little beast has turned out to be!" said the whole village.

Yes, if only there had not been a Cord Horacker. Later on then, everything could have taken its normal, smooth course.

But Cord Horacker existed and had already existed for a year and a half before Lottchen Achterhang first saw the light of the world, and from the very beginning he had been—just as were their parents—a scandal to the whole community. One day Widow Horacker found herself all alone in the world with her little boy; and since every human being needs company, even when it may be the worst possible, Widow Horacker and the Achterhang family clung to one another because there was no one else left who wanted to cling to them.

One does not choose for oneself the moment or manner in which one will stick one's nose out into the world. That Cord Horacker, in his nineteenth or twentieth year of life, still had a nose at all to show the world was in and of itself a miracle. His fellow villagers, old and young alike, had often, very often punched it for him—and done so now and again with only the flimsiest justification. A fatherless orphan—that sounds quite sweet, especially if mama is a widow living in very (or merely in something approaching) comfortable circumstances. But that good-for-nothing shrimp of a woman, Widow Horacker, hungry, cold, and sick, could lay little claim, even in her helplessness, to being considered touching.

So it happened that occasionally, driven by nothing but bitter necessity, the lad had had to help himself, with perhaps a prank tasting a little of sweet revenge (the poor fellow did not see much of any other sweets) thrown into the bargain.

Our manuscript is itself proof that we have no wish to speak ill of the good parsonage at Gansewinckel; but few people are capable of accomplishing much of anything contrary to their own dispositions. And the parsonage was quite simply disposed in Lottchen's favor. Pastor Krischan Winckler, at least, reproached himself quite enough afterward, and no other member of his flock appeared so often in his thoughts as Cord, whether as he paced back and forth between his warm stove and the curtained windows in winter or in the refreshing season of asparagus harvest. Every time, he would break off from his pacing or gardening to think, "I really am going to write another letter to my friend Trolle today and ask about that rascal Cord."

The proper authorities had, you see, at last taken an official hand in the affairs of the neglected lad and of the parish of Gansewinckel. They had taken the grown boy, washed and combed him, put him into a clean gray uniform and were now keeping him, much to the advantage of the world's future course, under their watchful eye in the nearest reformatory, where he was provided with adequate work and a just-adequate diet. One had to let the authorities have their way; however short their boarders' commons, they did not neglect their spiritual needs. Whenever the pastor of Gansewinckel did actually carry out his intentions and write his institutional colleague "on Horacker's behalf," there was always but one answer that came back. The last of these had read at its close—after the reverend correspondent had, of course, dealt with sundry other matters at its beginning—as follows:

"Concerning your Horacker, I can, God be praised, report only good things. The fellow still continues to behave in a most laudable fashion. The customary institutional melancholy (when I personally am absent *notabene,* the lads are merry enough among themselves) has likewise abated considerably, and I am quite content with what his gaze reflects of both his physical and psychological condition whenever I say: now look me straight in the eye, Horacker! I hope therefore to return to you an individual restored to humanity by your erstwhile humble roommate in Halle, vulgarly dubbed 'Housekey.' In return for which I would like prepayment in the form of a copy of your recipe for rheumatism salve; I gave mine away at the last clerical conference and cannot recall to whom.

With kindest regards to the lady of the parsonage, I remain

Your old friend and blood-brother

Trollius

P. scr. Have you heard nothing from our third confederate, good old Nöleke out there on the other side of Berlin?

I wonder if he's grown as gray as we two? I hope, I suspect not; on the other hand there was already some manifestation of a tendency toward baldness in our Halle days, and he probably has a right shiny pate to show off now. *NB.,* do you still recall how he loved to pipe long languishing melodies on his flute by moonlight and went into raptures over St. Filippo Neri's halo?[66] Both probably no longer a problem."

Oh, my yes, Nöleke! That name has appeared once already in our tale, and the man who bears it is of no little importance to it. . . .

"None of which helps in the least, as you can probably see, Christian. That you understand some things best, I don't doubt; but for now nothing is going to help here except for us to let her blubber it out of her system."

So spoke the pastor's wife to her husband, after he had talked for a quarter of an hour to the homeless waif now come home.

"No doubt of it, I'm to undergo everything one human can possibly undergo," continued the good woman. "Whatever troubles, terrors, and torments there are in this world land on my head here in Gansewinckel, and then afterward someone comes along, like that Assistant Master Neubauer that Eckerbusch brought with him not long ago, who tries to tell me that my life, and yours, too, Winckler, is idyllic—the perfect idyll of a parsonage! Oh, yes, ever so nice and idyllic, Winckler!"

"Assistant Master Neubauer simply viewed us subjectively, Billa," grumbled the pastor. "He teaches English at the gymnasium in town and probably is just now reading the *Vicar of Wakefield* with his lads."

"Objectively, subjectively, or perspectively, it's all the same to me. But even without my spectacles I can see you, me, and all Gansewinckel, plus this foolish thing here with her head in your armchair, my dear. You've tried to speak reason with her long enough, without accomplishing anything, dear heart; and now I cannot hold back any longer and I'm going to speak some unreason. You've held up your Gellert as an example to me often enough. Do you hear me, Lotte Achterhang, I'm now asking you very seriously to get to your feet at last, take your hands away from your face and to sit yourself down there on the chair beside the stove, and if possible to look me straight in the eye. Silly weeping and wailing never made the world any better, and you can't cry your way to a proper face, combed hair, and a mended skirt, either."

"Billa!" muttered the clergyman, shaking his head; but his wife had most definitely taken the floor again.

"Oh, go on, Winckler! Look, she's getting up and now she's sat down! So, my girl—take your hand from your eyes! Don't sit there waiting till I recall a verse from the hymnal for you the way I did for the chairman, the vestry, and the rest of the villagers."

"Good God, good God," whimpered the poor child, sitting now for a fact on the chair beside the stove, her hands between her knees. "I really do want to tell it just like a scholar, if only I could collect my thoughts again. There's the pastor's tobacco box, and there's the crucifix on the wall, and there's the sofa, and downstairs through all my tears I saw Wackerlos[67] and I'm sure he recognized me! Everything, everything is just like I remember it the day I set off for foreign parts, and now I've come back again from the other side of Berlin through all the heat and the dark nights and the great wide world. How was I supposed to collect my thoughts? I would have if I only could have. Every kind word the pastor spoke was like a hot coal straight from the oven laid to my heart, but I feel like I'll simply choke for the shame of being here again like, like *this*! Oh, dearest Lord God, I haven't been myself at all since that morning when I came in with the coffee tray and Herr Pastor Nöleke read it all out of the newspaper. I managed to put the salver down on the table, but then the floor slipped right out from under my feet and the ceiling swam off over my head.—Oh, if only I'd been the one he murdered, just me alone! I'll not survive it anyhow when they behead him. If I live to be a hundred, I could never survive that morning again when the pastor read out loud how the police and gendarmes and a posse from the villages was all out searching the whole neighborhood looking for the highwayman Cord Horacker. Oh, dear, dear Pastor and Frau Winckler, I would never wish for anyone else, oh, and certainly not for any other young girl or grown woman neither, to go through what I've gone through on my way here to Gansewinckel! Only once the whole trip did I look at my reflection in water, but never again; I was such an awful fright."

"Well, I'll hold up a mirror for you to have another look in just a bit," muttered the shepherdess, although apparently merely to conceal her growing sympathy behind the grousing. Christian Winckler, however, did not hide his feelings in the least.

"Who knows what one should say; one simply gazes deeper and deeper into nature and the human soul," he murmured. "There's a terror and a blessing in the sight!"

"And the closer I got to Gansewinckel, the more miserable I felt. I more or less grew up out there in the forest in my wicked youth; but I never really knew just how dark its heart was until this time when that first beech tree cast its shadow over me. It made me feel like I was a murderer and a thief myself, and I just had to call out; nobody'll ever know like I do what it means to have to call out like that in the forest. But there wasn't any answer from Cord Horacker. There I was all alone with just my voice and it seemed like the whole place was alive with gendarmes and troopers and—with him!"

"They'll be selling broadsides of this tale at the next fair!" groaned Frau Billa. "I'll buy one myself as a keepsake, you can be sure of that."

"The wind, the hedgehog in the thicket, the buck that ran across my path, were almost the death of me, 'cause they all might have been Cord or something even worse. And here I am now. I had intended to wait and then slip into the village after dark; but Hanneburg's boy, little Hans, caught sight of me instead, and then all the boys started in yelling; and then the farmers brought me in by broad daylight and the whole village tagged along behind them and had a fine time mocking and laughing at me and Cord Horacker. And here I am now, may God have mercy, and I don't know, I'm afraid even to ask if you believe me when I say that I'm still an honest girl or if you'll write Pastor Nöleke and tell him that it's so. If I knew for sure about Cord, then I'd gladly die and till then pay the price of my shame, too, by working for nothing for Pastor Nöleke. But I can't go to my grave before I know whether they've already caught him and if they have already chopped off his head. After I know that, why then I can be at peace again, I guess."

"And my guess is that you'd like to have a cup of coffee first, now wouldn't you, you silly goose!" cried the wife of the pastor of Gansewinckel in a strangely husky voice. "Winckler, now I ask you!"

"Does he still have his head? For the sake of our dear Lord, tell me that first!" shouted Lotte Achterhang, sinking once more to her knees, and with a savage energy she wrung her hands and held them up to the clergyman and his better half.

"Foolish girl, of course he has!" shouted the pastor with equal fervor. "Of course he still has that good-for-nothing, empty muttonhead of his! You heard it all yourself. They hope finally to get hold of the rascal's shirttails by using you. There must have been some other reason why he didn't answer you out there in the woods when you called him besides his usual lack of having something sitting atop his shoulders. Perhaps he was too far off. He's still out there in the forest leading them all, us all around by the nose.— Billa, Billa, the Lord is still preaching out on the highways and byways of this world! He still sits down at table with the sinners and the poor in spirit.—While we, we study at universities and take our examinations, and afterward, if we don't fail them, we find a position somewhere, and fret about adiaphora and argue about parochial remuneration,[68] because we only want to deal with the district treasury when it comes to our salaries. But what shall we do, here in the nineteenth century, so that we can find our way back again to deal with these children?"

"I'm sure I don't know either; but—but I still wouldn't claim that this tale belongs to this century," said the good clerical lady and blew her nose—the tingle in her heart having found its way up to that organ.

"Oh, but it is! . . . Yes! . . . Yes, most surely it is! . . . Thank God, yes, it is a tale of our own time," said Krischan, and then he stood up from where he sat and helped his Lottchen Achterhang to her feet as well. While the man and his wife had been engaged in this last exchange, she had been repeating the Lord's Prayer and had just arrived at the last petition. But the pastor was quite right in what he had exclaimed.

Even these days one can meet with and experience all kinds of reassuring things; one need only wait as calmly as possible for the next hour to roll around!

Chapter 10

For the second time in her life, Lottchen was led by Frau Winckler to the washhouse to be thoroughly cleansed of the dust from the roads of this world. But this time Frau Winckler did not perform the duty herself of applying green soap and a comb, but simply handed comb and soap in at the door, since "the girl was old enough to manage that much." But she did take a personal hand in things when putting the child, who had returned home in such a peculiar state, into one of her own discarded dresses, though it "had not exactly been waiting to be put to such a use." And while all this was going on, good Krischan finally, finally had the opportunity to drink his cold coffee in the bowery shade of the garden. One could not, however, say that he was puffing at a cold pipe as well, for he blew lusty clouds of smoke out into the late afternoon air with its riffraff of summer gnats. He had left both Voss's *Luise* and Voss's Homer upstairs in his study bookcase, having no need of any literary support whatever in the hour that was now gliding by. Homer's sun[69] lay warm and benign upon his gallant, reverend gray head. And, truth to tell, at such a moment as this, one is completely indifferent as to how many Ionians that sun may have shone upon so many years ago.

"Ah!" sighed the pastor of Gansewinckel, puffing out a new cloud, followed by a long pull on the next one, and putting a hand on yesterday's newspaper, which was also lying on the table.

Homer's sun shone as well upon the Luxembourg question,[70] and no less upon Frau Billa, who at the same moment was striding down the garden path between the bordering box hedges; and the pastor put yesterday's newspaper back down again. His spouse entered the bower, let herself sink down on the green bench, laid her weary hands in her lap and sighed, "So!"

"Hm!" replied the rector.

After a long pause, the rectoress continued, "She was very hungry. The poor thing! And now she's lying there sleeping like someone under ether. She fell asleep right in our hands, Minna's and mine. When all's said, it's a blessing that we can believe her. Yes, I believe she's told us no lies. What do you think, Christian?"

"I think I have already offered my opinion upstairs in my study, dearest. I believe her too. I believed it all, thank God, from the first word the child spoke."

"Hm!" said Frau Billa; but then she sat up straight, released another deep sigh while reaching for her knitting and said, "Yes, we are good folks at heart, whatever the village may think of us. Do you know, my dear, we have but one small shortcoming, and that is that sometimes I should be able to borrow your spectacles and sometimes you should be able to borrow mine."

"Don't we do that most every day?" the old gentleman permitted himself to ask.

His spouse, however, shook her head and said, "Not nearly often enough!"

And another pause arose, during which Frau Winckler brought some order among her knitting needles and Krischan Winckler took up the Luxembourg question anew. After five minutes, the pastor laid the paper back down again.

"Billa!"

"What's the matter, dear?"

"I have given long and repeated consideration to a matter and should like to submit to you the results of my reflection. Much— a great deal—a very great deal would not have happened in our lives, and in Gansewinckel in general, had not the Almighty in His wisdom denied us the joy of having children of our own."

"O dear Father in heaven!" stammered Frau Billa Winckler; but her husband went right on, not letting himself be bothered by this outburst.

"Children of our own, dear wife! We are, after all, an abnormality among the brothers of the cloth! We have time, leisure, call it what you will, for most everything. We have been, I'm sorry to say, neighbors only unto one another, and so there was nothing else for it but to adopt the cause of strangers. There's something to be said for celibacy, Billa."

That Lutheran clerical lady folded her hands atop the stocking she was knitting.

"Gregory VII was not only a pious man, he was a clever one as well, Billa.[71] He knew how to appraise human weakness. We, you and I, as a childless married couple, we live at least in a sort of half-celibate state. And so by just that much more it is our Christian duty and obligation to devote ourselves with all our hearts to the tasks Providence has found to be particularly appropriate for us. The counsels of the Creator are wonderful, and manifold are the ways by which He leads us to contentment within ourselves."

His spouse had edged her knitting from her lap onto the table; she laid both hands on the table and stared at him, her husband, in a way that she had stared at him only once before in her life— this having occurred as she was sitting in her church pew on the tenth Sunday after Trinity in the year of our Lord 1865, when in the middle of his sermon he had paused and, instead of a linen handkerchief, had pulled out one of her white nightcaps with which to wipe his brow.

"Krischan?!"

"I say, Billa, that Providence—"

"And here I sit flabbergasted and all I have to say is that you'll have to settle what you've said about the Pope and celibacy with Doctor Luther. What the consistory would have to say, you know best yourself; but as far as Providence goes, I shall grant you that you're absolutely right just as soon as I can be convinced that whatever Providence brings about along those lines is done with an eye to one's personal welfare and not always and ever to that of the village as a whole."

"Billa?! . . . Really, Billa!"

"Herr Doctor Neubauer came down on the side of the village as a whole. Oh, I heard it all, as I was passing back and forth when he was here recently with our friend Eckerbusch. You two, of course, took the contrary side; but it appeared to me, you know, if you won't take it amiss, my dear, that he gave you both a sound thrashing. You were the first to back out of the argument and went inside to have a personal look at how the punch was coming, and so I don't know how the vice-principal managed to handle the assistant master and what they finally agreed on concerning Providence, for in the meantime I was whipping sugar and you were down fussing about in the cellar."

The pastor of Gansewinckel placed the Luxembourg question in front of his nose and mumbled something about sending somebody off with a flea in his or her ear.

"Just mutter all you like!" shouted his wife, and who knows what all might now have been discussed in the shade of the hedges of the Gansewinckel parsonage had not a new phenomenon arisen there out of the clear blue sky of that summer afternoon, a phenomenon that lifted Philemon and Baucis[72] alike right up off their feet.

The phenomenon wore a light gray academic-holiday coat, a broad-brimmed straw hat and horn-rimmed glasses. So clad, it came down the lane from the woods, at a very hasty pace. As it ran it wiped the sweat from its brow and at the same time used its handkerchief to send up signals of great excitement in the direction of the bower.

"Isn't that Eckerbusch?" asked the pastor's wife.

And springing up and peering over the hedge, Christian Winckler called out, "It most certainly is, and moving at a pretty trot, no, at an absolute gallop! Billa, *something has happened*! Look at the old man run! What is he waving for? . . . Just look at those dancing-jack antics, Billa! He's just very lucky his fifth-formers aren't here with drawing pencils in hand to see such a galloping windmill."

The clerical couple were now likewise waving over the hedge to their good friend, and the pastor opened the gate in the hedge. The vice-principal hurtled through at top speed, waving his hat, his handkerchief, and his walking stick.

"Oh my dears! Oh my dears, oh my—a chair!" He collapsed into the nearest one, not an ounce of strength left in him.

"Oh my dears, what all can happen to a person! What all can a scholar meet up with on a holiday excursion!"

"Billa will fix you a glass of grog on the spot! We'll be bringing a sick man back home to Ida if you do not, *similia similibus*,[73] drink something piping hot at once," cried the pastor.

"Yes, you mustn't catch cold, Eckerbusch," cried the pastor's wife. "I'm off to the kitchen right now; but first—tell us quickly what in fact it is you've met up with and what has happened to you, both as a gentleman and a scholar."

"Windwebel is hot on his heels," gasped the vice-principal, gradually regaining his breath. "And I would indeed like that grog, dearest friend. The widow and I did everything we could to try and call him back. We practically yelled our lungs out for half an hour: Windwebel! Horacker! Windwebel! Ho—"

"—racker?!" stammered Krischan Winckler and his wife Billa as if with one voice.

"Who else but Horacker? Horacker the Captain of Brigands! . . . We—Windwebel and I and he and the widow drank a bottle of Château Milon together."

"With Horacker?"

"With Horacker and Horacker's mother, all quite jolly and peaceful, like a picnic in the woods with ladies and children. It all seems like a dream to me now; but I haven't the least doubt about the reality of the facts. That's how it was! . . . We would have descended together, arm in arm and in perfect harmony, to the village here, if that fool, Windwebel, had not heedlessly called out to the somnambulist and scared him back off into the bush by mentioning the public prosecutor. And then he, Windwebel, bounded off after him, Horacker, when he ran away from us.— The widow is still sitting there on her tree stump like a stump herself, and I finally decided that the best thing for me to do was to run here and ask you, Christian, if it is not our duty to muster the village and send a mounted messenger back into town."

"The universe is certainly in a spin. It's all simply stupefying. We've got Lottchen, and he—almost—had Cord! Well, why don't you say something, Billa."

"First he's got to get his breath and his wits back completely, and then tell the whole story once more from the start. As long as it's the universe and not me that's in a spin, I'd like to see things as clearly as possible and, above all, I'll not let myself be taken in by mirages and spooks."

"Just like my proceleusmatica!" said Vice-Principal Eckerbusch.

"Who God hath given a virtuous wife is like a tree planted by the rivers of water," muttered the pastor of Gansewinckel.[74]

"And sometimes like a mill!" muttered the vice-principal. Despite which he got his grog and then, starting at the beginning, he told the residents of the parsonage all that had befallen him and his colleague Windwebel out in the forest.

Chapter 11

If it was not the man in him that set out through hazelnut bushes on the trail of the dregs of humanity, then it was without doubt the artist, who had managed to capture on paper all but the last third of this German Rinaldini and who simply could not let the remainder get away. And nature had bestowed upon Herr Windwebel the legs necessary for such a chase in pursuit of the picturesque. Long, lean, and muscular, they were intended for this and similar tasks; and he used them.

"Stop, thief!"

At a distance of several hundred leapfrogs in front of him, he heard the highwayman's rustlings; and through brook and swamp, through thicket and timber, the chase went on ever deeper into the wilderness. Despite his long legs and despite the wasted and frail state the poor devil ahead of him was in, the drawing-master had to summon all his energies.

But nothing so lends wings to a pursuer's feet, nothing so quickens his confidence in victory, as does the rustling in the underbrush that comes from the fear the fugitive feels, be he man or beast. All hunters, warriors, lawyers, and lovely young ladies know this fact and its immediate application to the chase—the last-mentioned group, of course, only applies it with the consent and under the supervision of their mamas.

"Now the rogue is in for it!" panted Windwebel. "And even if it costs me the last scrap of lung power. Hey, Horacker, Horacker, give up, you scoundrel!"

But once more this was precisely the wrong policy. One should track down one's prey as quietly as possible. The banners of war, of the hue and cry, of love should display a mouth set under lock and key: *in hoc signo vinces.*[75]

Once again this last call lent wings to the fugitive's feet, much to the disadvantage of his pursuer. The rustlings sounded farther off now, and, setting his teeth, Windwebel had to stretch his legs further still.

They had wandered now rather deep into uncharted territory. All about them the forest was silent and filled with an oppressive sultriness from the setting sun. Had he not been fasting for several weeks, the highwayman would have escaped again this time, too, but all things, as we have said, must come to an end in this world, in this world full of fear and mad pursuit. The bandit ran on for another five minutes; but then in a new forest glade Windwebel caught sight of him, and with that the contest was decided.

They both flew across the clearing, stretching their necks out before them. Then a steep mountain slope, covered with bilberries and bramblebushes, rose up in front of them. Horacker groaned his way another twenty feet up among the overgrown rocks of a long-abandoned quarry, then he tumbled back to the ground in the middle of the gorge; and Windwebel, shooting right on over him, did likewise—and landed smack on his nose. But the highwayman lay where he had fallen, while the school's drawing-master got back to his feet as quickly as possible and taking his nose between thumb, forefinger, middle finger, and ring finger, gave an infuriated groan, "This, too, for art's sake!" . . .

It was a cool spot on that hot day, this hollow chiseled out of the mountain sandstone. Vegetation had long since reclaimed possession and as far as possible blotted out the traces of human activity. The area was shaded by bushes that grew high among the rocky rubble. Great ferns flourished among the mossy boulders, and down one side came moist and pearly drops where a tiny spring had worked its way through pebbled debris and now sought a path to the valley below by way of miniature falls. And the tall beeches further up the slope also cast some of their refreshing shade down into the clearing.

"The landscape around here is quite attractive," said Herr Windwebel, taking a seat on one of the rocks and looking about him with an artist's eye.

He sat there. But at his feet Horacker the Highwayman still lay with his face in the damp grass and moss, his feet stretched way out behind him, his hands clutching at old mother earth, "just as if he had obligingly thrown himself down to receive his just deserts from my hand," thought the artist, who still had not caught his breath.

"I'd take a certain pleasure in it, I admit, and the hazel switches are growing right here at hand. Horacker, you monster, don't lie there quite so temptingly; don't rely all too heavily on my basic good nature. I know dozens of people who in my present situation would already be hard at work on your backside. Turn yourself over on one side at least, man!"

"Oo-ooph!" moaned the criminal, burying his face still deeper in the earth, if that were possible.

"Yes, indeed. Ooph, ooph, ooph! Is that your thanks for the liquid refreshment we forwent on your account, you wretch? What was it that bit you like that all of a sudden, Horacker? A tarantula? Do you know what a tarantula is? . . . One has no more than shared one's last bite with such a creature, and in the next second—off he goes—away he goes, forcing one to chase after him, all in the middle of dog-day heat—"

"It'll most certainly never happen again! I'll never get up again from this spot!" groaned the highwayman, biting into the ground.

"You'll never rise from this spot again?"

"No, good sir. Go on ahead to the village and fetch the farmers. I'll still be laying here waiting for you, you can be sure of that. Just go right back to town and fetch your gendarmes and your public prosecutors. I'll let them drag me off like a log. I swear by Almighty God, I've had enough and I'll run no farther."

"Well, you could have spared me this last chase then as well, Horacker," grumbled the teacher, fanning himself with a frond of fern to cool himself as best he could. "You're a cool cucumber, Horacker; I don't suppose you've ever had a conscience?"

The highwayman sobbed softly into the moss and grass, and the drawing-master gazed down at the poor fellow with a look that showed he was increasingly at a loss to know what to do.

"When all's said and done, this is more than just a joke," he muttered. " 'Always count slowly to fifteen first before you fly off the handle,' Hedwig says. 'We always end up the butt of other people's jokes easily enough as it is, Victor!' And the dear thing is right—absolutely right. And now my fleetness of foot has landed me in yet another nice mess. Good heavens, what shall I do now with this fool? This is almost worse than the old maid's discovering someone has left a baby on her doorstep! That woodpecker up there in the fir tree is the only reasonable creature here; he's worried only about his own business and hasn't bothered to throw one sidelong glance at us down here in this dell. And not a soul far and wide whose opinion one might ask . . . If only I had my colleague Herr Eckerbusch here right now, but he's sitting there and comforting Widow Horacker, if not already calmly on his way with her to see the pastor of Gansewinckel. Must it really always be me who once every half hour at the least plops into this sort of botheration, not to use a stronger term?! Oh, Hedwig, Hedwig, he's got me in his clutches now, this Horacker the High-wayman. Not without reason you warned me against him before I marched off!"

He put his head between his hands and tried to think the matter through. To the sweat from exertion and the heat of the day that was on his brow was added something very like the sweat of anxiety as well. Cord Horacker went on lying there just as before.

"If he doesn't perish right here under my nose out of pure contrariness, the next thing I know he'll start snoring. This fellow is capable of anything! Horacker—hey there! Hello, Horacker; I am asking you for the last time now to show me your sweet face just once more. Horacker, I swear I'll give you a thrashing if you don't at least turn back over on your side for a good five minutes."

Such insistence helped at last. The callous villain gave another heartfelt groan and turned halfway over on his side, displaying his unwashed, savage, emaciated physiognomy to the drawing-master.

"Just let anyone ever talk to me again about the miseries of humanity!" muttered Herr Windwebel. "What we need here is a doctor, an apothecary, and a few sisters of mercy, and not the gendarmerie and the farmers of Gansewinckel. Hm, Horacker—Cord, my boy, unfortunately I can't offer you another pull of red wine—but tell me now, that was in fact your mother, was it not, the old woman who led you out of the wilderness to us by one corner of your jacket?"

The brigand now sobbed aloud as tears streamed down his face. "This here is the only half of my suspenders still buttoned on; the other half got lost in the woods another time I was chased. And I swear I would have hanged myself on the first branch that was handy long before this if it wasn't for the ol' lady—and—for someone else."

"Someone else?" whistled Windwebel. "Oh, if only my colleague Dr. Neubauer were sitting here now! I'd not begrudge my colleague Dr. Neubauer the pleasure in the least. And he's just the right fellow, too, for he wouldn't let the slightest nuance of such an experience escape him. This is the very stuff that idylls are made of! What hexameters could be got from this! Someone else?"

"Yes, someone else!" said the highwayman, gnashing his teeth. "My Lottchen! What it is that you want to make of that, I can't say. But her, Lottchen Achterhang, and the ol' lady and me—we're a threesome. The whole rest of the world don't count for me anymore."

"Greet my sweet Lottchen, friend," [76] muttered the drawing-master, displaying with this quotation that, even in his perplexity, he was a classically educated man. "So you three are as one? . . . I wish I had Hedwig here, but she's home putting up fresh curtains."

Upon the unpleasant distractions of the moment shone a ray of bright, agreeable light that came from the charming home life so new to him. Windwebel shook himself, and then banged his fist down on the nearest boulder and cried out, "If I could turn all this into verse, it would make me feel a lot cozier as well, I'm sure; but for the moment I'll even toss my sketchbook away. Horacker, here we sit, totally undisturbed—sad to say. You've gradually managed to get your breath back to some extent, and I feel increasingly compelled to believe more in your harmlessness than in your wickedness. Tell me about you and your Lottchen. Most anyone can land in a reformatory, but the average mortal, at least among people like ourselves in a region such as this, doesn't come up every day with the disreputable notion of constituting himself as a gang of thieves. I'll not tell tales out of school, you can depend on that, my friend."

"And you really and truly have nothing to do with the court?"

"As I informed you before—most certainly not! In His wrath, the good Lord hath made a schoolmaster of me."

"And a highwayman of me, even though I was learning to be a tailor!" cried Cord Horacker and sat bolt upright. "Dear, kind sir, how can a person help it if he becomes what he was meant to become? Going to school and church don't help change that at all."

"With ever more fervor do I wish my colleague Dr. Neubauer were here," muttered Windwebel. "He calls me 'Herr Draughtsmaster,' because he considers 'ght' the historically more correct grammatical form. And he is a philosopher, skilled in all the nuances of this world. He could tell me what he thinks of this philosopher here."

"I can tell you all on my own what I think of myself, sir, leastways as much as I know about me," said Horacker. "Other folks don't know a person all that good, not even the gentlemen of the court, nor even Pastor Winckler.—But I was put in the reformatory all legal-like. For somebody like me it's all the same in the end, and if I know my Lottchen it wouldn't have made any difference to her neither, specially since it was meant to make a better person out of me. I really did enjoy learning to be a tailor in the reformatory, even though my talents along those lines had never exactly been encouraged in the village. Oh, how I'd love to be making my way in this world as a tailor right now and helping my ollady out, too. You see, kind sir, folks like us, we play around with ideas in our heads sometimes too, even if our notions aren't so fine like those of learned folks and rich farmers. It's like with hemp thread and silk thread. It's still thread. And the reformatory chaplain helped me spin it out for myself, so that I could become a respectable person again, first inside my own head and then out in the real world. You see, after I was released with good marks, I was first to go out into the wide world as a journeyman. That way I could get the reformatory smell out of my clothes—and I would have made a success of it, I know I would! And once I was there in foreign parts, and I'd have gone off to America if I'd had to, I would have worked till I had a nice stack of hard cash, and if my Lottchen had waited all the while for me like she promised she would a thousand times over, why then—why then—"

The thought of what might have been overwhelmed the poor wretch completely. He wept bitterly and wiped away the bright tears with his haggard, dirty hands and the sleeve of his jacket. It did not make him any more attractive physically, but in Windwebel's eyes he grew ever more handsome in spirit.

"Take your time, Horacker," said the drawing-master. "Men like myself haven't found a place in the world without a struggle, too:

> Ah love, dearest love, a journeyman's life
> Is not a country walk!" [77]

"So you know that verse, too? Sure, but you can sing it easy enough! You've a handkerchief in your pocket to use whenever you want; my Lottchen had just bought the first half dozen she'd ever owned when the troopers came to take me off to town."

"A salary of four hundred thalers and a handkerchief in your pocket!" murmured Herr Windwebel. "Oh, if only I had Hedwig here!"

And he saw the sun shining in over the tops of the flowerpots at his window and heard the soft, merry voice calling after him, "You haven't forgotten anything, have you, Victor? You went out yesterday without your cravat!" He was once more given real cause to use his handkerchief to mop his brow, for many things were going through his mind, all of them reminding him of younger, rather disorderly days when he had been a journeyman himself, firmly convinced that he would still amount to something in this world.

"Go on with your tale, my friend," he said somewhat abstractedly, and the highwayman continued his general confession.

"I was pretty well familiar with what all a man's hide and heart have to put up with, and Gansewinckel had taken my measure for it all ever since I was little. Slowly but surely I'd been suited up, so to speak, with hunger, thirst, cold, heat, sickness, abuse, thrashings, cussings-out; but there was one thing I wasn't prepared for, for going crazy I mean. And I came pretty close to it, and just when things had taken a turn for the better for me. What would've you said if somebody came to you and whispered in your ear, 'Here you sit, you ass, getting reformed at public expense, while *she*'s walking around out there free and easy and doesn't give a fig about you. Just the opposite, she only laughs at you and calls you a jailbird, and says an honest girl who can get married whenever she wants can't think enough bad things about you.—Pastor Winckler and his wife have made much too fine and proper a miss out of her for a louse like you. Cord Horacker, she doesn't care a pin for you anymore!'—And now, sir, you're probably going to say, 'Why didn't you ask about it closer, Horacker?' But—you just try asking closer inside a reformatory!—The director and the inspector and the chaplain and the supervisor are only human, too, and nobody can really sit inside somebody else's skin. Everything that's done in this world, the good and the bad, gets done with words, and it's the bad and the wicked that gets done first. You try asking a director or a chaplain about a girl sometime if you're in a reformatory, and then listen to the answer you get. And afterward you'll be glad to turn right back to the skunk who whispered in your ear without you ever asking, even if it's all a pack of lies. 'Cause he's got things bad too and he's just as crazy as you. Typhoid sent the fellow who made me crazy to the graveyard; but I ran off to see with my own eyes and hear with my own ears how faithful my Lottchen is and to prove he was a liar. If he was still alive, I'd have to strike him dead like a mad dog, and he's just lucky he's already a goner. Sir, a man's only too happy to have someone weep over him, but he can't bear to have someone laugh at him. And they laughed at me a lot in the reformatory, behind the chaplain's back and the director's and the inspector's, and so here I am, here I lay on account of them laughing, and it's all so awful and so laughable, isn't it! You'd have to say so yourself."

"You're a very curious fellow, Horacker," said the drawing-master, gazing, chin in hand, at his bandit with utmost seriousness. He, Victor Windwebel, likewise belonged to those people over whom others "amused themselves royally," and especially on occasions when he felt there was nothing to be amused at; and so in this instance he was aptly chosen to give a considered opinion.

"Actually, you don't seem laughable to me at all!" he asserted.

He saw himself making his own way through the world, and could taste it all, sour, sweet, and bitter on his tongue. One didn't get to be a mediocre painter and a good drawing-master without having been buffeted about a great deal.

"Oh, Hedwig, what haven't *we both* put up with for each other's sake!" he lamented. "My poor little girl, what thorns fate placed along the path that led to *our* bit of comfort within our four walls! What would have become of us today in that wretched little town on the other side of this forest had it not been for old Eckerbusch? The skittle club would still take the greatest pleasure if it only could to laugh us right out of town and into the wilderness, me as Rinaldo and you as my Rosa! Yes, it's true, Horacker; and I, too, have laughed at you along with old Wedekind and the other gentlemen in the club. Give me your hand, friend. Men like us must suffer because there are all too many sensible people in this world; were we in charge, were we the majority, things would certainly be tidier, steadier, and more peaceable. But do me a favor now and pull yourself together! It is really high time we took that walk down to Gansewinckel and accepted the world just as it is, and the people in it just as they are."

"I'll never be able to face the pastor again, and still less the pastor's wife. I'm going to just go on laying right here!" wailed Cord.

"Because everything your chum in the reformatory whispered to you was a shameless lie from beginning to end? Because those good folks in the parsonage have earned the softest couch in heaven for what they've done for you and your Lottchen?"

"Sir, you're worse than all the rest, and you'd probably even call it mercy!" sobbed the highwayman. "It's just because everything was a shameless lie and because the pastor and his wife were kind enough to arrange for Lottchen to wait for me at the home of nice folks three miles on the far side of Berlin, it's because of that that I'm laying here like a stone or like that raspberry bush there and don't want so much as to feel anything anymore, don't want anything, and will just lay here till they come and fetch my corpse. My mother would've brought me down to the village from the forest long ago if that would've helped! Just three months and a few weeks more, and I would have been out, a free man and an honest one—and—now this! The talk of the town, chased by gendarmes, damned all over the place as a murderer and a cutthroat! Why should I care about anything anymore?!"

"If only I knew what I would do if I were in his place!" said Herr Windwebel to himself in the stillness of his heart. But aloud he said, "You're an ass, Horacker, if you don't mind my saying so."

"You can say that easy enough," groaned the brigand captain, who appeared to have every intention of reburying his nose deep in the moss and grass of the old quarry. "You are somebody and have no more trouble taking care of yourself than some fat farmer from Gansewinckel. But ten horses can't pull me up out of the swamp of my misery, and it'll take a force of at least six troopers to haul me back into town, even if I am only a poor starving tailor. Oh Lottchen, my Lottchen!"

"My Hedwig laughed at him, too, every time I would bring home some new story about him," cried the drawing-master. "My colleague, the vice-principal, intended to portray him on amateur night at the casino, and now—here I sit with him like *this*! . . . So now, Horacker, won't you be reasonable and come peaceably with me down to the village?"

Horacker mutely shook his head.

"Fine! I can't lug you there piggyback; so I shall go alone to Gansewinckel and describe to the pastor's wife where you can be found. And then she can send your old schoolmaster, Böxendal, out here, and he can bring you home."

"The schoolmaster?" stammered Horacker, Brigand Captain.

"My good colleague Herr Böxendal. He had you in school, I believe . . . What? You'd rather come with me after all?"

"Yes! Better with you than with old Böxendal!" howled Horacker mournfully.

And Herr Windwebel said, "You see, that's the honest thing to do. You're a real crackerjack fellow, even if you're not the first person who needed his imagination to open up the back door for his courage to slip in!"

Chapter 12

At approximately five o'clock in the afternoon, Vice-Principal Eckerbusch had capered out of the forest and into the parsonage garden. A quarter hour later, Chairman Neddermeier was halloed from over the hedge by Pastor Winckler, who shared with him all the latest news in the Horacker affair. And already at half past six that evening, a field mouse from Gansewinckel spoke through the crack under the town gate to an urban mouse, who listened of course with ears pricked high in terror, as follows:

"Haven't you *heard*? Horacker murdered two old schoolmasters out in our neck of the woods today!"

But before we follow this dreadful news in all its effects any further, as it spreads across the community lying there drowsy in the evening sun, we must still go a bit further into the events transpiring out at the parsonage in Gansewinckel. That is indeed the nice thing about any rumor—one can peacefully leave it to itself. It thrives as bane or blessing, without any action whatever on the part of him who wishes to be left undisturbed both in what he is doing and in his opinions and beliefs.

At that moment the folks in the pastor's garden were engaged in praising Windwebel, most heartily in fact.

"He's a fine man," said the pastor's wife.

"That he is," seconded her partner in marriage.

"Actually, he's too fine a fellow!" suggested Eckerbusch. "I'll tell you, ever since he joined the faculty of our illustrious gymnasium, with each passing day I've become more and more like some old nurse watching over his feelings, fears, and difficulties, so that in my mind's eye I always have got a grip on the back of his

77

trousers in an attempt to keep him out of harm's way. 'Be careful there, Windwebel! You almost fell on your nose again. And you almost bumped up against that philistine there again, too! Exactly, and now you're going to stumble right over our colleague Dr. Neubauer! Didn't I tell you?'—And just as I have my hands full with him, so my good Ida has hers full with his young wife. But as far as Dr. Neubauer goes, I can only congratulate his future bride, for come that noble gentleman's silver wedding anniversary, he will most certainly be able to recall the mosquito that bit him as he made his declaration of love."

"Please, for once spare us your everlasting colleague Dr. Neubauer, Eckerbusch!" cried the pastor of Gansewinckel, and there was even a trace of crossness in his voice.

"With pleasure, if only he would spare me; for the fellow has formed the same deep attachment to me that I have for Windwebel. Whether awake or in my dreams, I always see *him* right behind *me,* looking out for me like some nurse—the son of a gun! It has never once dawned on the fool in his whole life that it is a man's own fault if he wastes so many of life's finest hours. But he hasn't any need whatever to realize the fact, since he has his fun no matter what. By which I mean, he spoils other people's good times as often as possible. But the real hijinks come when he mixes with my proceleusmatica, and for that reason alone he'll always be counted among the dearest guests in our house. It's just too heavenly to watch how each tries to get around the other with kindness, spite, irony, and rage."

"And you still claim that you're a decent sort of a person, Eckerbusch?" asked Frau Billa Winckler. "Oh, I should be your Ida!"

"What do you say to that, Krischan?" wondered the vice-principal.

But the pastor reached up to resettle his cap on his head, though with a smile this time, and turning to the chairman, who still happened to be present there in the bower, he asked, "Don't you think so, too, dear friend and neighbor, that, though we know we live in a world of curiosities and perplexities, we also know, I would hope, that in the end it's not all too difficult to find our way along in it?"

"That we two have found a good way for getting along with

one another for what is nigh a half century now, Herr Pastor, is a
fact, God be praised, well known to you, to me, and to the parish,
your dear wife included. And I hope that it will continue to be the
case."

"Ah, you don't say, Neddermeier," concluded the pastoress.
"Well, I hope you mean that in all earnestness, Herr Chairman.
I'd be glad for it, and you know me and that I'll do whatever is
possible on my side to maintain peace and harmony. But now let's
get back to Horacker!"

"Yes, I'll grant that's the most pressing matter at the moment,"
stated the chairman. "Everything in its time; though there may be
a crackling frost come New Year, that's no reason by a long way
to be heating the house in the dog days."

"Shouldn't we perhaps actually follow Drawing-Master Windwebel out into the forest with a few steady, reliable parishioners,
Herr Neddermeier?" asked the pastor.

"No indeed!" said the upright chairman of Gansewinckel parish
with the greatest possible emphasis. "It's a handsome thing the
gentleman has done in going after the rascal, as this gentleman
here said he's done. But that's all the more reason for him to bring
him in himself if that's possible. It's a great relief to a person to
know that for once someone else is running his legs off a-chasing
him. I'll vouch for the village that it's done its part—in that department there's nary a one of us what hasn't earned a general
medal of honor. So that now if someone takes up the chase after
such a scamp out of the pure goodness and kindness of his heart,
then in my opinion that's his own sport and no one should disturb
another man's sport, as long as it don't result in harm done to the
community or some other mischief. The schoolmaster's surely not
going to bolt with the scoundrel if he does get hold of him. Just
let him bring him right along back to us; we'll know well enough
afterward what's to be officially done with him."

"The child's still sleeping, I take it?" the pastor asked his wife,
who during the chairman's lengthy speech had gone to have a
look and a listen in the house and had now returned to the bower.

"Dead to the world!" came the answer.

"Then she'll be just that much more pleased later on when she
wakes up and the schoolmaster arrives with the rogue, and then

we can confront the two vagabonds face to face," suggested the chairman, and—

"We shall certainly request your presence for the occasion, Neddermeier," said the rectoress of Gansewinckel with a strange sort of courtesy, which the good man unfortunately knew how to appreciate from only one of its sides—and that the courteous one.

It goes without saying that Vice-Principal Eckerbusch had one of his own long pipes standing at the ready at Gansewinckel. At the moment he had already filled it for the second time and was puffing away vigorously while constantly waving the aromatic clouds from his eyes so that he could look over the hedge toward the forest. And the forest threw ever lengthening shadows across the meadows and fields that bordered it.

"If only I could get the old woman out of my mind. She's most assuredly still crouching there on her tree stump!" sighed old Eckerbusch. "A person thinks that at long last he has supplied and furnished himself properly enough with all the humor necessary both to survive the vexations and shortcomings of daily life and to take his leave of it; what nonsense! Every moment something brand-spanking new comes along that he was not in the least prepared for. Compared to which, the tricks the weather plays on a meteorologist are nothing at all! So here I sit, after looking forward for eight long days to sitting here, and have to chew on the tasteless hardtack of that old woman! And then there's the little girl up in the house whose story you've explained to me. Is that supposed to make a summer evening any cozier, do you suppose? . . . And Windwebel! . . . If only I weren't responsible to his little wife for him, why, he could run off as far as he likes for all I care. But wouldn't that be a lovely tale, if I were to return home without him. Friends, I tell you, you don't have to believe in ghosts and nevertheless at the right moment and in the right state of mind, why, the first best white towel behind the door or the nearest old willow tree can drive you crazy. What's the alarm bell ringing for? . . . Oh, my dears—what if—he's gone and murdered him?!"

"Oh, but Eckerbusch?!" cried the whole Gansewinckel parsonage.

"I'd not want to vouch for the contrary!" said the chairman of Gansewinckel parish.

"You see, you see, even he'll not give you a guarantee," continued the vice-principal, pointing with his forefinger and rapidly becoming more and more excited. "I wouldn't want to say he's done it because he's the bloodthirsty creature the whole neighborhood and beyond suspects him of being. But try trusting a person who's totally beside himself! Oh my, you need only ask one of my lads what even the best-natured person is capable of when aroused! If I were completely in my right mind, why, I would never throw old father Zumpt or uncle Madvig[78] or Cicero's *De officiis*[79] at anyone's head, either."

"Yes, indeed. Know it well. That's how it happens," the chairman assured them gravely. "But folks like us usually prefer a pitchfork or a fencepost to bring the world to reason."

"My husband uses the Word of God, the Holy Scriptures, in such cases, Neddermeier," asserted the rectoress. "Whereas I, my dear Eckerbusch, both Ida and I, we gather up all our patience and try to change things by reasonable argument, Eckerbusch!"

"If only every dumb beast that walks on two legs and has its eyes, snout, and mouth in the right spot didn't jump to the conclusion that it was a human being," grumbled the chairman. "That's easy enough for you to say now among reasonable folks, Frau Winckler. But there's a time and a place for everything, for flies in August and for waxing wroth when a man's at the end of his wits. Just remember that, Frau Winckler—"

"I shall let you know immediately when I'm smitten with a fondness for your wise pronouncements, Neddermeier," came Frau Billa Winckler's brief, sharp, and cutting answer. "And now, please, we weren't quite finished with your anxieties, Eckerbusch. For what reason, do you suggest, might Horacker have wrung our friend Windwebel's neck?"

"Out of pure and simple fear, my good woman! I simply put myself in his shoes and consider what I, in that same abject condition and after having been through all he has been through, would be capable of. You know me, Winckler knows me, and I know you both. But who really knows that beast on two legs the chairman was just speaking of? But let them raise the hunt, dear friend, for me or for you, and either of us would be capable of tossing his or her head, if that were possible, between our pursuer's legs to send him tumbling. Now suppose this unfortunate Horacker believes that my long-legged colleague Windwebel behind him there is the very personification of the Last Judgment and of our friend Wedekind to boot. Desperation seizes him, and he seizes my colleague! Merciful heavens, what shall I say to his sweet wife if I come home without him? And to my own wife! . . . *Medius fidius*,[80] will she ever make a face if I don't bring her friend Windwebel home with bones and hide intact! *Mehercle,* it's one thing to join in with the other philistines at skittles when they laugh at some fellow who's lost his wits, but it's another to—"

"Be laughed at for the same reason while sitting in the parsonage garden in Gansewinckel," said Frau Winckler. "No offense intended, Eckerbusch, but the world has got itself a curiosity in you, and I don't understand government policy at all. It is at any rate most unjust of them if, as Christian informs me, they want to do away with vice-principals."

And now the pastor of Gansewinckel, Christian Winckler, laughed too; but it sounded rather cheerless nevertheless.

His was normally a fine, honest, loud laughter; and he knew how to speak up and add a word to the conversation, too. Today, however, he was quiet, and he remained that way, and sighed more than he spoke or laughed. What he said gave the impression that he was thinking of a hundred other things—and yet he thought of only one. He laboriously got up now out of his chair, left his friend merrily skirmishing with his wife, and crept off toward the house, sighing and shaking his head. And at once they began to talk about him.

When he had returned and silently retaken his seat, they waited with a certain shyness for him to start up the conversation again. And they had to wait a good while.

Finally he remarked, "The child's still sleeping, but very, very uneasily."

"When I looked in before, she lay quiet," said Frau Billa.

Chapter 13

A nd now our tale has become almost too jumbled even for us
and threatens to come crashing down all around us! The
bright bricks and stones go thumping over our heads and with
little effect do we pant and brace back and elbows to prevent ourselves from being buried in the pulsing rubble. Oh, what clever
businessmen the Dutch once were in the Moluccas! They would
rather set fire to a whole harvest of nutmegs than let the market
price of that noble spice sink. Let us take our example from them
and keep at least two thirds of the fine things growing for us in
the present chapter all to ourselves!

Let us restrain ourselves, let us restrain ourselves in the midst
of the abundance of events and above all in our description of
them! Let our account be as believable as it is true. There will
always be enough people, we are sure, who will believe the work
of an honest craftsman. But one must grant that it is strange how
many people there are who, in every question they raise, in everything they say, in every opinion they express, quite candidly—
though, of course, quite unconsciously—let it be known that they
wish to be included in the Windbag family. We count among their
number people on the public payroll, very respectable, well-to-do
people, people who have accomplished something in life, and who
for no amount of money would ever be willing to bear some other
individual's head upon their shoulders—and his coat still less.

"Horacker has murdered again! A man from Gansewinckel just
told the dyer Burmeister all about it at New Gate! . . . Horacker
has slain an old schoolmaster! . . . Horacker has slain two
schoolmasters!"

"Were they carrying papers identifying themselves as school-masters, friend? . . ."

"Can't tell you, friend; perhaps you could tell just by looking at them."

"Yes, they found them in a thicket with their heads bashed in—it was horrible! And the murderer left a note on a bush making fun of them."

"An old woman from Dickburen found them while she was out pilfering firewood. And then they brought them into the village on stretchers.—They say one of them lived for a quarter of an hour, and the chairman of Gansewinckel parish himself rode into town with the awful news just now, and the mayor and the court officials already know about it. Oh, wouldn't I ever like to know what they're saying right now. I mean, can you even call something like this human? What sort of civilization is this? Is it even conceivable with the taxes we pay? And the education in the schools? I ask you, what good are police and government to me if it may very well seem to them to be a joke that something like this can happen to someone in our century? Sure, but just don't sweep in front of your door at the right moment, and you'll certainly have no doubts about there being authorities whom the Lord hath set over you! . . . Well, in the end I for one don't lay the blame on Horacker if he keeps on getting wilder and wilder!"

"You're probably right about that. And when all's said and done, a person feels jealous of his own dog, because once it has got a license tag dangling around its neck, it at least can go for a quiet walk in peace! . . ."

And so the grisly tidings, with all the commentary arising therefrom and appropriate thereto, spread abroad in the little town as it lay there in the loveliest evening sunshine. Since the battles in Bohemia of the previous year, Fama[81] had not made such use of all her resources. From house to house, from lane to lane rumor flew, though now and again, like a conflagration in a strong wind, it leaped over a house or an individual. But she who watcheth and sleepeth not, she, the youngest daughter of Earth, born of her in angry revenge upon the gods for the murder of her stalwart sons, her dearest Titans, she, Pheme,[82] the goddess of sagas and reputations, espied our friend Hedwig Windwebel at the right moment, too, and whispered this most recently engendered nonsense in her ear.

"Oh, God, my Victor!" cried the little woman, atoning now with the Olympians for the overthrow of the giants. *"He*'s the one who went off into the forest with the vice-principal!"

Let us preserve for posterity the name of the dear friend who gave her this information. Ühleke was the man's name, and he has every right to be satisfied with the effect his news had. By helping to spread a rumor, an ass always has the opportunity of suddenly becoming an interesting fellow—and of feeling like one as well.

Taking down her parasol with a trembling hand, the poor little thing gazed for a moment into the comfortably benevolent and insidious face of the philistine, only to stumble off at once on tottering legs—most assuredly, however, not to her own dwelling, but to the home of Vice-Principal Eckerbusch.

"Poor woman," said her upright friend and neighbor, shaking his head as he stared at her scurrying off. "Well, I myself still consider the whole story utter foolishness. People are simply too gullible! Well, there will probably be a detailed account of it all in tomorrow's paper. I for my part can wait till then. I myself am in no hurry about it, but—of course one is always a bit curious, isn't one."

A bit curious, too, was the nose Frau Vice-Principal Eckerbusch raised above the flowerbox at her window to sniff out the epoch-making ramifications of great historical events or of a story such as this. But whatever that hoary old sinner, Herr Eckerbusch, might say of it, it was one of the most courageous noses in town or country, and, as we already know, in no way unfamiliar to either town or country.

"Now what is this all at once, all this putting together of heads and running and dashing about?" asked Frau Ida, lifting her horn-rimmed spectacles from her nose and letting her knitting lie in her lap. "My God, there's not a fire somewhere, is there? No—praise be!—because in that case one would have already heard the alarm bell and the tooting of the siren, I suppose. Lord, what has got into that child Frau Windwebel again? Just let someone try to preach reason to her about walking sedately down the street! Look there, she's tripped again; and I've told her a hundred times al-

ready she just brings the whole town down on her by doing that.
Oh, her and my husband both! I'll not even speak of her husband—he was simply born with the fidgets. Well, at least she is
headed this way, and I'll have a chance to hear in peace what's
suddenly taken hold of this nice summer evening."

And a woman who once more could calmly pick up the stocking she was knitting, although she had just seen how outside her
window the whole world was seized with excitement, such a
woman was called by old Eckerbusch his proceleusmatica:

U U U U !

And indeed she came, the wife of her husband's youthful colleague; pale with terror and somewhat disheveled, she stumbled
into the good woman's room and cried in a voice that she had
only partially recovered, "Dearest, dear—Frau Vice-Principal—here
you sit, and I'm perishing! . . . Horacker! . . . Two schoolmasters murdered!—And my husband and your husband—oh, if only
I had made mine stay at home! Oh, my Victor, my Victor, my
poor Victor! . . . They've found them both in the middle of the
forest, murdered by Horacker!"

"Balderdash!" said the old woman, pulling herself up stiffly
where she sat. "It looks like folks have come up with a really fine
bit of foolishness this time. Do you know what, silly goose? When
you have taken a seat and have completely got your breath back,
you can tell me all the details of this nonsense they've taken you
in with. And so first, in a word, who told you this?"

Sinking down onto the nearest chair, Hedwig exhaled the name
of her bird of ill omen, and—

"Ühleke!" repeated Frau Eckerbusch with a truly devastating
contempt for that name. "Well, my girl, he's the very man I would
have selected myself for that inevitable occasion when humanity
decided to visit its folly upon me."

"But he didn't just invent the news himself!" sobbed the unhappy young woman, springing up again and wringing her hands.
"You have only to look out the window! You can see how in
every doorway the whole town is saying the same thing. Just look
how people are looking at you! And with looks and faces like
that, you can just sit still! Oh, God, oh, God, I've been so afraid

of this, have felt it hanging over me like some heavy cloud for months now!"

"Stuff and nonsense, child!" grumbled the old woman half in sympathy, half in annoyance. "I advised you some time ago on what to do about such symptoms, to avoid all unnecessary upsets whenever possible. I beg you, Hedwig, be reasonable. How can you imagine that my husband—that old Eckerbusch could be murdered while on his way to visit Pastor Winckler in Gansewinckel! Why, the idea is simply ridiculous!"

"Not to me! My husband went with him, and I know my Victor. No one would ever find it strange for him to end up in the hands of a murderer. Everyone would believe that of him, and I—oh, I shall die!"

"So shall I here soon, but for vexation," muttered the matron.

"Look—just look there. There goes Judge Nagelmann with Officer Fünfrad. The very stones, the walls and windows and doors shout it at me from all sides. There—there, look how they're crowding into Müller's shop and clapping their hands in dismay. Oh, Victor—my Victor!"

"Something has happened," muttered the old woman. "But what it may be, the Lord only knows. Well, we shall find out for ourselves at once. If only it's not another one of my husband's practical jokes. He looked much more suspicious than usual today when he said good-bye. God help us if he's the one who's made us the talk of the town again with another of his escapades. Oh, I'm almost certain he has perpetrated some foolishness again. I've noticed for some time now, he's felt there's been much too little talk about him in town of late! . . . No doubt of it, here we go again! Linchen—Linchen!"

It proved unnecessary to call for her maid a third time, for the girl was already tumbling in at the door, her face a bright red.

"Is that you, Linchen? Fine, then you can run on over to Herr Müller's shop and give him my compliments—"

"I've been there already—O dear Lord, Frau Eckerbusch," the girl wailed. "Oh, God, oh, God, oh, God, everything they say is true. The poor master! There he lies stretched out on a table at the inn in Gansewinckel. The forester from Birkenhof found him

out in the woods with his brains all running out. And Herr Windwebel was lying twenty paces away and he was battered about
even worse still. One of them lived, though, for a half hour and
had them write it down that it was Horacker that done it. The
troopers are already mounted, and the court has ordered an extra
coach from the posthouse, and it was just today noon that he
praised me for my veal roast, the master did—oh, who would
ever have prophesied this would happen to us, Frau Eckerbusch!—He even approved of the gravy this time; but it was meant
to be his last."

"If he could hear all this he would dissolve with delight right
here in front of me," said the proceleusmatica. "Would there ever
be some cavorting about the room then! . . . Good heavens, if
only I didn't have this child here fainting half away and convulsed
with sobs and in her delicate condition besides! . . . Dear Hedwig, come, come, be reasonable, and conduct yourself like an intelligent woman! Have you still not comprehended that it is only
my old husband and he alone who is behind this April Fool's joke?"

"And my husband—where my husband is lying now, did no one
at Müller's say anything about that?" cried the wailing young
woman, clasping Linchen by the arm with both trembling hands.

"No, Frau Windwebel, but I suppose he's at the inn, too. When
the messenger left from Gansewinckel, they'd only brought the
master, Herr Eckerbusch, into the village."

"Ah!" groaned Frau Hedwig now, and as tears streamed down
her face, she sank onto the bosom of the dear older woman.

"They'll force him into retirement for all this commotion,
whether he caused it or not," muttered Frau Ida. "They'll get their
hooks into him this time and pitch him out, just as they've been
yearning to do for years now! And far and wide not one cool head
to offer a body some support in all this madness—not even a doctor for this poor silly goose here! . . . Sooner or later the child
will manage to get me rattled as well . . . I can't say what all I
would give right now for someone with a cool, reasonable head."

"There goes Alderman Bockböse, why don't you ask him, Frau
Eckerbusch?" called Linchen from the window. "After all, I know
him, you know—I left his service to come here—and he's a man

who stays cool, because every third word he says at home to his wife is, 'I'm not going to get upset over this.' "

"That dunderhead! The next thing you know they'll be making Ühleke mayor," said Frau Eckerbusch as she gently set her young friend down on the sofa, shoved her Linchen away from the window, and took a look out over the stems of roses and geraniums, searching now herself for a cool head.

"Good evening, alderman. Just a word. Tell me what you think of this silly talk going around town."

"What I think, Frau Eckerbusch? Well—as you know, I much prefer to keep a cool head whenever and for as long as possible; but—sad to say—people do say it is really true this time!"

"Please give my regards to your lovely wife," replied the proceleusmatica, turning back to the two women in her room and calling out, "There you are! Didn't I size him up just right?" But in her heart she added with muffled rage, "A person has to draw the line somewhere, and I shall not forgive my Eckerbusch for this evening's amusements."

At that same instant, Herr Dr. Neubauer came around the corner of the marketplace, arriving for once at precisely the right moment—even for his colleague's wife, Frau Eckerbusch.

Man truly does not live amid the hubbub that he himself makes or hears all about him, but in the stillness that he carries within his own breast; and whoever saw Assistant Master Neubauer as he walked along—his hands behind his back, his face expressionless, his eye calm and bright—would have had to admit that here indeed strode a man who on principle desired to maintain an unshakable tranquility of spirit. There the assistant master came around the corner, tapping out on the back of his left hand a hexameter but newly created for his Epos of '66 and tasting yet once again how the word *Predsmirzitz* [83] scanned. And if not as handsome as "he who strikes from afar," [84] he nevertheless shared with Apollo the same total diving contempt about the nostrils.

"Here comes Assistant Master Neubauer!" cried Frau Eckerbusch, for the first time in her life breathing more easily at the sight of him. "He could not have chosen a better moment! He really does have the only other cool head in town besides my own!

That man has always been an abomination to me until today. But—that's how things go! Fate presumably sent him here to our gymnasium for the sole purpose of proving to me how many different sorts of apples there are that can still a thirst . . . Herr Dr. Neubauer! Herr Doctor! Herr Doctor! Might I ask you to come up for the briefest moment.—And now, Hedwig, pull yourself together, don't make either yourself or me look ridiculous in Dr. Neubauer's eyes. You know him as well as I, so be a dear, reasonable child. There you have a fresh handkerchief; now dry your tears and try to look like a sensible young woman. I hear him on the stairs already—tap, tap! He is the only person I know who never lets anything alter his pace. So—that's right, my dear! I most certainly have not called the man in on my own account. Knock, knock! There he is! . . . Come in, dear Dr. Neubauer! Oh—just wait until that old sinner, my Werner, gets home!"

Assistant Master Dr. Neubauer, who had been interrupted on his poetical journey to Sadowa[85] by Frau Eckerbusch's strangely cordial call from her window, had of course at first glanced about to all four quarters of the globe before turning to the spot from which the request that he come up for a moment had rung out.

Raising his high-crowned black hat and then letting it sink again, he had nodded his very curly head and replied, "With the greatest pleasure." And had added a quotation:

"Alas I must admit what seemed impossible,
That Sabine charms do murmur and disturb my heart,
That Marsic spells do well nigh burst and cleave my brain.
What does she want of me?"[86]

While climbing the stairs of the house of his colleague Eckerbusch, however, he cited the quotation in Latin.

"Actually I've called you up here only for the sake of the child, dear Doctor," said Frau Ida. "My counsels of reason are of no avail. Now *you* talk to her, Neubauer. For once you are my man. And as you were coming around the corner there just now, it was as if all Greece and Rome were calling out to me: 'We would have sent for him right away. We would have sent for him first thing.' "

"You're very kind, dear Frau Eckerbusch," said the assistant master with his most amiable smile. "And as soon as I know—"

"Just look at the child. There she lies quite beside herself on account of this silly rumor that is making the rounds."

"On account of what rumor, if I might ask, dear ladies?"

"That Horacker has gone and murdered her husband and my Eckerbusch along with him," said the old woman, casting a brief sidelong glance at the assistant master.

"Really? I hear this with some astonishment myself for the first time," replied the doctor, tugging his shirt collar back into place. "Well, let us hope the rumor will not be confirmed."

Frau Hedwig whimpered softly; Frau Ida stared at Dr. Neubauer, her eyes growing larger and larger. "You do not consider this story then, as we do, as I do, to be a contemptible, disgusting, preposterous fable?"

"You will permit me, I'm sure, to take a seat, dear lady," said Dr. Neubauer gently and without expression. "When was it, then, that we last made jokes about Horacker? If I am not mistaken, here recently one evening. And afterward your husband, our good vice-principal, in his waggish fashion offered us his fine imitation of a tomcat caught in a door, much to everyone's amusement! Worthy Frau Eckerbusch, may I take the liberty of speaking to you as if to a colleague—I would hope you are convinced that I share your opinion completely as to the nature of this ludicrous adventure; but—"

"But?" cried Frau Ida Eckerbusch, keeping rein on her impatience with only the greatest difficulty.

"But in point of fact, as I made my way through town, I likewise noticed, without paying the matter much attention, of course, that the prosecutor together with his amanuensis were just climbing into a coach at the posthouse in order to drive to Gansewinckel."

A loud scream was emitted by the younger woman, who ran about the room wringing her hands.

"Didn't I just say that?" cried Linchen the maid.

Frau Eckerbusch, however, smiled grimly and said, "Please don't be offended, Neubauer, but you do appear to me now to be a bit too composed, I must say! But after all, I ought to have thought as much from the start, that you would be even worse than the others in this instance, too."

"I can't bear it! Oh, I can bear it no longer!" lamented poor Hedwig. "I'm driving out to Gansewinckel, too! I want to go to Gansewinckel, too—I'll go to Gansewinckel on foot if I must! Oh, my Victor, my dear, dear Victor!"

"You have all taken it into your heads to drive me crazy," cried the old woman. "Is it really possible that humanity can be so stupid and so wicked at the same time?"

"Preeminently wicked—and stupid, too," whispered the assistant master, his voice, if anything, friendlier and milder still. "One must only study philology, one need only be a scholar to find the fact not merely confirmed by daily experience, but multiplied as well."

"To Gansewinckel, O God, to Gansewinckel!" whimpered Frau Hedwig; and now Frau Ida Eckerbusch likewise began to wring her hands and to pace up and down the room.

"I have seen many things in my life and been through a great deal with my Eckerbusch, but never would I have thought this possible," she cried. "All this idle chatter goes to one's head like a fever! As for you, Neubauer, old fool that I am, I should have let you go peacefully on your spindly-shanked way. But since you are here now, I shall hold onto you, my good man, and—*you shall come with us to Gansewinckel!*"

The young wife of Drawing-Master Victor Windwebel was already hanging at her neck, sobbing convulsively, "Oh, yes, yes, yes—please at once, at once—let us go at once, they shall drive us there just as we are!"

And the old woman cast a matron's expert eye at the sweet, trembling newlywed standing there buffeted by calamity and dampened by tears, and murmured, "She'll fret herself away, and I love her too dearly to bear the *entire* responsibility myself later on."

Aloud she said in a vexed and whining voice, "So calm yourself now, silly goose. I told you, we shall go. For your sake for once I shall actually be as stupid as the others. Hooo, but if I find my old Eulenspiegel still alive and kicking, then . . . Arrange a coach for us at once, Dr. Neubauer."

Assistant Master Neubauer, who thought himself equal, yes, divinely indifferent to all human blandishments, stood there for a moment totally dumbfounded.

"Me? Me, my good woman? You wish to take me along with you to Gansewinckel?"

"Yes, you, Neubauer! You most assuredly do not wish to let us two poor worms be driven out in a coach by night, all alone in a forest full of murderers and Horackers. Your face, you see, shall be a comfort to me all the way. Now please hurry. Fricke shall drive us. Linchen, you go along now with Herr Doctor Neubauer and make sure they don't foist off on him that green rattletrap with the yellow wheels."

Chapter 14

"Lord Almighty, are all my worst forebodings to come true?! Here they come lumbering up with it all the same!" cried the vice-principal's wife, as, despite the voice she had raised in warning, the "yellow-green coach" came tottering around the corner with a hollow rumble. "Didn't I suspect it? But that vehicle of abominations certainly does fit in with the rest of this affair and expedition."

"The postmaster offers his sincerest apologies, Frau Eckerbusch, but it was the last coach we had in the yard," Fricke called up to the window from his coach box. "But I'll give my personal guarantee it's been well greased, and I beat out the cushions yesterday, too, and had them in the sun. Not a trace of moths now, nor the least chance of getting stuck to the seats, neither."

"We did all we could, Frau Eckerbusch," called Linchen, springing down from her seat next to Fricke, "the Herr Doctor and me did. But Prosecutor Wedekind is off with the brown coach, and one is at a wedding and another at a christening, and the one with the blue cushions is at the saddler's. Herr Doctor Neubauer is sitting inside."

Herr Doctor Neubauer was indeed seated inside and now stuck a rather doleful face out the window of the yellow-green coach.

"The driver says we shall hardly arrive in Gansewinckel before dark, ladies."

"As far as I'm concerned it can be black as pitch," the old woman growled down from her window. "That four-wheeled monster will be the death of me, not to speak of the shame of having to bump our way through the streets inside it. Oh, Eckerbusch! Eckerbusch! And you, miss, you see that you take good care of the house for me. We shall be down to you in five minutes, Dr. Neubauer. Take one of my shawls, Hedwig. We cannot possibly drive by your place in that coach—it's a scandal to the whole town and the countryside too."

"I only want to get to my husband as quickly as I can," sobbed Frau Windwebel.

"And so do I!" said Frau Ida with some energy. And in ten minutes they, too, were actually inside the yellow-green coach, with Assistant Master Neubauer seated, obedient and sulky, across from them. And closing the door, off they drove, right after Frau Eckerbusch had inquired, "Why didn't you at least take down the top, Fricke? Are we supposed to suffocate, too, on such a perfectly fine evening?"

"Just try and take it off," Fricke had replied. "Just you try sometime to make this turn-out do something against its will. Everything about the critter bucks and kicks like it was alive. Not the first trace of tractability, Frau Eckerbusch. When it gets on in years, a contraption like this has its mind bent on retirement same as you and me. Well, the wheels is in pretty good shape, thank God, and with His help—well, gee—gee-up, gee-up—and we're on our way!"

They were on their way. And half the town joined in the departure, though this time without the comments and jokes that usually accompanied the notorious old yellow-green coach out the town gate. Popular emotion had been moved too far in another direction, and the fact that these two ladies were setting out into the evening air had raised the level of excitement considerably. As we know, Horacker had more than once already given a strange churn to the feelings of both town and country, but indeed never before one like this.

Everyone—friend and enemy alike—was at the windows and doors or in the street as the yellow-green coach lumbered by.

People had already begun to sing the immoderate praises of the murdered gentlemen. We need, however, repeat only what a very astonished Herr Ühleke had to say.

"Lord, Lord, just listen to that," he said. "I mean, I knew Vice-Principal Eckerbusch myself and have always held him in high regard, but considering what people generally thought and said of him, and considering what fun they made of him, I never knew till today what a credit to the town, what a fine and learned man he was! It would certainly have pleased him could he hear how well he is spoken of now all over town and how sorry we all are. And if the world has that sort of thing to say afterwards, why then it may have its joke and amusements right along! . . . Just listen to that! . . . And I feel so sorry for Frau Eckerbusch, too, and then there's that poor young woman.—The drawing-master was, I'll grant, somewhat new here. But it's a comfort that they have the new assistant master, Dr. Neubauer, there with them in that old green-and-yellow terror of the roads. Has a keen mind, they say, and will know how to comfort her by the book. Just look at all the pupils from the gymnasium that are still in town during vacation, how they're running after that old rattletrap and would love to hop up on it if they only could. All because he made himself so well liked among them. Well, it's the last straw! If this doesn't bring down this Horacker, then he can just walk up bold as brass and knock the Superintendent General[87] over the head on his way to church next Sunday! Till the end of my days, I'll see that poor little lady shaking and trembling. And it's a comfort to me as well to know that she is the reason the new assistant master, who's so clever and highly praised, is sitting there in the coach, too."

We leave the town now, and Ühleke, to follow the "shay," as Fricke called the thing—in addition to all its other names. The critter, the rattletrap, the terror of the road, the yellow-green scandal rolled smoothly enough along the firm highway, in the wake of the dust cloud raised by the public prosecutor. The clock struck a quarter till eight; the sun hovered on the horizon still, but not for long. The evening was splendid, though Assistant Master Dr. Neubauer could not bring himself to make a remark to that effect. He initiated no travel conversation whatever. The situation he had so suddenly and unexpectedly got himself into did not suit him in the least. It takes a great deal of human misery to touch the feelings of an ironist who thinks he looks ridiculous.

And the Herr Doctor thought he cut an uncommonly absurd figure. Without the least bite of conscience, he could have throttled both these females. He had friends in several capital cities of Germany, and like himself they had all liberated themselves from the trivialities of the workaday world. To his chagrin, he saw them all laughing at him. With a shudder he coughed daintily into his fine white handkerchief, having glanced yet again into the clever, but far from aristocratic face of Frau Eckerbusch.

Could I not have pretended as if she were calling someone else? he thought—just as you, for example, dear neighbors (male and female alike), have thought when you likewise all too readily responded to some friendly request for help, only to regret having done so.

"From today on, I shall not listen to anything or anyone in this awful hole of a town. More than that! I hereby swear never again to open my mouth to—"

"Shall I tell you, Neubauer, what you're thinking at the moment?" asked Frau Eckerbusch quite unexpectedly.

"Me? . . . You?" stuttered that gentleman, who had been so rudely interrupted in the midst of his listing of good intentions. "I—with greatest interest, I would be—"

"Good! But if afterwards you tell me, 'Eckerbusch, you're wrong,' you'll merely be telling a lie. You are quite simply pondering how it came that you—you, such a clever young man who stands above all such things and who came to us purely by accident—how you got involved in this affair! . . . How did I deduce that? you ask. Well, I shall tell you. I've brought you along for precisely those reasons. And had I had the choice, I would have picked no one else but you. And now you had best put the best face on it! You'll not escape paying me your dues today, for both the comedy and the tragedy."

"My good woman—"

"Oh, my good man, the Ministry of Education shall not have sent you to us all in vain. That is, after all, what people are here on earth for, to learn something from one another. And since modesty becomes a lady, let me tell you quite candidly that till now I have in fact never known a person like you, but that I count it a true joy to get to know you better at every opportunity. Whatever my old husband and I have to offer you in return has long since been at your disposal. And that you have already made some very jolly use of it, too, is something you perhaps know best yourself."

Herr Doctor Neubauer, as an elegant philologist, had hobnobbed with the very finest people in Berlin, Heidelberg, Karlsruhe and Munich. Privy councilors, and not just honorary ones, had called him "dear friend," and the wives of such genuine privy councilors had addressed him as "dear Doctor," and countesses had referred to him as "our interesting young scholar." And now this dreadful person, the wife of Vice-Principal Eckerbusch, called him "my good man," and at the moment he had not a single weapon to use against the ghastly old lady. There he sat in the sultry closeness of the coach, his shoulders hunched and bent over, leafing page by page through his book of life's experience searching in feverish haste for something that might make an impression on this absurd person.

But this time, here in the yellow-green coach on the road to Gansewinckel, the proceleusmatica proved a match for every one of his privy councilors, for his countesses, for his bankers' wives both Christian and Jew. This frightful old woman would have flustered Juvenal[88] or even M. Henri Heine[89]—not to mention the latest fashionable satirists! Herr Eckerbusch's imitation of a tomcat caught in a door was nothing compared to the rendering his wife knew how to create by trapping her victim, the assistant master, across from her knee to knee and putting him on display.

Ooph, what a journey! And this old spider, this Canidia,[90] this concoctress of poisons, appeared in fact to have been looking forward to this, preparing it for months! And having once begun to share her opinions, she did not cease doing so for some considerable time.

"Did I not tell you from the start what a rhapsodist, in the classical sense, I got when I got her? She knows what improvisation is, does she not, good colleague? I boldly call that talent, a talent that should be heard out in the marketplace and not just in a coach, don't you agree? It pours out and inundates even the Epos of '66, does it not, Neubauer?"—Which is how old Eckerbusch would have chortled and rubbed his hands had he been there. Herr Doctor Neubauer, who was there, was at the moment incapable of uttering a word, other than one left within the depths of his heart: "I'd give that drunken fellow up on the box an extra thaler if he would topple us all into the ditch!"

He expressed this inmost wish or resolve, of course, only at the moment when Frau Ida turned away from him for the first time to address her poor little companion crouched anxiously in a corner.

"And now, my dear, how are you feeling?"

"Oh, fine, fine! If only we were there already."

"Fine? Fine? To be sure, you certainly do look it! . . . And now, Neubauer, I ask you once again, do you still not feel a twinge of conscience? Are you still not sorry that you gave the final shove that sent this poor, dear, foolish child here—who by rights should now be lying on her sofa all comfortable and quiet—that sent her, I say, tormented out into the night, into the wilderness, and into such stupidity? Did you really have no mother? Did you truly just plop down full-grown out of the moon and into philology, into the art of poetical hexameters, and into our new North German Confederation?"

Assistant Master Neubauer felt nothing, except a violent lurch of the yellow-green coach and the even more violent wish to be allowed to give Frau Ida Eckerbusch, the wife of his colleague the vice-principal, a slap.

"I beg you, for goodness' sake, tell me what I have—"

"Nothing, that's what you did! You chose to do nothing with your authority, your remarkable authority, to tip the scales in favor of my reasonable position. As usual, you wished to have your little joke with us, and as a result here I sit now with you and with this little creature in the midst of the aforementioned stupidity, and here we are at the forest now and darkness is coming on! Oh, just you wait, my good man, that bump was nothing! The journey has only just begun. Oh, I shall see to it that you remember this pleasant excursion to Gansewinckel with Frau Eckerbusch, Herr Doctor!"

They had indeed reached the forest and the road had not held to the promise of its beginnings, meaning that it had most certainly not got any better. It appeared to take on an increasing resemblance to the path of vice, which according to the song likewise begins as a "broad, fine way through meadows," but proceeds then to bring one into all sorts of difficulties and in the end to run out "in gloom and shadows."[91]

Tenderly and solicitously the old woman now laid her arm around the young thing entrusted to her care.

"There, there, my child! Fricke knows me, he knows whom he's driving. And fortunately he also knows whom he'll have to deal with at all events. Hello, Fricke!"

With these last words she had leaned out of the coach window, while Fricke bent back down from his box to her.

"Something wrong, Frau Eckerbusch?"

"We're in the woods now, old man, and here's where the highway department should be most contritely ashamed of its roads. But tell me, Fricke, what's that squeak I hear below and behind me?"

"Nothing to worry about, Frau Eckerbusch! Those squeakings ain't coming from you but from the coach. I noticed it from up here a good while ago myself. It's only that cursed rear left wheel. But we had the wheelwright rerim that blessed cracked spoke nice and tight. The road still runs right smooth through here, but once we get to the cross put up for Forester Rauhwedder, I'd be obliged to you, Frau Eckerbusch, if you and the other lady and gentleman was to hang on a bit tighter to your seats. There's a gully there along the left side of the mountain that can often play the tolerable devil."

"It would have to be the worst sort of emergency before a body would ask you for any solace," grumbled the old woman, pulling her head back in, but not without a repeated warning to drive slowly and some other words of caution.

"You can rest ever so easy, Frau Eckerbusch," Fricke called after her. "As an experienced driver I know the spot well enough! If worst comes to worst, I'll pull nice and easy up against the mountain on the left. Can't say I'd be fond of going off on the right head over heels down the gorge neither."

Now at that time, the cross erected in honor of Forester Rauhwedder was an ominous sign along the road, and on this trip it seemed to be an outright sinister one.

About fifteen years previously, Forester Rauhwedder had been shot from his horse by a poacher. At the spot where the murdered man's body had been found, the tall black memorial still stretched its eerie arms out from the underbrush that had since reclaimed the area once cleared around it. But it was just this quasi hide-and-seek aspect that made the object seem more terrible still. No one from the region ever came by without his glance moving involuntarily to one side in search of the cross in the woods; and as soon as he had found it, he would look straight ahead and try to think of something other than of that gruesome deed of long ago.

"That's all I need, to have that standing there beside the road!" sighed Frau Ida Eckerbusch softly. "As far as I'm concerned, it doesn't bother me in the least, despite nightfall and a hundred Horackers. For all I care, I could drive with an easy conscience through any old forest full of homicidal crosses, even through those piratical Neapolitan mountains, the ones with the name like the sniffles—Abruzzi, that's it. But this little thing here, with this absurd Horacker in her heart, I do wish I had her well past it. Well, let's hope a timely diversionary maneuver will take care of it!"

"Fricke!" Herr Assistant Master Neubauer shouted at exactly the same moment, leaning out of the window on his side of the coach.

"What can I do for you, Herr Doctor?"

"As soon as we get to the site of the murder, I mean to the monument erected in honor of the huntsman who was shot down, would you be so kind as to halt for a moment—"

With a low moan of distress the younger woman looked toward her older friend and grabbed hold of her arm.

"Just by way of precaution, I should like to climb out and walk alongside the coach. It may well be, ladies, that I can lend a more practical hand should it become necessary to direct this vehicle, which certainly is emitting stranger and stranger tones, to the left or right. Did you understand, driver?"

"Yes, sir, Herr Doctor! Very good, Herr Doctor!" Fricke called back to him from his box. Frau Eckerbusch, however, who had sat there struck dumb with anger and indignation for a moment and a half, now reclaimed the gift of speech with redoubled energy.

"We are stopping nowhere! No one is getting out! Do you hear me, Fricke? Do you understand? Do you—understand—me?" she shouted out her window. "You are to drive straight on and not stop before we get to the parsonage in Gansewinckel. Have you understood me, Fricke? I ordered this coach and the Herr Doctor is to stay in the seat assigned him, whether this rattletrap squeaks fore or aft, whether it falls apart fore or aft."

"Very good, Frau Eckerbusch," rasped Fricke in reply, and the assistant master did indeed stay in his seat, but with a look such as Pallas Athena bestowed only upon the dumbest of her and his pupils at moments of their most extreme perplexity and cranial vacuity.

"But my good woman—"

"Yes, indeed, my good man, the whole world has always known me till now to be an exceptionally calm, even phlegmatic woman, and my husband picked out his vexatious nickname for me for precisely that reason. But the Father in heaven would lose his patience at this, I declare. Just because this child here is almost perishing in my arms for foolish fear, it naturally seems to you to be an increasingly favorable opportunity for practicing your shameless jokes on us. What you'd most love is to drag Rauhwedder's cross right into the coach with us, correct? Well, just bring it on! But I'll tell you this much all the same, Doctor Neubauer: though goodness and mercy may have an end, it is still a long way from there to humor, and if this is supposed to be your idea of humor, then you should know that, sad to say, all too many people have humor like that up their sleeves. Heaven knows you needn't flatter yourself that you've been blessed with a patented talent for it. Have you understood me, good doctor?"

Now that was a question! The good doctor, who, of course, under normal circumstances held whistling to be a terribly common practice, whistled the first best melody that popped between his lips. He sought once more in vain for an answer, for words sufficient to preserve or, still more, restore his dignity and self-esteem. Frau Eckerbusch, however, devoted the next quarter hour exclusively to her companion.

"Don't worry about that silly cross, my dear," she whispered. "And still less about that dry-as-dust and shameless fellow there on the rear seat. Forester Rauhwedder, bless his soul, hasn't the least to do with our husbands, though we'll see to it that those scamps are duly rewarded with crosses of their own to bear in an hour or so. But it was the goddess of revenge herself who put Neubauer in this yellow-green coach with us. I have waited a long time for an opportunity to have him directly across from me like this. And now, if on my account, he's waiting with redoubled scorn for my husband to be pensioned off—why, it's all the same to me! Just let him take over my husband's chair! Just let him deal with Vice-Principal Eckerbusch however he pleases. But he's not done dealing yet with old lady Eckerbusch, not by a long way! They are always carrying on about how the battle of Königgrätz[92] last year was won by Germany's schoolmasters. But now I ask you, Hedwig, which ones? The old ones or the new? As far as I know, by the old ones and no one else! . . . It still remains to be proven what sort of a generation of heroes the new ones are going to produce with their

'Rush, rush, rush;
Tar them all with just one brush.'[93]

It's all the same to my husband and me. *We*, thank God, have a sense of humor that lets us enjoy most everything. But I pity these poor lads now who'll not be able to rid themselves of a drillmaster in one form or another their whole lives long, from the cradle, on through school, and finally to a cold, numbered grave. Oh, I know well enough that they call my old Werner the Last of the Learned Mohicans, and I know that he's the last vice-principal as well. But, thirdly, I know that even as a fifth-former he would have joined the procession up the Wartburg[94] if he had been able to come up with the money for the post coach and the other expenses of the trip and if they had let him march up with them, and I know that it perhaps took a clearer mind, deeper thought and more heart to do that than it takes nowadays to march in step row on row with a hundred thousand others."

"I only want to have my dear, dear Victor back again alive and well! I can only think of my Victor and of Horacker," moaned Frau Hedwig Windwebel; whereupon Frau Ida turned abruptly to the assistant master with a most unexpected, calm, and cheerful question.

"What are you sitting there so mum for, dear Neubauer? After all, you have your good Horacker alive and close at hand, and *you* need not worry yourself about anyone else."

Now this stream of words, this strangely irenic digression, had been poured out in purest proceleusmatica. But despite its whispered tone, the doctor had been able to scan the meter of a good portion of it on his fingers, quite possibly not to the prosodic detriment of the Epos of '66.

It was miraculous how much the assistant master's answer, both in tone and expression, resembled that of one of the boys in his classroom upon suffering a total moral defeat. And it was miraculous as well that in answering he did not first rub the back of his hand across his eyes and then wipe it under his nose.

"Up to now, my dear lady, you have steered this conversation in the most admirable fashion," he mumbled. "All I could do was listen—listen—and listen some more. Who knows so well as you how to join pleasantries with didactics? Were not the air in this coach so unspeakably sultry, I'm sure I should later recall this droll journey as one of the most amusing experiences of my life. But recall it, I most assuredly shall."

"I would hope so," said Frau Eckerbusch, and in his innermost heart the assistant master was moved by the notion of allowing himself the pleasure of wringing the nasty old witch's neck right there on the spot.

"And she calls herself phlegmatic!" he muttered. "And what shall I call myself now after this?"

Thus they passed by Rauhwedder's cross without accident or injury. The hunched-up assistant master cast it only a glance, but Frau Ida at once sat up very erect and stated, "Don't trouble yourself, Herr Doctor—we have eyes in our heads, too."

Dusk grew ever deeper; the evening breeze, though warm and gentle, began to rustle in the forest; owls and bats took flight, seeking out their hunting grounds. And up on his coach box, Fricke said, "I really do wonder which of the folks down below this evening will give me the handsomest tip. Well, the entertainment and the catfighting on the way have been right lively and pretty, specially from Frau Eckerbusch. But the mill finally seems now to have stopped turning. It's grown wondrous quiet and peaceful inside, and all I can say is, if it wasn't for the little teary wife there, I'd sure love to call down from my seat here and turn the talk to Horacker. But I know the vice-principal far as that goes. That'll be some joke when I drive up with this whole household of his and him not suspecting none of it. I wouldn't have missed driving this party tonight, not for the handsomest tip! Well, by God's grace we'll be at Pastor Winckler's in Gansewinckel in a quarter of an hour. And the best thing is that, with or without Horacker, that's a right proper and respectable house, that is, where they don't leave you sitting high and dry out front, but are reasonable folks and know the decent thing to do and that it ain't decent to sit there in the parlor thinking of no one's pleasure but their own. An honest old coachman always does his part to get folks over-land to their happy reunions, does the most important part in fact. And all that kissing afterwards and the "dear" here and "dearie" there, and the "so you're finally here," why, they can take care of all that and still see to it that they send the maid out with a tray for the coach box, with something warm in winter and on an evening like this with whatever happens to be handy. And no thanks to him what don't like it."

If we wished to chronicle every bump and thump that our trio in the yellow-green coach still had to withstand, both in body and mind, for the continuation of the journey—i.e., for the last sixth of their adventurous expedition—we would most certainly not ar-rive to join the merry party at Gansewinckel before midnight. And we do feel more and more pressed to get to the place. Whether the calendar registered moonlight, we cannot say. But both heavens and earth had veiled themselves in the most charming summer-night dusk, though, to be sure, this made neither the forest nor the road any brighter. Besides which, the road ran steeply down-hill several times, and each time it curved around a sharp outcrop-ping of the forest. And like the wilderness around it, the "vile vehicle" emitted ever more sinister tones, until among these latter there was uttered such a terrifying "crack!" that Herr Assistant Master Dr. Neubauer himself cried out, "Oh, sweet Jesus!" and Frau Hedwig Windwebel screamed aloud, while Frau Ida Ecker-busch said, "Too much is too much! I shall soon be at a point where I shall take great pleasure in personally holding the ladder when they hang that rogue Horacker on the gallows for his crimes!"

"Gansewinckel, ladies and gentlemen!" called out Fricke from his seat. The doctor stuck his head out the right window, his colleague's wife hers out the left one, and they both spotted a light flickering up ahead through the trees.

"Oh, my Victor!" murmured the young wife.

"Well, Eckerbusch—Eckerbusch!" growled the old woman.

Doctor Neubauer sneezed, something many people do whenever they feel a great easing of the mind.

Chapter 15

A real storyteller is quite another sort of potentate than that erstwhile braggadocio, the King of Spain, with his paltry: "The sun never sinks within this realm of mine!"[95]

That the real sun, the genuine planetary sun dare not sink entirely from this realm of ours goes without saying. And as for the other one—well, we can let the other one rise or sink just as we please.

At this moment, though sinking fast, it is still shining down on Gansewinckel and on the black velvet cap of our current Patriarch of the Two Indies,[96] which is to say, on the head of Pastor Krischan Winckler of Gansewinckel. Not half a minute has elapsed since he returned from the house and informed the group gathered under the bowery, "The child's still sleeping, but very uneasily."

"When I looked in before, she lay quiet," Frau Billa had remarked; and we—we shall follow the lovely fiery red rays that both our suns are sending into a low window of Gansewinckel parsonage, a window located just beneath the gutter along the roof.

There lies the child who had lain there so quietly earlier and a moment later lay so very uneasily. At the moment as we approach, she is lying still again, but with her eyes open—on one side, her hands folded before her, absolutely motionless. She is looking at something, but at what? Who is so wise that he can explain this dreadful gravity in the eyes of animals, of children, of the common people, this terrible gravity that in the ordinary course of things only truly surprises us and gives us great pause when we encounter it in the eyes of some unfortunate man or woman from our own social class?

Lottchen Achterhang stared out before her into the lovely rays that had glided to her from a sea shimmering in the setting sun, across forest and fields, village rooftops, trees in the parsonage garden, and into her little room. Fragments of images from real events that had truly happened, and then of things that she had only dreamed, thronged inside her poor head. And the wilder this dance of visions grew, the less it seemed possible to her that she would ever again take joy in her work, be industrious, quick, prompt, busy with hands and feet, ever again lie happily down to rest as she once had, so long, long ago.

Yes, so long ago! How distant it all seemed, that world she had known before she set out on that terrible journey across such vast, vast lands full of strange people, from the other side of Berlin all the way back to here—to Gansewinckel, to this little room that once, oh, ages and ages ago, had been the domain granted to her.

Now she felt her feet began to ache, though they had stood up so well along all those endless dreadful country roads. But the sun had been almost too kind to her the whole way—making the nights just that much colder, of course, despite its being summer, and darker, too, despite the stars.

What had that old man said who had suddenly sat bolt upright in the straw inside that old tumbledown brick cottage?

"In a hoarse voice he called me 'Comrade!' right there in the gray and frosty light of morning. Maybe he really had meant no harm with his hoarse voice, maybe he had miseries of his own, but I ran something awful anyway down that narrow path through the wet fields of grain . . .

"That was the path where that hamster stood up on its hind legs and chattered and looked like he was going to jump right *at* me . . .

"Those are nasty beasts when they're angry, Cord always said, but then he knew all about all kinds of critters; that was the only thing the village ever gave him credit for . . .

"Then I screamed and ran right across the field and trampled down the grain—may the good Lord forgive me the sin! And the fog was so thick. So that the hot sun was a real comfort when it came out again at last . . .

"And now my name's in all the newspapers, too! I'm sure it is!

Pastor Nöleke must have put it in all the papers! Oh, Cord, Cord—at least now, thank God, they'll search for both of us together all over the world along with the other black sheep! . . . Dearest Cord!"

"So then, thus far and no farther, you monster?!"[97] cried Drawing-Master Victor Windwebel at the very same moment of the day, as he stood beneath the last trees at forest's edge and propped himself with both hands holding tight to the handle of his walking stick. "It once again becomes quite clear to me what a wretched thing it is to get to know another person all too well! If that were not the case, I would certainly think that you, my lord, still deserve a thrashing. Well, Mother Horacker, what do you say? Shall we take his chaste bashfulness into account or do we drag him on in in spite of it?"

The gray and ragged old woman, who with her last bit of strength was propping up the wobbly brigand on the other side, gazed at the drawing-master with a woefully pleading expression and said, "Oh, kind sir, you are laughing at us, it's true, but only because in your heart you're weeping for us. On my deathbed I'll not forget you and all your kindness. What trouble you have had with my boy—and with me in the bargain all the way here from Mäuseberg's Brake! Who else in the whole wide world would have asked so little in return for lending a helping hand to such a dirty, filthy fellow, to such a wretch like him, and with nary a sign of disgust? But then, when things go bad for you and your spirits are low, why, remember me. Yes, dear, dear sir, when there's neither king nor kaiser to turn to, just remember Widow Horacker! . . . And now, kind sir, show us one last bit of mercy, leave us sitting here, me and my Cord, and you go those few steps into the village alone and advise the pastor that *we are here*!"

Herr Windwebel sneezed, something people do now and then out of embarrassment but without the least sense of easing the mind. It was not to be denied, moreover, that he had had his hands full with his friend Horacker all the way from Mäuseberg's Brake. And without the widow even the repeated threats of calling in Böxendal would not have sufficed to bring the rascal along. But they had found the old woman still on her tree stump, and in the end she had proved the best helpmate the drawing-master could have met on his way to Gansewinckel with the highwayman. The old woman contributed tears of encouragement in great abundance, while immediately moving in to lend a supporting hand on the other side.

"If I had captured it all life-sized in oils, the three of us stumbling along that day arm in arm, you would be the wife of one of Germany's most famous men, Hedwig!" the drawing-master had often said afterwards as he paged through his sketchbook with a sigh.

He said it, however, apparently only so that he could once again hear the reply: "I like you just as you are, Victorchen."

Stumbling, falling, rising again, they had arrived, as we now know, at the edge of the forest, and the drawing-master had not once found time to concern himself with local color or the various other hues of the landscape. But at his first glimpse of the light of the open fields shining in through the trees, an involuntary cry escaped him, "God, what a refreshing sight!"

What then was said, we have already reported. The brigand captain lay stretched out once again with his nose buried in the earth, the Widow Horacker crouched beside him while keeping a steady hold on one corner of his jacket. And Drawing-Master Windwebel declared himself—after he had eased himself with that sneeze—willing to go on ahead and inform the Reverend Christian Winckler that, as Widow Horacker had put it, "we are here." . . .

Excited, but striding slowly and peering constantly back over his shoulder at the pair he had left behind, Windwebel descended from the forest's edge toward the village and the narrow path that led to the gate in the hedge of the parsonage garden. But the further he left the forest behind, the more his feet took wings. He had already demanded much of his long legs that afternoon, and now they demanded something of him in return, for they began to fly off without him; and only much later did he remark to himself, "If only I knew why I ran so fast at that point."

His long legs did indeed run away with him, just as his much longer shadow hurried on ahead of him.

"Here he comes! And just as I suspected—*solus*![98] And as if the devil were after him!" Vice-Principal Eckerbusch cried suddenly, springing up from the bowered bench. And they all sprang up after him, sticking their heads over the hedge in tiptoed nervous expectation.

"He's stumbling! . . . He's down! . . . No, thank God! . . . There he is!"

The pastor of Gansewinckel had flung the garden gate open as wide as possible, almost tearing it off its hinges. With a final bound, six paces long, the new arrival leaped through it, waving his hat.

"Hurrah!!!"

"What? . . . Hurrah? . . ." asked those assembled.

"Hurrah!" repeated Windwebel, and then they all fell on him, grabbing at him here and there, tugging him here and there, while each shouted, "Let him be! Let him catch his breath at least!"

He was bullied most voraciously, if not to say viciously, by old Eckerbusch, of course, who had at once shoved both thumbs into the top buttonholes of both lapels, sinking his claws in, as if never again to release him—or so it appeared. And when all the others had at last let go of him, he still sawed away at him, rocking him back and forth, trying to shove him into a present pregnant with great events.

"Do you really have him, my friend?"

"I do!"

"Ah!" said the Gansewinckel parsonage.

"Where do you have him?" puffed Vice-Principal Eckerbusch.

And Frau Billa, pushing in very close again and taking her guest by his lapel, cried, "Yes, that's what I should like to know, too. But stop shaking him so, Eckerbusch! . . . And you, Windwebel, you can stop leaving us dangling! Where do you have him, if, as you say, you have him?"

Gasping for air, the drawing-master pointed with one thumb over his shoulder toward the forest, and all eyes followed in the same direction.

"Ah!" said the assembled company for the second time, but now with such a droll mixture of sundry feelings and sentiments that here, more than at any other point in our story, we regret that every single reader was not personally present.

"And that's the reason you're shouting like this?" groaned Frau Billa Winckler.

"Hm, hm," murmured the *pastor loci*,[99] shifting his cap. Then, having pondered for a moment, he added with a smile, "Yes, yes, to be sure. That's where we've had him for a good three weeks now."

"No, you don't say!" said Neddermeier, the parish chairman. "Now isn't that just like a gentleman from town! But our schoolmaster, Böxendal, already made that joke, Herr Windwebel."

For his part, Vice-Principal Eckerbusch gave his colleague one last shove that almost landed him in the hedge, then let loose of his coat collar with a final, grim jerk and sat down—not uttering a word.

"I beg you most earnestly for some moistening drop. It is absolutely impossible for me to enter into any details until then. Running after him was nothing, my friend, but dragging him here— let me tell you, ladies and gentlemen, that presented difficulties," said Victor Windwebel, with all the dignity of the unappreciated genius who has accomplished great things. "You just drag, shove, heave, haul, pull, and tug him for me sometime, if you please, all the way from Mäuseberg's Brake to the edge of the forest primeval. Had it not been for the widow's assistance, there would hardly be anything left of me right now."

Chapter 16

Our good Windwebel had, you see, erred mightily in the effect he expected from these last words. If he had mutely shown his parched tongue before uttering another word, then at least Frau Billa Winckler would have had some small interest left to devote to his needs. But now he had thoroughly diverted all friendly and hospitable concern from himself and directed it toward another. They all fell on him anew, but most certainly with none of the refreshment that table, house, and cellar might have offered. It was most assuredly not for his own sake that they fell on him yet a second time, and at a very considerably heightened level of excitement.

"Where? What? How? . . . No, you don't say! . . . Can it be! . . . Windwebel, you're not pulling our leg? . . . You're certain that you've not had too much heat or seen some forest spook?"

"Yes, go ahead and shake me. Whatever falls off is yours to do with as you like," laughed the drawing-master. "Stand me on my head if you want. The fact itself remains irrefutably upright. I'm your fellow! I'm the one who has brought him in! He is sitting there at the edge of the forest with his mama. And now—will you finally give me the chance to speak to you all intelligently."

"Speak! Speak, Windwebel!" cried the pastor, his wife, and Vice-Principal Eckerbusch as if with one voice.

The chairman said for the third time, "No, you don't say!"

Drawing-Master Windwebel, however, wiped the sweat from his brow once more, and glancing with delight from one to the other, he did indeed give a brief speech, directing the greater part thereof, strangely enough, to the chairman.

113

"Dear Neddermeier," he said, "when my dear departed father was angry with people, or worse still, with one single person, it was his custom to curse dreadfully. No word was too exalted or too debased, too good or too bad, to serve as a vehicle for him to vent his fury. Oh, could the old man ever deal out insults. All Gansewinckel would come creeping to him with their heads tucked between their shoulders! And nevertheless, I ask you, Herr Chairman, how did he curse? Very simple: 'Here *we* are, good-for-nothings on the roster again?! Here *we* are, the whole damned bunch! Here *we* are, unmitigated scoundrels! Here *we* are, fatuous fools!' That was the beautiful thing about it, he never excluded himself—never excluded himself but always wanted to be added to the roster. Now I am my father's son, Herr Neddermeier. But I have just struck the name of that cruel captain of brigands, Horacker, from the roster and have come out of the forest with him. And *we* (including the Widow Horacker) have taken counsel on the matter, and *we* have come to the conclusion that it would be best for *us* and for everyone if above all no alarm were to be raised in the village, if the vestry and all the fine, brave lads were not to trouble themselves to go up into the woods on *our* account—in brief, if you would take us, just as *we* have offered ourselves so completely of our own accord: that is, very quietly."

"Without any scandal," growled Vice-Principal Eckerbusch. "But proceed, my friend. Once again I'm getting to know you from yet another side."

"Without any scandal."

"Dear Windwebel, before you say anything more, might I really not offer you some refreshment first?" asked the wife of the *pastor loci* with truly maternal tenderness.

"Please do! So then—without any scandal, as a poor wretched sinner, Herr Neddermeier. At this moment, in this affair you are the most important man in the North German Confederation, and it lies with you to do the proper thing and land this fish, and you'll do that best by keeping Gansewinckel entirely off our backs and by laying your hat down beside you and sitting there stuck as fast as possible to your chair. He has requested that the pastor come alone to fetch him. If the rest of the village comes along, he'll be off and gone again, taking hook, line, and sinker with him.

Whoever wants to watch him swim in the pond afterwards, may do so. For my part, I shall take my bait and go home."

"May I ask you, Billa, to fetch me my hat and walking stick!" said the pastor of Gansewinckel.

"I'm already on my way, dear!" cried his wife, who was indeed already on her way.

Neddermeier grumbled, "I'm sitting here quite comfortable, if I've heard and understood you rightly. If I can have something delivered to me, then I'm sure I'll not go and fetch it for myself, Herr Art-Instructor."

Vice-Principal Eckerbusch cleaned his spectacles and paced up and down between the rows of bushes lining the nearest garden path. He was ruminating. Now if we consult a Latin dictionary, we find the following: *rumen* the gullet—*ruminare* to chew the cud, to think over, to ponder, to consider carefully. He was ruminating audibly. Until with a sudden start, he put his spectacles back on, planted himself firmly with legs apart in front of his hiking partner, took hold of him by the lapels once more and said emphatically, "My friend and colleague, I must offer my renewed congratulations to the faculty on the acquisition they have made in you!"

And with chin, nose, and bespectacled eyes directed heavenward to express to vespertine Zeus his general sàtisfaction, he added, "My, but he is a most curious fellow!"

Frau Billa left four cautious, sensible, deliberate men behind her in the bower. She, of course, had abandoned herself to the inspirations and emotions of the moment as she walked back to the house—and even more so as she entered it.

Her Christian had sent her in to collect his walking stick and hat; but she would certainly not have been a woman as the good Lord created them, had she confined herself simply to fetching the items she had been commissioned to bring.

She lost one slipper on the step at the threshold and did not take the time to bend down and slip it back on. There was time for everything, except for the great need she felt to indulge her emotions! Words—uproar—scandal, fire in the village! Oh, to be sure, there sat the upright parish chairman—there sat her stalwart neighbor Herr Neddermeier, and he was peaceable enough now among the other gentlemen there in the bower, was waiting, in fact, with exceptional imperturbability for the hat and walking stick of his pastor. Horacker? Why should he, Neddermeier, go to any trouble to cause an uproar in Gansewinckel?

"Horacker!" groaned the pastor's wife at the door to the house. At the door to the kitchen she simply shouted, "No one is to move from the spot. In fifteen minutes my husband will bring *him* in! It never rains but it pours!"

With that, she had already reached the stairs leading up to the second floor. In the next moment she was in her husband's study and had grabbed his hat from its nail, his walking stick from its corner.

Another, more ladderlike stairway led to the parsonage attic and garrets, and Frau Billa paused to consider for a moment, her hand on the shaky banister. But the temptation proved too great.

"If only she's still asleep!" whispered the good woman. "The best thing would be if the silly, foolish thing would sleep quietly right on through it all. Her squalling is all I need."

And she was already up the second stairway, opening the door to the chamber as quietly as possible. Cautiously she stuck her head in.

"Oh, good heavens!" she cried when she spotted Lottchen sitting upright on the bed and staring back at her with wide-open eyes. "Just as I thought! Wide awake as an owl when evening falls!"

And evening had indeed fallen. The purple ray of vibrant light had vanished from the little chamber, and Lottchen Achterhang had been sitting up on the edge of the bed for some time now. Our friend Wedekind and his companion had just rolled by the Forester Rauhwedder Memorial Cross; Frau Eckerbusch and company in the yellow-green coach were out of town now, having arrived at the forest's edge. And we are most anxious to be as precise as possible about times, just as we also would ask the reader to come to our aid by doing some calculations of his own while leafing back to previous pages.

When the prosecutor arrives in Gansewinckel, Krischan Winckler will then be just on his way back to the village from the edge of the forest, with Horacker and the widow. When Frau Ecker-

busch arrives with Herr Dr. Neubauer and Frau Windwebel, he—
the arm of the law—will have already collared him—the criminal.
And the story will, or so most people would say, be more or less
at an end.

"If I want my hat, gentlemen, I fear I shall have to fetch it
myself, otherwise I shall, it seems, have to wait a rather long time
for it," said the pastor of Gansewinckel.

Pastor Krischan Winckler was waiting for his hat, our readers
are waiting for the end of our tale, and whenever anyone stops to
look peacefully in on the confusion of this world and its life, the
scene about him always leaves the impression as if the world, too,
were waiting for something. But what is it waiting for? Why, of
course, merely for some absolutely necessary bit of reality—though
often a remarkably minor one that lies very close at hand—to walk
in the door or to drop from heaven. All that needs to take place,
to happen is this or this, this or that, and for all eternity one will
be very happy, will be prepared to be completely content with
oneself, with the world and all the traffic one has with it. For our
part, however, we have found that it always makes a powerful
impression to find a human being who is *not* waiting, or who even
merely leaves the impression that he is not waiting for anything.
We are usually quite taken aback by the eyes of the individual
who has achieved such peace. There is something in them that
impresses even the normal, the indifferent observer, forcing him
to declare his surprise.

"Gracious, child, why are you looking at me like that?" cried
Frau Billa Winckler.

It was difficult to find an answer for that question; but the rectoress was not expecting one anyway.

"It's pure craziness to stare at someone in that dumb way, child.
Did I let you have your sleep out so that like some silly goose you
could make a face at me as if this were Judgment Day? Courage,
girl—Lottchen! When you're on your feet again, come down to
the kitchen. A proper supper will do you more good than anything
else. And as far as that foolish lad Cord—that scamp, that Horacker—goes, he evidently got wind of your arrival in Gansewinckel right off. He's sitting up there at the edge of the forest,
playing coy for just a bit yet before he comes down here. There's

never been anything like this since old maid Schnelle called in my husband to console her when the doctor prescribed an enema for her. Child—he sent word that he wished the pastor personally to come and fetch him, and my husband is down there now in the bower waiting for his walking stick and his hat. In my opinion the stick alone would be sufficient. I would simply put it behind my back and bide my time beside the garden gate with the utmost patience, peace, and tranquility."

"Billa, what's keeping you?" the usually patient shepherd of souls shouted at the same moment in an exceptionally impatient voice.

"Here I am! . . . Just a moment!" the shepherdess shouted back, and pattered down the stairs again in great haste, without once looking back to see in what state she—despite all her kind intentions—had left her ward, still sitting there on the edge of the bed. Fortunately, Pastor Christian had no notion of it either, as he climbed the path through the fields just as fast as his years allowed him.

Those two eyes, that before had waited for nothing whatever, now closed completely for a considerable time.

Chapter 17

Now, more than at any other point, these idylls begin to resemble a truly fine book. The latter, namely, must be written in such a way that neither a handful of errata, nor a miserable binding, nor silly advertisements, nor stupid reviews can harm it. From out of all the chaos, absurdity, and stupidity of this world, from out of all the encompassing confusion of hate, envy, spite, and wrath, it emerges ever and again, joyous and free—so gaze, now, upon Gansewinckel lying there! Does it not still seem idyllic? Has it not remained an enchanting thing despite all that we have reported from and concerning it?

Is there a human passion that was not given full, wicked play as the afternoon progressed? Is there a shameful deed that was left unmentioned in the course of these sweet, smiling hours, or one that we have perhaps overlooked but which the men and women inhabiting this corner of the earth did not think themselves incapable of?

Have we not heard of rape, pillage, and murder? Did not jealousy and the sorrows of love buzz loudly above the chirping of the birds? Have we not seen the green eye of malice shimmering through the green foliage, enjoying the woes of others? Did not the past itself put out its scrawny, dusty paws in the form of musty parchment to disturb the gentle air of summer, spreading vexation and enmity from house to house?

Was there not almost too much hunger and heartbreak to be borne on that long journey from "the other side of Berlin"? And, through it all, were not more verses of the Epos of '66 composed by none other than Assistant Master Dr. Neubauer?

119

Almost too much yeast has been added to the epic, tragical brew, too many human failings to these idylls, and still, still how idyllic! What a cloudless ether above the world's hubbub! And here and there the heart senses such a cool and peaceful breeze coming from a strangely different world, one free of errata, advertisements, and reviews!

"How do you construe the verbs of emotion and emotional expression: *gaudeo, delector, admiror, glorior, gratulor,* and *gratias ago,*[100] Windwebel?" asked the vice-principal "dreamily," and Windwebel replied with a laugh, "You have me there."

"*Sequens!*[101] Do you still recall, Winckler?"

And the pastor of Gansewinckel likewise answered with a smile, "With *quod,*[102] if I'm not mistaken, Eckerbusch."

"Or with the accusative *cum infinitivo.*[103] Friends, what a wonderful evening! Makes one want to melt into cheese and sugar, when one stops to consider that one sits down to correct exercise books, while all around lies a universe full of blunders and beauty! Out of my mind? No, merely extraordinarily moved and charmed! Of course you would blame that on your country air, Herr Chairman, though you know as well as I that the wise Seneca says in one of his epistles: '*Ideo peccamus, quia de partibus vitae omnes deliberamus, de tota nemo deliberat.*'"[104]

"I don't blame anything on anything, Herr Eckerbusch," said Neddermeier. "And as far as epistles go, I only know them from the schoolmaster, and from the pastor, the ones in and out of the New Testament. Ask me straight out in German if you want me to give an answer to your Latin there."

"And therefore we err because we all rack our brains about the details of life, but there is no one who concerns himself with the whole of it," said Vice-Principal Eckerbusch.

"Is that supposed to be a jab at me as chairman of the vestry in this village?" asked Neddermeier.

"Heaven forbid! The subtle Lucius Annaeus meant the phrase for me alone. Just look at how the pastor is laughing. Oh, he can laugh easily enough."

The sun had sunk behind the forest. But the sweet clarity of the summer evening was left hanging in the air for some time.

Prosecutor Wedekind and that poor little woman, Frau Hedwig

Windwebel, rolled on toward Gansewinckel. But Krischan Winckler at last was given both his hat and his walking stick, with the
following words:

"So! Now God go with you, dear. And don't keep us waiting
too long. It really is high time this comedy came to an end. I've
just hinted to Lottchen that you've taken matters in hand, Winckler."

These last words almost held the good man up for a while yet,
but after giving his wife a doubtful glance, then casting a second
glance at the little window beneath the roof, and without taking
any further farewells, he strode quickly out through the garden
gate and up the hill.

"I've never noticed so clearly in all my life before today how
barren and sorry many a patch of earth would look if weeds didn't
grow there, my friend," said the vice-principal, turning to the
drawing-master. "Green is green, no matter what! Just look at
how he is legging it up the path. I am firmly convinced that in all
of Gansewinckel there is no proper garden vegetable, no sober
fruit of the field that at this moment provides him with such melancholy pleasure as the useless stuff running rampant among his
cabbages and carrots. Satan sowed it there, you say, Neddermeier?
Try to tell him that! I'd stake my life he would offer you just the
opposite explanation and thank the good Lord for the pleasure it
gives him, and—by the immortal gods, so do I! And may Satan
himself simply sit here doing nothing! I'd prefer three days of detention! . . . Hallo, Winckler!"

He gave a shout, picked up his own hat and walking stick once
more, which fortunately he did not have to have brought to him,
and strode out after his gray-headed friend.

"Naturally!" said Frau Billa. "Don't anyone say it's not just
what I expected right along!"

Shall we, however, wait in the quiet bower now with her, the
chairman, and Drawing-Master Windwebel for the arrival of the
prosecutor, or shall we go with the pastor and Vice-Principal
Eckerbusch?

De tota vita deliberamus! We'll go with the vice-principal and
the pastor.

"Hallo, Winckler!" shouted the vice-principal. "On second

thought I'm against the separation of church and school in this instance, whatever my usual opinions in the matter may be. Here I am and I'm coming with you. And why not, really?"

"If Horacker raises no objection," said the pastor with a smile, waiting for his scurrying short-legged friend to catch up and then offering him an arm. "You know, dear friend, with what pleasure I accept your company along all of life's paths."

"And over the years we have wandered many of them arm in arm, Christian—you, it's true, generally as Mentor and I as Telemachus, but now and then vice versa, too. How would you have lasted so long in Gansewinckel without me, or I without you for so long in that cursed little town on the far side of the forest!"

"We have indeed stood by one another now and again in all sorts of trouble and adversity, Werner."

"And do you know what the finest part about it is, old fellow?"

"Well?" asked the pastor somewhat expectantly.

"That neither of us shows the tribulations he has suffered."

"Do you think so?" asked the pastor very doubtfully.

"I don't just think so, I know it for a certainty. As a matter of fact, there's hardly a week goes by without someone's announcing to me in the most flattering terms how he rejoices in both my lively exterior and interior. We have remained young. I assure you, Krischan, we have remained young, despite the transiency of all things—not excluding our wives!"

"And how much of this remarkable youthfulness, dear friend, do you think can be credited to our good wives?"

"Now just look there. I haven't once given that a thought!" said Herr Eckerbusch, coming to a full stop where he stood and pensively crossing his hands and holding them at his belly. "*Vivat* my proceleusmatica!"

"So you agree with me, dear friend?"

"But of course! Only yesterday I crept in before her and called her attention to what all may happen to her come the Last Judgment simply because she has been flesh of my flesh."

"For example?"

"For example, I said to her: 'Think of your death, Ida. Think of the fact that there is an Everlasting Justice. Have you ever once thought of what you will answer when on that day the Lord God asks you, "Well, Ida Eckerbusch, née Weniger, what use did you make of your good fortune in my giving you such a jolly fellow for a husband?" ' "

"And what did she answer you, Werner Eckerbusch?"

"Pah, the old woman!" groaned the vice-principal.

"Did she then retire to consider the question in private?"

"After she had slammed the door behind her? No, not this time. She grew very calm and brutal, held one finger up under my nose and replied: 'Just look at that, if you please, my boy!'—'Well?' I said.—'Yes, look,' she said and I had the impression that in leading her to the altar I had really led all three Parcae—Clotho, Lachesis, and Atropos.[105]—'Yes, look, Eckerbusch, just take a glance at how I have worked down this wedding ring *peu à peu* [106] over the years, just so that you could go running after your tomfoolishness with no one to disturb you, making clowns of both yourself and me.' "

"Splendid!" cried the pastor of Gansewinckel, coming to a halt himself now.

"Tit for tat at any rate. Oh, my yes, Christian, it's not been without due cause that we both have devoted ourselves to our hobbies—I to my meteorology and you to your Christian Fürchtegott Gellert. But at that moment I could not call on the weatherman in Haparanda for assistance, but he's an undependable sort anyway. Fortunately, however, my colleague Dr. Neubauer knocked at my door just then, and so I quickly called out 'Come in!' and helped myself out of my embarrassment by letting fly with every sort of aesthetic, sentimental, and literary porcelain possible, pelting the idealistic fellow's head till his ears hummed."

"And after he had taken his leave again, Werner?"

"I, of course, likewise took mine as quickly as possible and went to play skittles. To be frank, however, I did not play in prizewinning form, and more than one miss and gutter ball were tallied onto the score of that foolish female I'd left at home."

"And when you got home again?"

"Oh, I had all my pockets so full of town gossip and Horacker tales that there was no more talk about our private affairs."

Horacker tales! That name sent them on their way again toward the forest at a faster pace, one they kept up for some time amid a most thoughtful silence. Until Winckler suddenly spoke up.

"That will do in town, no doubt, but what would have become

of me here in Gansewinckel without my Billa? There are almost too many conditions attached to the bargain here for me ever to have a life of my own now and again. If I should have to begin to deal with every single vexation myself, I would be totally lost, even with Professor Gellert in my pocket. What good luck it is then, that one person splashes about with gusto quite in his element, where the other one would be out of breath at once! Without some tribulation to visit her, my good Billa can hold out for a week at best. In the second week she will without question appear with a cloth on her brow, suffering from a nervous headache. But that usually only lasts till Wednesday, since by then we normally have found what was lacking—and know that once more there's yet another battle here on earth for us to fight. The white cloth disappears and the banner of war waves until Saturday evening at least, when I write my sermon, by which time—up until now, thank God—the house has always grown quiet.—Oh yes, dear Eckerbusch, against our best intentions our important affairs are constantly bedeviled by unimportant, inconsequential ones. Just take for instance this confounded matter of quarter-money and felicitations! Here we are on our way to bring this pitiful Cord Horacker back to civilization. My whole heart is full of this strange human misery, and nevertheless—nevertheless, I cannot rid myself of the question of how in the world we shall deal with this other stupidity, how we shall disentangle ourselves from this new and absurdly wretched briar patch. Here we are on our way to resolve, as best our poor powers allow, one of the many great tragedies of this world, and all the while I live in pure terror at the thought that she is sitting again now in the bower across from Neddermeier. Ah, Werner, we wear peace no better than if it were a garment—"

"One that we mend in front while it rips in two up the back. I know your dressing gown well, Christianus! You sit in it till it is worn through and Billa patches it up every now and again. Yes indeed, it is a curious thing about peace in this earthly vale of tears. The cloth simply does not last. For my part I wear mine in the most cheerful, colorful patterns, but the padding doesn't show through just at the elbows, let me tell you. Yes, the padding! Images and metaphors come thronging in, and we had best break off here, Krischan, before we drag the education ministry and the consistory into the tailoring business. But as far as the current squabble with your pious congregation goes, you can always consider yourself lucky that you don't have to count me as a freeholder or cottager among your lambs. Would I ever make you cry out then, like Moses to the Lord because of the frogs.[107] That story fits my humor perfectly. And our friend Böxendal would likewise have to sing his New Year's song before an expert. I am completely on the side of the chairman and your farmers. Oh, you would definitely have to come to me; you would most certainly not pocket those parochial fees without first providing in return the spiritual and artistic services stipulated by the patriarchs, that I can assure you."

"Entirely unnecessary, Eckerbusch," said the rector of Gansewinckel, patting his companion on the shoulder. "I need no further assurances from you. I'm certain I should hear your voice loud enough in all that swampy chorus. You'd peep out at me there, very green and very big-mouthed, and I suppose Billa would have to write to Ida to get you to dunk under again. But here we are at the forest; let us drop this vexatious subject. Here comes the widow hobbling toward us. Oh, Werner, how could I ever begin to deal with this Horacker, if my wife, my Billa, had not brought up Lottchen to be such a respectable young girl?"

This was a serious, a risky question that the pastor of Gansewinckel had posed, but the vice-principal did not manage to reflect even briefly on what to answer, before Widow Horacker came up to them at a quick hobble, sobbing, whimpering, the tears streaming down her face.

"Pastor! Dear pastor! There he is! . . . Oh, good evening, pastor! Have you really and truly done us this kindness as well and come out here to us? There he lies, just like he promised the other kind gentleman he would, and he's ready to submit to everything. What have you to say now?"

"What's Hecuba to me?"[108] muttered the vice-principal, who *had* to say something. "For God's sake, compose yourself—compose yourself, my good woman! Everything will turn out all right! . . . Just let anyone ask now what Hecuba is, with something like this running about the world!"

The pastor of Gansewinckel, to whom Widow Horacker had addressed her question, did not reply. He just gently took her hand

and walked with her back under the first trees of the forest.

"Cord! . . . Cordchen!" shrieked Widow Horacker. And eating his humble pie, having eaten his humble pie, the poor sinner whimpered, "Here!"

"There you are indeed, Cord," said the pastor, "and my heart aches just to look at you."

> *"Pidget, pudet, poenitet,*
> *taedet atque miseret,"* [109]

grumbled the vice-principal, rocking the upper portion of his body back and forth. "A nice jumble of emotional states of excitement! All with the accusative of the afflicted person. O dear Lord!"

The first bat fluttered through the gray of evening. Horacker raised himself up from the grass onto his knees and extended his emaciated arms. "Then the comical gentleman did give you the message about how I'm so hungry and miserable I don't care anymore? Thank you for believing him, Herr Pastor, and thanks for coming here without any farmers. There my mother stands, weeping away! So now just tell me everything at once! The whole world can whale away at me—I don't care. I didn't get to be a bad fellow for the fun of it, but since I've turned out to be one, why then that's what I want to be! . . . Damn the—"

The pastor of Gansewinckel had grabbed the scrawny arm of his poor prodigal son of Gansewinckel by the wrist. "Cord Horacker!" he shouted; and the reprobate raised his other elbow up over his head as if indeed a blow were about to fall that would make his well-deserved end.

But the blow did not fall. Krischan Winckler put his walking stick under his arm, patted the sinner on the shoulder, and said, "Why you have turned to me, my poor boy, is something you know best yourself. We'll go together now quietly down to the village—you, that gentleman there, your mother, and I. You know the gentleman already, and me as well. Who's to be damned, Cord Horacker? The whole world? I'm part of it too, you know, an old man who has come here to talk with you like one friend to another—like a father to his son—"

"To a scamp of a son!" muttered Vice-Principal Eckerbusch. "As if I didn't recognize that tone of voice and know what it's good for! But get on with it; it's as if I were watching my double. There I stand in front of the school benches, giving the lad a talking-to myself, while—here I sit with this captain of brigands letting myself be touched with all kinds of remorse and won over to his side."

"Now come along, Cord Horacker," said the pastor, smiling as he considered that never before had it been so clear to him what a poor orator he was, and that he himself was most assuredly to blame if his congregation let him preach to an empty church so often. "Come, my lad, we want to help you if possible, without any unnecessary speeches, out of your troubles and misery, out of this forest and onto the firm, broad path. It's getting dark; the lights will soon be going on down below. Take one last look behind you, and then let us return to where there are people. That's the best thing. The village is busy cooking its evening meal and no one is lying in wait for you. My wife is sitting down there and so is Drawing-Master Windwebel—"

"And Chairman Neddermeier and Miss Lotte Achterhang," cried old Eckerbusch; and Horacker the Highwayman clutched at Christian Winckler's arm.

"Oh, my dear Lord, Lottchen?!" cried Widow Horacker.

"She ran away from her employers on your account," growled Eckerbusch. "And when you've become a decent, respectable fellow again, then you'll have the right to thank her personally for it. *Allons,*[110] home! Though how I'm ever going to get home today yet myself, the gods only know."

"Mother, Mother, did you hear what he said?" sobbed Cord.

"Yes, my boy."

"Is it true, really true, Herr Pastor?"

"It's true, you hopeless vagabond, you! She gave us all quite a start. But I hope that you will die an honest old man after you've spent a good long life making that girl's life easy and her road straight and gentle."

And now at last, praise God, they were indeed descending through fields filled with chirping crickets. Smoke ascended straight up from the chimneys of Gansewinckel, and in the air was the pleasant odor of all sorts of pleasant things. Vice-Principal Eckerbusch took deep, delighted sniffs of that sweet aroma at several points.

Chapter 18

"And you'll carry those shoes out of my house right this minute and toss them in the creek in the village with all the
other leather goods the parish has thrown out. There are already
enough old boots and broken crockery there as it is, and it's an-
noyed me many a time when I've crossed by there, but I don't
even want to see these miserable scraps of leather in our rubbish.
You'll get them out of my house and into the creek this minute.
The poor creature will have to lie quietly in bed for three days
anyway."

So had Frau Billa Winckler spoken to her current maid approximately an hour after Lottchen Achterhang's arrival, and, naturally, her orders were carried out. Both shoes, which is to say, the
pitiful remains of them—both shoes that the "poor creature" had
worn all that great journey were long since in the creek at the end
of the village lane among the other cast-off footwear of Gansewinckel. And never, even during the days when she had been on
her way here from the other side of Berlin, had that young girl in
her attic room imagined herself so in need of a pair of shoes as
now.

To cry above the battlefield for a horse and to offer a kingdom
for it [111] sounds more tragic perhaps, but in such a case it is not,
than for someone appearing in his or her own tragedy upon the
stage of life. A kingdom for a horse—the whole world for a pair
of shoes!—

We know that the former parsonage maid had closed her eyes
tight upon the breathless announcement of impending events; we
know, too, that the pastor's wife had departed from the chamber

in the same haste in which she had entered it. The two friends, Winckler and Eckerbusch, had long since begun their walk up toward the woods just as we have described it and were still deep in the charming conversation we have also shared with the reader, when Lottchen Achterhang again became aware of this world and its affairs.

"They're bringing him in!"—

Then she sat up, her eyes once again open wide. But the astounding peace of nonexpectation was truly no longer in them. With trembling, groping hands, the girl reached for the clothes that had been assembled out of the wardrobes of the female population of the house. She stood there swaying dizzily on her feet, and yet she felt not the least weariness or weakness in those poor— and in reality quite exhausted—limbs of hers.

"They're bringing him in!" . . .

They're bringing him in! . . . She murmured the words over and over again, while with pounding heart and trembling hands she dressed. And who of us has not at one time or other been very much a part of the multitude, has not stood on tiptoe like everyone else in the crowd when the cry went up, "They're bringing him in now!"

When has that cry—whether in anger or mockery, in love or hate, in fun or in dead earnest—ever failed to have its effect on the crowd or the individual? Who has not at least once somewhere, somehow, been a part of it, with all his heart and with all his soul, when—they finally brought him in?! Even in the theater, whether in a tragedy or a farce, even in the worst of plays, that moment never fails to have its effect on the audience, from the orchestra to the top balcony. But each real door or street corner, each churchyard, each marketplace or courtroom supplies, after all, an entirely different sort of showplace for the loud cry, for the whisper:

"They're bringing him in now!"

One can hardly bear it to remain in one's chair, at the workbench, at the kitchen stove, or at one's desk. Wise Socrates always went to see when they were bringing someone in. Kant laid down his pen at once and walked to the window. On such occasions, the writer of these words always sticks his neck out as far as possible to look over the heads of the others standing in front of him.—Lottchen Achterhang did not worry herself in this instance about the missing shoes, did not even feel her sore feet on the steps as, with both hands to her ears, she slipped downstairs in order to be there as well when—they brought *him* in.

No one in the house heard her soft footfall. She made it to the entry hall without being discovered; and so suddenly there in the bower she stood ("Like a ghost!" remarked Frau Winckler), facing the two gentlemen, Chairman Neddermeier and Drawing-Master Windwebel. From Frau Billa she elicited a low screech, and she wept and got her words out only with the greatest difficulty. And even then they were very hard to understand.

"Oh, please, please, let me be here when they bring him in! Oh, please, please, please, I'll die if I can't be here."

"Oh, my soul, what a get-up! Lottchen, can it be?" cried Frau Winckler as soon as she recovered herself the least bit from being confronted with this unexpected apparition, though she alone had conjured it up. "Girl, do you know what you look like? How can you appear in public like that? It's a pity we have no mirror up there in the garret! You look worse than a hoot owl! You will now march right back into the house and crawl into bed. Don't you laugh, Neddermeier, I warn you, even if you see a thousand items from my wardrobe hanging on that scarecrow there! Dearest Herr Windwebel, I beg you, for heaven's sake!"

The chairman rubbed his nose with his knuckles and only laughed as much as he dared in the presence of the rectoress, particularly after she had warned him—which means, he grinned very broadly. It was Herr Windwebel who once again, amid loud and unbridled laughter, found the best solution for this deplorable situation.

"This is the girl—the darling—Mistress Lotte Achterhang?" he cried, inching gradually from fullest mirth to fullest seriousness. "This is the famous Lottchen? Well then, she will suit my friend, my catch out there in the wilderness, perfectly, and she's decked out pretty enough for me, too! No, my dear, my pet, my sweet girl, you are of course the main character in the drama, and must be present—under all circumstances! No one else has as much right as you, and Frau Winckler has nothing at all against your being here when he comes with the pastor. But he's not being brought in, Lottchen; because I renounced the pleasure of doing so. He is being fetched, and by the pastor. And now you may boldly peek over the hedge with the rest of us. Who knows, Neddermeier, when they may bring us in sometime in one fashion or another? It would certainly be a comfort for me to have Hedwig with me in that case, dear Frau Billa."

"Well, at least I shall go fetch you a pair of old slippers, my girl," called out the rectoress of Gansewinckel. "It's just my fate, I suppose, Lotte! You know this is not the first time you've appeared barefoot under my nose. There's an old worn-out pair of my husband's on top of my clothespress."

"But first a *vivat*! There they come, by my soul, in triumphal procession right down out of the woods!" cried the chairman, pointing up to where the path began in the fields. "The vice-principal at their head with the banner—yes sir, that fits the occasion! Shall I proclaim that the village should be illuminated, too, do you think?" And good Christian's worn-out slippers were forgotten for the present.

The first to emerge at the top of the field was Herr Eckerbusch; and what the chairman had termed a triumphal banner was only his hat, which he held high in the air at the end of his walking stick as a symbol of the final, complete success of the expedition.

Behind the vice-principal strode the pastor, leading the sinner Horacker by the arm, and at parade's end came Widow Horacker. The four figures were etched sharply against the evening sky, still clear, calm and grayish-blue in that direction.

Herr Windwebel was swinging his hat in the air again, too.

"Hurrah!"

"Will someone please tell me what to say!" said the pastor's wife, abandoning herself, with no will of her own, to the events in the distance.

"In spite of it all, I'd still say it was a gruesome occasion," grumbled Neddermeier. And Lottchen Achterhang—bolted, and so fast it was as if that long, sore trip from "the other side of Berlin" did not lie behind her.

"Let her go—please!" cried Windwebel, taking hold of Frau Billa Winckler's hand just as she was about to catch hold of the girl's fluttering skirt.

Out on the path, the pastor had likewise let the parish scapegrace go, and he stood there now with the vice-principal watching Cord run. Widow Horacker sat down on a boundary stone and put her head in her hands. One does not easily rid oneself of such an old habit, the result of a battered and tormented life; and in such cases the most uncompromising instructors and moralists often end up giving instructions to and moralizing with themselves all in vain.

And yet in this world of dust and clay, what a tender and lovely creature circles about the light of the flame! They gave the pair of vagabonds a full five minutes to exchange their greetings. And there are few works of art in this world to be compared with the smiles old Winckler and old Eckerbusch smiled while watching the event. We, however, shall describe it just as the trusty pen in our hand directs us.

"Oh, it's you!" sobbed Lottchen Achterhang.

"Yes, you see me—don't you?!" wailed Horacker, that captain of brigands. And with that they appeared to have completely exhausted all words. And we have the suspicious feeling that over the years we have wasted a great many words in too many situations.

Yes, do you see it now?! . . . Our only consolation is that all our caution and precautions have not helped in the least, that the whole village suddenly knows that Horacker is back, and that we can lose ourselves and our own emotions among those of the crowd without anyone's noticing. But who was it that brought Gansewinckel out of its evening lethargy and to its feet with the cry: "They've got him! They're bringing him in! They've got Horacker. Horacker is back!"

Of course afterward no one would have known exactly, if that question were to be posed. One whack to the swamp immediately silences every last frog. One stone thrown on the manure pile sends all the sparrows fluttering off with a noisy scream.

Everything in Gansewinckel, so to speak, got to its feet—not just the people, but the animals too! Young and old poured from the houses. Every dog in the parish was beside itself. The cattle lowed in their stalls. The weariest plowhorses raised their heads. Geese and ducks hissed and cackled, and every single farmyard rooster led all his ladies, who had already retired for the night, back down out of the roost to be a part of the excitement and to inquire about what had actually happened.

"Huzzah, there he is! And the best part of all is that Lottchen Achterhang, that perfect model of a princess, walked here on foot all on her lonesome besides! . . . They're both sitting at the parsonage. The pastor's wife said it was truly touching, and we all know the pastor. But, thank God, Herr Neddermeier is there, too, to deal with the matter. They'll probably be sitting in very different quarters come tomorrow, and then maybe they'll leave a body in peace again."

"He's sitting in the parsonage, your honor," said Schoolmaster Böxendal with pedagogical gravity and courtesy, as he stepped up to the door of the carriage carrying the prosecutor into the village. "I've known him since he was a lad. He had the pleasure of my instruction. And it was only a rumor that he had murdered Vice-Principal Eckerbusch and Drawing-Master Windwebel. I've been teaching in this place for fifty years, your honor, and know them all—oh, yes, I know them all—every one!"

"To the parsonage," Herr Wedekind shouted to his driver, and turning to his youthful companion in the law, he said, "You don't know old Winckler of Gansewinckel yet? Well, then, you shall have the pleasure of making his acquaintance, and in the future you'll never need avoid the chance for an outing to visit him, whether on official or unofficial business. I, too, have been a civil servant in these parts for many long years and know them all—oh, yes, I know them all—every one. Neither Horacker nor Krischan Winckler are the worst of the lot! . . . And good old Eckerbusch! And that curiosity, the drawing-master—what's his name now—ah yes, Windwebel! . . . This will be a most extraordinarily genial evening, depend on it, my friend. For a person in my position nothing can beat an excursion like this out to visit the likes of the honest Voss, the venerable Gellert, grandfather Gleim[112] and the *Wandsbecker Bote.*[113] You, good Herr Nagelmann, are of course still young and are a devotee of Heine and will have to add a few years, I fear, before you are quite mature enough for an official tour of duty like this one."

Chapter 19

For the most part, humanity deals with world history the way a good housewife deals with the daily events of her household. She is stirred by great emotions only when the holiday bell rings and her cake is lying ready on the table or when the coffin is lifted onto black benches. Then she starts in. But till then she slaves away quite unemotionally and could not even endure her harrowed existence if it were not so. Now and then, to be sure, a person is overcome with emotion even while making preparations for the great moments and crises of life. Let us peer now into the second coach tottering toward the village three-quarters of an hour after the arrival of the prosecutor. Since the moment Fricke bent down from his box to point with his whip handle at the first lights of Gansewinckel in the dusk, Frau Hedwig Windwebel has been beside herself. Fully overwhelmed by the emotions raging within her, she lies there in Frau Eckerbusch's arms—who likewise gives vent to her emotions, but to ones peculiarly her own.

"You're sweating, Neubauer, so am I! Go right ahead and sweat, sir. I only wish you would have to sweat the cold sweat of fear for a whole year! Here this child is hanging in a swoon about my neck, and too much is too much. Hedwig, Hedwig, you need hold on for only five minutes more! In five minutes we shall meet those shameless tramps head on, and thank God I have my speech down by heart. You may depend on it, Neubauer. If you think I've made things hot for you on the way here, wait till I get hold of my old Catilina [114] beneath the bower in the parsonage garden. He'll remember me and this evening every time he teaches Cicero from now on."

"So shall I!" muttered the unhappy assistant master and traveling companion. "Every man must perish, but it were to be wished that each might meet his end in a manner appropriate to him. That I am perishing at the hands of this *lamia*,[115] this *venefica*[116] is too much, by God. It's sport of the gods, it's a foul trick of the fates!"

Somewhat more loudly, but with uncommon reserve, he said, "You will not say one word too many beneath that bower, Frau Eckerbusch, for every word will be as if spoken from the bottom of my heart."

"What's that you say? Stuff and nonsense! I'll say nothing from the bottom of your heart! I'll speak my piece just as I see fit.— Stop, Fricke. Stop here for a moment. Lift your head up, Hedwig! There on those planks next to the sawmill sit our first two Gansewincklers. Hey, you there. Come here! Which of you can tell me what's been going on with Horacker today?"

It was a pair of Gansewinckel turtledoves, who at the shrill, inquisitorial call of the proceleusmatica started up from an oak stump beside the sawmill and, after some hesitation, came over to the coach through the evening twilight.

"Say now, what's this about? You speaking to us?"

"What's this business with Horacker, I'm asking you?"

"Oh, with Horacker! . . . They got him, madam! He's sitting tight!"

"He's sitting tight?"

"Yes, in the parsonage kitchen. Surely you've heard that Lottchen Achterhang's suddenly back from the other side of Berlin, haven't you? She's sitting in the rectoress's kitchen too."

"And the pastor and his wife? and the—the gentlemen—from town?"

"They're all sitting by lamplight under the bower by the garden hedge. They're having great fun, it seems."

"All of them alive?"

"Well, you can hear them all from pretty far across the fields. You going to the party, too, is that it?"

"You might say that!" said Frau Eckerbusch. "Drive on, Fricke, and drive as quietly as possible. What's meant to be a surprise should stay that way right up to the last minute. Well, Hedwig?"

The little woman made no answer. She sobbed away very softly on the bosom of her kindly old friend, until all at once she lifted her head, sat up straight, and cried with a long, deep sigh, "Oh, it's horrid; but—I'm so happy! . . ."

After a pause she added, "But I'm going to give Victor a piece of my mind."

"Well, you don't say, my dear!? Haven't you given him that already? *Quousquay abbutteray patsientsiam Catilinam?* [117] You still have to learn, my sweet, to bring a calmer patience to matrimony than you've shown today. But after you've been employed at our gymnasium for half a century, you'll gradually learn, I suppose, to get the knack of life and to quote the old Greeks, Romans, and other classical writers. Unfortunately, it's easier than one imagines as a young girl. Well, my young classical author there on the front seat?!"

The young classical author on the front seat, rhapsodist of '66, assistant master and doctor of philosophy, Herr Neubauer, had also sat up straighter. With arms folded across his chest, he brooded as follows:

"An abomination! Truly, an absurd abomination! But this hideous afternoon was also foretold at my birth. Cooped in with these two vapid creatures, knee to knee with all this female impertinence and epithalamial despair—and despite the best motives for it, I have not committed suicide. The wise man emerges from this fussing and whining, too: *totus, teres atque rotundus* [118]—whole, smooth, and round. But just let someone try to get me to take the step! *Vates sum et poeta,* [119] a searcher of hearts am I and a poet. There will be no marrying—none—never! So does fate lead her chosen ones through quotidian trivialities toward knowledge. He alone can be a perfectly genial husband who concentrates his entire selfhood in his wife, and so a true poet has never been a totally genial spouse—just the opposite as a rule. O muses, guard your son henceforth as well. Let that frump there, the old town matchmaker, let her have at me just once more with her hints, intimations, suggestions, and insinuations! I swear that in the future I'll not let matters rest with a demurring smile. I shall coolly tell her my opinion of her insipid sex, and—thus it was not without purpose that I've been dragged to Gansewinckel along with these two geese."

Meanwhile Fricke had driven on into the peaceful village, ford-
ing the village creek, right over those poor shoes that Lottchen
Achterhang had worn out on her long, piteous journey. One last
jolt, creak, and groan, and the yellow-green coach halted in front
of the Gansewinckel parsonage.—Frau Hedwig had had her trembling hand on the door handle for some time now. Before the two
old nags had even been pulled to a halt, she had thrown open the
door and was about to be the first to dash from the coach, when
her older friend grabbed her by the skirt and pulled her back in.

"Easy does it, my child! You're certain now yourself that *he* is
still there, so go ahead and let Herr Neubauer climb out first. It's
always a comfort to have a pleasant, urbane gentleman at one's
side. Careful, Neubauer! Be careful with such a delicate lady . . .
So, here we all are, and now drive off as quietly as possible and
without any fuss to the inn, Fricke. And as for you, children, I beg
you for heaven's sake not to spoil the effect for me. Softly, softly
through the house, Hedwig. On tiptoe—please, on tiptoe, Neubauer, so that we fall upon them like the clap of doom. Oh, will
I ever proceleusmaticize *him* now! You write very pretty verses
and poems, doctor, and so I beg you, walk on tiptoe, do me the
kindness and tread as softly as swift vengeance itself, and afterwards you can put us all into proper poetical meters. The whole
company is sitting out in the bower, not giving us a thought, and
it would be a pity if they were to get wind of us ahead of time in
the hallway. Softly, children, softly, so that we have something in
exchange for the scandal and are repaid at least in part for our
journey. They're sitting there in the lamplight, thank God, so I
can see my husband's face. Merciful heavens, till now I truly never
knew that such feelings as I have at the moment could exist with
such purity and perfection in this world!"

"Nor I! Oh, Lord, I am so happy!" sobbed Frau Hedwig.

"Then contain your sweet self for just one tiny moment yet, my
dear. You needn't explain to me in detail what's going on inside
you. Yes, we still have them on our hands and they'll continue to
make our lives miserable for a good long time, let us hope. Please,
on tiptoe, Neubauer, and then like thunder we shall burst over
their heads."

"You know how I share your feelings in the matter and the
pleasure I take in pursuing all such intentions," said Herr Neu-

bauer with a smile, and it was, thank heaven, his old smile. There must be smilers such as he as well, and it would have truly been a shame if on this trip to Gansewinckel he had lost it completely, never to smile that irresistibly pleasant and easy smile again in the circle of his acquaintance.

And now they were creeping along the hall of the Gansewinckel parsonage—the two ladies first, the gentleman behind them! They made it through the house, unheard and unseen. No one leaped out to greet them, and we—we shall let them creep, thinking it best that we should be surprised along with the others in the bower. We are all firmly convinced, one would hope, that their cause is just.

They brought him into the midst of the varied group in the bower of the parsonage garden and so back among humanity—Horacker, that is. They pressed around him and almost knocked him down yet again. One important person, however—Lottchen to be precise—did not let herself be pushed away from him. She held him upright in her embrace, right in front of Chairman Neddermeier and Frau Billa.

"Horrible! I didn't imagine he would look like this!" shrieked the latter, clapping her hands together over her head. "Oh, my dear, my dear, it would melt a heart of stone to look at you! Christian, I ask you! Neddermeier—Eckerbusch, I ask you, is that possible?"

"A great many things are possible in this world. But, secluded as we are, we don't always meet up with them," said wise old Eckerbusch. "You need only ask Windwebel about that; he's done some traveling."

"He's to be put to bed right this minute! A message must be sent to the doctor right away. And you, Lotte, yes, you—it's a miracle you're still on your feet, or on them again. See that they light a fire in the kitchen at once and put as much water as possible on to boil. Wait! We might as well have a fire in the washhouse. And in the kitchen tell them I said to start making chicken soup right away. Have them wring the necks of three of them, because I swear all this would make a walking stick weep. For the rest of my life I'll think of nothing else in church, Christian, when you read the parable of the prodigal son!"

"He'll best be kept in the firehouse until we've notified the authorities in town about him," suggested the chairman. But he was already shoved to one side—Chairman Neddermeier was, that is.

"In the firehouse?! . . . If you had brought him out of the forest yourself, then you could do as you please. In the firehouse? For the present, *I* have him here at the parsonage. In the firehouse! Oh, certainly, and we can talk all about that come New Year's, but for now you'll do me the favor of sitting down again, chairman, and not bothering yourself with things that don't concern you in the least right now. And you can sit down, too, Frau Horacker. She's the mother, and I know only too well what that means under the present circumstances. Don't everyone crowd in so close! Be reasonable, Lotte. You talk to her, Christian."

Which is what Christian Winckler attempted to do, as best he knew how, and Eckerbusch and Windwebel added many a good word as well. But for a quarter of an hour it was merely verbiage lost in the babbling din. The whole household had, of course, taken a most active interest in these events from the very first. And then— as we have noted—the village descended upon them as well.

"Horacker is back!"

Head to head, they peeked over the hedge. The vestry came, Böxendal came. And Lottchen Achterhang sobbed on, not without some cause.

"Oh, Cord, dear Cord, if they execute us, then they'll have to execute us both. Don't be ashamed, Cord. I'm not ashamed neither. Let them put us to death. That's the only reason I walked all this way when they read out loud about you from the paper, Cord. The pastor and his wife here are my witnesses."

"I'll witness to nothing except that you are a silly goose, Lotte—"

"And a good girl," interrupted the pastor of Gansewinckel. "And now, dear Neddermeier, which of us two, do you think, is better capable of assuring our good neighbors and friends that they have now seen all there is to see at the moment, that our Horacker has indeed returned to us, and that you and I will most certainly see to it that it was not without some use both to himself and the parish, not without some use—"

"That he caused such a stir in our idyllic existence!" cried Vice-

Principal Eckerbusch. "Excuse me, Krischan—don't trouble your-self, Chairman. I would like finally to speak a word or two my-self! Go on and lead the brigand captain, our Furcifer Rinaldini and his Rosa, off to the kitchen. Take Widow Horacker along with you. Go ahead and feed, wash, and trim the hair of the beast, just as your kindly heart moves you, woman. I'll take it upon myself to say the few friendly words that need to be spoken here *coram publico*,[120] before the village and surrounding universe. Help me up onto the bench, Windwebel, so that people can see me as well."

"I don't even seem to exist today," grumbled Neddermeier.

"If you want to, dear Eckerbusch," said the pastor a bit doubt-fully, "then go ahead and speak."

"Yes, speak, Eckerbusch! Speak right from your heart, old friend. I can use the words!" shouted the rectoress as she tugged the high-wayman, Lottchen, the widow, the parsonage servant, and the parsonage maid off toward the house.

"Climb right up on the table and speak out loud and clear!" she called back from the steps that led down from the door and into the garden. And Eckerbusch was already standing on the ta-ble, and he spoke ever so audibly to all Gansewinckel gathered there. "Providence Herself sent him to us that day," it was fre-quently said in the Gansewinckel parsonage later on. "He knows how to do that sort of thing."—"It's not for nothing that those who sit in higher positions are so very hostile towards him, one may suppose," old Krischan would add, shaking his head and smiling. "Because it is well known that he knows how to speak when he wants to."

It is an equally well-known fact to us that Vice-Principal Eck-erbusch was blessed with a talent for imitating all creatures, both animal and human, and presenting them in their joys and woes. And he never so resembled a crowing rooster as he did now at this suspenseful moment.

"People of Gansewinckel!" he crowed away. "Inhabitants of Gansewinckel here assembled! In Kashmir where the cradle of hu-manity lies [121]—no, that's going back a bit too far and would also lead us too far afield! For I am speaking to you now not only because I wish to speak, but because I want you to hear and, if possible, to understand me. Everyone knows that you—all of you old enough to wipe your noses or have them wiped for you—are shrewd folks, and Kashmir is no concern of yours. So then, dear neighbors and old friends, do me a favor and hold your tongues for at least five minutes. Above all, don't push and shove so much, and those of you on the other side of the hedge can stop howling. And leave the young ladies in peace as well for a moment; no one could put up with that squealing and giggling. Where is Böxendal?"

"Here, Vice-Principal Eckerbusch," came the voice of the man he sought from the crowd. "How can I be of service?"

"Please step up to the front, friend—come up here to the table, if you would. Out of pedagogical respect, I'll not ask you to climb up on this chair. But you, who have educated this village over the generations—have known its backside, so to speak—I most definitely must have you here before me at this moment. Permit me, dear friend, to point to you and ask those present here: Do you know this man? . . . I see faces all around me saying, 'Yes.' Despite the growing darkness I can see more than one person hunching his shoulders and reaching with one hand for his—backside, and I assume that that does not mean 'No!'

"People of Gansewinckel! Here before the eyes of your honored and respected teacher, here under the very nose of my worthy and dear colleague, Herr Böxendal—a man so highly esteemed by you all, though I'm sure he can never be esteemed highly enough—are you so outrageously—naive that here and now you can look down in contempt at my friend and your *profugus*, [122] Horacker?! Do you really dare, right here under Böxendal's nose, to speak of scamps, scoundrels, rascals, and scalawags?! You speak to them, good Böxendal!"

"Most honored Herr Vice-Principal, if I were to say—"

"Say not another word, my friend! I know what you wish to say and that is sufficient. It is evening now, to be sure, and darkness deepens. But I have indeed come out here to Gansewinckel often enough by day, by brightest, clearest light of day, Sundays and weekdays, seeking refreshment, and have found it every time. I know each and every countenance about me here in the dusk. Natural candor, honest sincerity, unadorned simplicity, unaffected good manners, and a remarkable innocence and virtue are in all the smiles I see. And—my worthy colleague Herr Böxendal—oft,

oft when I was constrained—being given no other choice—to tan a pair of breeches, I have thought of you and gathered strength in the thought, gained renewed vigor for myself!

"Oh, Hor—acker and still no end![123] Here I stand and ask you all once again as your dear friend: do you know your old Ecker-busch? Would you all be kind enough to steal away now with no fuss, one after the other, or do you really want me to make myself clearer still? There, for example, I see Herr Schaper grinning. Well now, shall I explain to him more precisely that I know something about the timber business myself, and that an old schoolmaster from town still can tell the difference, after all, between a cord-foot and a cord?—And there he goes, heading for home! . . .

"Friends, friends, that I am supposed to know something about literature, you can see from my spectacles. But I also know very well what village gossip is, and it has not been in vain that I have wandered out this way to you my whole life long. Do you know what comes of getting a schoolmaster's dander up? There stands Böxendal, my colleague. You tell them, Böxendal."

"If I might say so, honored—"

"Get to the bottom of things! And you're absolutely right! And with emphasis. I share your opinion completely. Yes indeed, my friends, I too could climb down from this table and write up more than one tidbit of village gossip, all correct and proper, too, and with the names of more than one of you added onto the bottom of the page, with emphasis! . . . Heavens, Herr Guckup, do I spy you here, too? Is that pleasure really mine? Well then, my wife sends her best regards, and if you should ever have another greasy old gander to sell, then she says you should—ah, there he goes. And so I'll not find out today either where he learned the trick of refurbishing such an old vandalized skeleton by stuffing an inhuman amount of clay into the unfortunate and worthless creature's stomach! Oh, yes, thank God we have Horacker back. But in the deepening gloom I see here and there persons whom, sad to say, we've never managed to lose as yet. Which brings me to the point in my speech where I would like to pose a question to my old friend Chairman Neddermeier, who is standing there scratching behind his ear to signal his agreement. And the question is: who among the parishioners of Gansewinckel he knows for a certainty will one day wing his or her way to heaven as angel?! Take your time to think about it, Neddermeier, and don't forget to include yourself in the evaluation."

"Vice-Principal Eckerbusch, in all my life—"

"It has never been so clear to you till now what a very curious science statistics is. Windwebel, the pastor is standing behind you— step aside and let my old friend Krischan Winckler up here—"

"I really must beg of you, Eckerbusch—" cried the rector of Gansewinckel, but he, too, got no further.

"Do not beg, but rather be assured that it is truly a blessing for your parish that the shadows of night have gradually removed from your eyes the sight of the flock entrusted to you, of those cheeks red with shame. People of Gansewinckel, whoever among you still wishes to slip away now, should do so quickly. Because I wish to say a word about the only true angel among you—and there he goes, probably to take a look in the kitchen to see how they are treating Horacker!—And the night cannot grow black enough to cover your shame, you threefold Horackers of Gansewinckel! . . . I thank God that he has departed, too!—Now we are among ourselves and none of us needs to stand on ceremony. So then—to come back to you, my dear friends! What? A man like that, who turns his back on us only because he does not want to hear himself praised, and you want to spoil still further the pleasure he takes in helping you to earthly and eternal salvation? You want to make the life he must live out here among you still more wretched than you have made it thus far? Out of the goodness of his heart he no longer wanted to allow the lure of mammon to thrust itself between him and your callous sinful souls, and for that you come to him with your old parchments and privileges? For that you send his good wife, the rectoress God has seen fit to provide you with, back to her room, spoiling her disposition even more?! Depend on it, Böxendal, I shall help you sing come New Year's. Depend on it, dear friends gathered about this table, I'll be here to start the year by offering my felicitations as well! I most certainly will not let a scrap of paper come between you and my old friend Krischan Winckler. Did I not study theology, too, and did it not hang by a single thread whether or not I, old Vice-Principal Eckerbusch, would become pastor of Gansewinckel?

Verily I say unto you: just as a man yearneth now and then to roll in grass, clover, and thyme while the sun shineth overhead, so do I pant on this occasion to lie down right in the midst of—something else . . . There they go! . . . All of them! And they know well enough why it is they are slipping off! . . . Do you really want to leave us as well, Neddermeier?"

"If in fact I thought you still needed me here, then I'd probably stay a bit longer—confound it all!" grumbled the chairman. "You do know your business, Herr Eckerbusch. Anyone would have to admit that. But inasmuch as Horacker is in good hands now, I'd say, why, we'll let the other matter rest. That is my opinion, and each party should take his time to consult with his lawyer and then with his conscience."

He left and took the rest of the village with him.

"You spoke those words as if from the bottom of my heart, Vice-Principal Eckerbusch," said Schoolmaster Böxendal. "You truly know what man is and what great patience his Creator must have with him. You know precisely the point where vengeance shades off into foolishness, and I have regrets on only two accounts."

"And what two accounts are those, Herr Böxendal?" cried Windwebel.

"First, good sir, that we stirred up all that old rubbish in the first place; and secondly, that my wife wasn't present to hear that speech. She's been beside herself as well."

"I wonder if our wives are equally beside themselves at this moment? What do you think, Windwebel?" asked Eckerbusch. "I would indeed love to have had the proceleusmatica here, too, by the way—to hear my speech."

"How are we to get home? When are we going to get home? And what will my poor girl say?" muttered the younger husband anxiously—and justifiably so.

"There you had best first consult your conscience and then only afterwards—me!" said the older man with a grin, for he was a hardened rogue. He was, in a word, "Eckerbusch"—"about whom the whole town has the right opinion," sad to say, as that better half, whom he had just expressed his longing for but who was more like his better five-sixths, now and then contended.

But now the pastor emerges from the house again, bearing a garden lamp under a full white glass dome. He holds it up to illuminate the gentle summer evening and cannot hide his surprise at finding the garden empty and only his friend Eckerbusch, Drawing-Master Windwebel, and the schoolmaster alone there in the bower. He lets it shine to all four quarters of the globe and then with raised eyebrows into the friendly but somewhat pinched face of his friend Eckerbusch. Hesitantly he sets the lamp on the table at last and says, "Our Horacker is still wolfing down the food. I was detained by the fascination of watching him eat. But what has happened here, my dear Böxendal?—Eckerbusch, I fear—"

"Fear not, pastor," cried the schoolmaster. " 'Tis only a pity you did not stay when the vice-principal got round to speak of you! I am convinced your wife would have rejoiced had she heard it as well. People went home without another word after the vice-principal said what needed to be said about you and me and about the quarter-money, too, and it was high time the parish was made aware of the things that needed to be said."

"Very simply, I extolled you mightily, Krischan, and with all the languor at my disposal I indicated to your flock of goats, to your infamous Gansewinckel farmers, that in your place I would certainly play my pipes of Pan at a different tempo. As you can see the words of my mouth bore fruit. I too regret that your wife was not present."

His alarm steadily increasing, the pastor shoved his cap back and forth on his pate and said, "You are quite sure, Eckerbusch, that you have not been cooking up a stew that I can choke on until my retirement?"

The vice-principal muttered something about "rice pudding to the strains of organ music," and there was something suspicious at least in the fact that suddenly Böxendal, too, rose up from his worthy and grave meditations and with solemn shakings of his head asked that he be excused to return home.

He left. He strode off and, as we have reported, it was from the door of his schoolmaster's residence that he provided the prosecutor as he drove into town his first information about the current situation in Gansewinckel.

"Well, at least no one can deprive me of one consolation," said the pastor. "We have my Horacker safe in hand, and that's the main thing. The rest will be settled in due time as well, I suppose, with the help of God and old Gellert. Above all, dear Windwebel, I must once again offer my deepest thanks to you."

"Me?" asked the drawing-master in great astonishment. . . .

"And he's sitting there in your kitchen, Frau Billa?" asked the prosecutor only a few minutes later that evening. "Splendid! And I would hope that all Gansewinckel has been convinced by ocular inspection that we have him?! In fact one ought to issue an official summons for the whole region to come have a look! . . . Good evening, Eckerbusch. Good evening, my dear Herr Windwebel. Things look quite cozy here, I must say, Winckler! Does the parish chairman know all about this, gentlemen?"

"Eckerbusch sent him home some time ago," cried the pastor's wife. "And he's just as safe under our two pairs of eyes as in that firehouse of his. Besides which his mother and my Lottchen are looking after him. What can Neddermeier do with his firehouse that I can't take care of equally well on behalf of public security and morality?"

"You appear indeed not to know, my dear, what people are saying in town."

"Well?"

"It is known for a fact that he has murdered not only Vice-Principal Eckerbusch but Drawing-Master Windwebel as well."

Vice-Principal Eckerbusch leaped into the air, whereas his colleague Herr Windwebel sat down.

"Merciful heavens—*Hedwig*!"

"In consideration of which, let us proceed to the taking of evidence, Nagelmann," said the prosecutor, turning with a melancholy look to his younger colleague in the law. "We shall probably have to summon the chairman here again, don't you think? Bring me the criminal! . . . This evening air truly works like a balsam, Winckler."

Chapter 20

"**S**oftly, softly, softly," whispered the proceleusmatica. "You've something of the pussyfooter about you on other occasions, Neubauer, so—on your tiptoes again this time, like a bloodthirsty Indian, sir. Each walks in the other's footsteps, Hedwig, and then— we fall on them like a trio of tigers . . . There they sit around the lamp—sure enough, and the prosecutor's already got a lemon and Billa the sugar hammer. And my husband, as was to be expected, has the punch ladle in his hand and big words in his mouth. What's he talking about? About me? And he's nudging your Windwebel with his elbow and pointing with one shoulder at nothing in particular? . . . Child, they are even making fun of us! No holds barred now! At them! You take yours, and I'll take mine, and you, Neubauer, the whole pack! . . . Oh, you sinners, you wicked, unscrupulous, god-forsaken sinners, have we caught you red-handed? Is this what you call murdered? One of your tomfool tricks is what I call it, Eckerbusch. You—you—yes, you told the farmers what to say and sent them into town with the news you'd been murdered, Eckerbusch! Oh, why didn't it strike me right at the start!"

At any rate she had struck now, and her surprise was a complete success. Never had the peaceful bower of the parsonage garden seen such commotion.

Frau Hedwig Windwebel hung at her Victor's neck sobbing and kissing him to death. Frau Ida held her Eckerbusch by the collar. The prosecutor sat speechless, the two halves of a lemon in his hands. Christian Winckler simply sat there rigid. Nagelmann bowed and scraped in the shadows, and Frau Billa Winckler raised her hands to the dark, cloudless ether above Gansewinckel and said, "This beats everything else I've been through today! Did you come out of thin air? Did you fall down out of the night sky?"

"Oh, Hedwig, my darling, my child, my poor sweet wife, I just now found out—not a half hour ago—what a fright you must have had!" stammered Windwebel. "But it has done you no harm, has it?"

"No, no, oh no, I'm so happy. I still have you after all!" sobbed the young woman.

"Stop smothering me, my dear. You still have me, too," said Eckerbusch with a grin.

"Admit it, you put the rascals of Gansewinckel up to it, coached them, egged them on, and sent them to town to play this trick."

"Do you still regret, dear Nagelmann, that as a matter of chance, duty, and profession you rode out to Gansewinckel with me this evening?" said old Wedekind, turning to his young companion in the law. "Didn't I tell you that at my friend Krischan's one always meets up with—all kinds of people?"

"Oh, Victor," whispered Hedwig, "don't you think it really was too mean of you?"

Herr Windwebel likewise attempted to free himself, though gently, from the hands his wife still had clasped about his neck. He had as little success at it as the vice-principal.

"Stop smothering you? You bet I'll smother you!" cried Frau Ida. "Do I still have you? Sad to say, I do indeed, you—you, oh you—Ho—racker! Ask Neubauer there what I've suffered on your account, you impudent sinner, and ask him what he had to bear on the way here, and then—tell me to stop it just once more. Oh, and this is the man who is supposed to teach young boys wisdom, good manners, tidiness—and, in sum, common sense?! Yes, ask your colleague Dr. Neubauer how all the way here I had to apologize to him time and again for more than one reason."

Up to this point Assistant Master Dr. Neubauer had found himself incapable of contributing to the din. It was his custom to remain silent on principle whenever he could not keep his dignity completely intact. Only the most refined gentleman sees his own life as his work of art, whatever the situation and amid all babble, bedlam, and blubbering; only he can hold fast to the thread by

which, strangely enough, fate holds him as well. Herr Dr. Neubauer held his peace now, too, despite the question posed directly
to him. He smiled silently and gladly let his hand be shaken in
welcome by the pastor of Gansewinckel, who began to enjoy himself more and more.

"You don't like it too sweet, do you, doctor?" cried the pastor,
with an eye to the punchbowl. "My, but it's wonderful how everything seems to fall so splendidly into place at once. You don't like
it all that sweet, either, do you, Frau Ida? Frau Hedwig can help
herself to some extra sugar on her own. My dears, isn't this splendid! Since I've finally unburdened my soul of this Horacker, I feel
as if I'm quite another person."

"No, she doesn't like it too sweet!" groaned Eckerbusch, still in
the clutches of his proceleusmatica. "It's wonderful, it's splendid—there's no way to express it. Embrace me, my love, but please
let go of my neck! . . . What? Under the very eyes of the law?
. . . Has there not been bloodletting enough as it is? Wedekind, I
call upon you to take immediate action. Nagelmann, you'll be taking down evidence a second time. Here, hold my spoon, please.
How can a man whose nose has just been bitten off pay adequate
attention to the punch?"

"Why don't you do an imitation—show us your pug-dog with
a bellyache! Oh, I'll see to it that your favorite role turns out
absolutely lifelike this evening! An old woman plucking a live goose
is one of your great achievements, isn't that right? You do the
gaggling very prettily, Neubauer tells me, and also manage a strik-
ing imitation of my voice—when I'm not there. Thank God I'll be
there this time, Eckerbusch, and I'll show you just how well I can
pluck a goose."

"Help, Winckler! Help me, prosecutor! Assist me, O spiritual
and temporal swords! Wedekind, she's serious about this!" cried
the vice-principal, gasping for breath. "Give my best to that fellow
in Haparanda when this old body has wiggled its last, and—not
too much lemon in the pot, Wedekind. Otherwise tomorrow
morning no one will be able to open his eyes for headache! Hah,
now there's a kiss, my dear. And now that's enough of this, otherwise the fellow there will spoil the whole brew."

"And now before anything else, a very good evening to you

all," said the proceleusmatica, her face beaming brightly as she stretched out both hands to those in the circle. "Children, this whole affair is perfectly glorious. Why, just to see the two Windwebels there makes amends for the trip. We came in the yellow-green coach, Eckerbusch, and we've sent it on to the inn. The whole town watched us pull out. And my only consolation is that we brought Neubauer along with us, and he'll set it all in the proper light for everyone come morning."

"I shall do my best, Frau Eckerbusch," said that gentleman. And then they all began to greet one another in a proper fashion.

We have described how Cord Horacker and his Lottchen, after their unfortunate separation, were reunited there in the fields on the path that ran down out of the forest, out of that grim and grievous world, to their home village. The educated folks were not so speechless when reunited after their droll separation. They had no end of things to say to one another, and Nagelmann and Neubauer were finally the only ones who remained masters of their emotions and who found a knowing wink sufficient for calling one another's attention to the main events in all that noisy emotional exchange.

"I can assure you that I had quite an experience with those two females," whispered Neubauer to Nagelmann. "How I actually came to have the pleasure still remains a mystery to me. The gray sorceress picked me up, carried me off and set me down here without releasing me from my stupor for even one brief moment. That woman, I am certain, once lay inside the egg of a roc and was hatched by a griffin. I have never before felt myself to be such a helpless baby as this evening in her clutches, or better, in her talons."

"You too, doctor?"

"Yes, me too! . . . Given my current mental state, I can make that confession without the least embarrassment. Distraction—yes, distraction is the word! I shall beg you to excuse me for at least the next month for chronic mental incapacity and please try to explain my condition to the other gentlemen of our mutual acquaintance. Above all, however, you must explain to me how you came to allow yourself to cut such a ridiculous official and professional figure?"

Nagelmann cast a cautious glance at his superior before he supplied the information. But at the moment the prosecutor was moved most by feelings both gastronomical and sentimental, dividing his attention between the young married couple and the preparation of the punch, which latter had gradually devolved upon him. He had neither an ear nor an eye free for his younger colleague, and thus Herr Nagelmann whispered back with impunity.

"For some time now we've been driving about through every town and village in the district looking for his favorite snuffbox. He left it lying somewhere but has no idea where. It would certainly be a welcome relief if he finally would decide to abandon the hope of finding it again."

"And Horacker?"

"Bah!" laughed Nagelmann with a disdainful shrug. "Horacker?! Permit me, please, to attribute the use of the name to your mental derangement as well. We would most assuredly not have driven out to fetch him had it been raining!—You don't know Wedekind, if that's what you think. By the way, the local divine seems not to be a bad example of the species. These jaunty gray-haired fellows hereabouts all hang together in a remarkably friendly fashion. I think it rather unlikely, sad to say, that we chaps nowadays will sustain things with the same naive jollity. What do you say, Neubauer?"

This time Assistant Master Dr. Neubauer shrugged, but said not a word.

"For the drive back I'll surrender my seat with the chief, and you can give yours beside little Frau Wedekind to me in exchange. And I'll accept Madame Eckerbusch and the drawing-master as part of the bargain. The vice-principal is sure to ride with the prosecutor. Would you want to do that, Neubauer?"

"I am only too well acquainted with the witticisms and adages employed by those two, but—I'll make the exchange," sighed the philologist. "Hm, who can say what divinity has placed me across from the spouse of that dreadful old woman? I shall at any rate use the opportunity to praise him for it. And, dear Nagelmann, for my part I'll most certainly do what I can to continue into the future the harmless state of affairs we've known in the past."

"Ladies and gentlemen, dearest friends," Prosecutor Wedekind called out, thank God, and raised his full glass. "To your health! I call your attention to the fact that this potion, as best I can judge, corresponds to the ingredients provided. Fill your glasses, all of you, and please taste for yourselves, so that from the abundance of individual testimony we may come to a resultant verdict that is as objective as possible. I look around me here and my soul is filled with delight. I behold my *old friends* and enjoin the younger folks, for their own good, to do as we have done and to take life seriously, tragically, only at the proper times. (I didn't by chance leave my snuffbox lying here recently, did I, Winckler?) Duty demands, of course, that tomorrow morning I shall have Chairman Neddermeier deliver our mutual friend, Horacker, to me in town. But duty does not demand that we receive him tragically, as you also know, Herr Nagelmann. And in regard to this criminal whom we have finally been successful in nabbing, I would hope to see you there as well, Winckler, and I hereby invite you to lunch with me afterward. Have the glasses provided by our honored hostess, Frau Billa, all been filled? Good. I therefore shall now take the liberty of drinking my second glass to the health of the ladies. And bring one to that brave little girl of yours, to Lottchen, as well, *hospita*,[125] and tell the poor sweet child that old Wedekind never haphazardly travels the countryside on official duty, but always first gets to the bottom of the matter at hand and usually lets reason speak its piece, too, along with all the documents. Eckerbusch, you will lunch with me tomorrow as well. The other three gentlemen are also invited."

"That's the way it always turns out," said Frau Eckerbusch in the protracted rhythm that the world and Vice-Principal Eckerbusch had come to expect of her. "Besides which, I would finally like now to make the personal acquaintance of the monster, your Horacker. You have him under lock and key, Billa?"

"In my apple cellar. He fell fast asleep there in the very hands of the law. His mother and my Lotte are keeping watch over him. Do you want to examine him as well, my dear Frau Windwebel?"

"If you please," said Hedwig Windwebel with a glance to her Victor that could only mean: but shall I find you here when I return?—And so the three women went to view Horacker the Highwayman in his sleep. We, however, cannot repeat it often enough: it was a lovely night, the most pleasant in all that year of 1867.

As the three good souls entered the apple cellar of the Gansewinckel parsonage, Widow Horacker pathetically laid a finger to her lips. A little oil lamp shone upon the straw and all sorts of pillows and blankets that had been used to make a bed. There the fearful sinner had let himself fall in complete passivity and torpor. He lay in the very deepest sleep, and next to him, her head in the lap of the very alert widow, lay Lottchen Achterhang whose sleep was just as deep, almost that of a brute beast, after all the sore trials and terrors of the last few days. And outside the sweet scent, the rapture of summer, and the soft rustling of leaves filled the world, while Assistant Master Neubauer, epoist of '66, filled the glasses once more.

"Oh, dear heavens!" whispered the two faculty wives from town.

And the proceleusmatica added in dismay, "I really didn't imagine he would look like that, Billa."

The young woman sobbed softly into her handkerchief, saying in a broken voice, "And—my Victor—was the one who—who—"

"Now, children," said the rectoress of Gansewinckel as decidedly as she could, holding her hands behind her back. "I hope, children, that a year from today everything will have turned out better than we can imagine it will now. Don't cry, Frau Horacker. Whatever we three can do will most certainly be done. He'll have to finish out his time in the reformatory, Wedekind says. But that won't do him the least bit of harm. I know what everyone in this parish is worth, and your lad, Frau Horacker, is not the worst soul my husband will have to offer New Year's felicitations to. So stop your crying, Frau Horacker."

"Yes, do stop crying, Widow Horacker," said Frau Eckerbusch. "I don't want to have come out to Gansewinckel for nothing, and I give you my word, my husband's not going to have had his fun this evening, either, without first having done something useful in return! He can come lend me some help right here—in both word and deed."

TUBBY SCHAUMANN

*A Tale of Murder
and the High Seas*

Back on board.

Before I proceed with the setting down of this narrative, I would like it understood that I still consider myself an educated man. What I mean is that I have made my fortune in South Africa, and the people who do that best are not usually trained in dead languages, literature, art, or philosophy. All of which is, no doubt, proper and useful for the spreading of culture since you can't ask every German professor to go to Africa and apply his knowledge—use it on the bushman or leave it in the bush—in order to make his fortune.

"Let us prove to them, Edward, using Platen's[1] Fateful Fork, that we still know our literary p's and q's." Edward, I should explain, is my first name, and Mopsus is the name of the shepherd in Platen's Arcadia who "wanted to buy an estate some day at the Cape of Good Hope and was saving all his money for the purpose."

"Where did he get that idea?" asked Damon, the magistrate in Arcadia, and the world is fully entitled to ask the same of me.

But perhaps it is the world that can give me the answer. How *do* people sometimes come to be in places where, when they stop to think, they wonder how they got there?

All I can say at this point is that I honestly think Störzer ought to be held responsible. My old friend Störzer, the country postman. My dear old friend from the highway of childhood wending its way about my home town—in Arcadia—and so my friend from all the highways and seaways of the wide, wide world.

Well, having laid my credentials on the table to show that I am entitled to speak my piece at home, in the Fatherland, where men of culture converse, I hope I can now proceed with my story. But I must warn you that I am quite unable to say whether I can spell correctly by present-day standards. During my absence very important little people have been at work in the field: they can, with the authority of the police to back them up, quote that wonderfully ironic adage of our old enemy the French that says, "Nous avons changé tout cela." [2] What the Germans never admit, of course, is that they have taken hold at the wrong end; they are always so heavy-handed, especially when their advantage or their ambition or their vanity is involved.

But it's nice to be at home in the old country, and if it weren't, I certainly shouldn't be writing this down to entertain myself on my return journey on board the *Hagebucher* across the broad waves of the Atlantic. But at least if the weather holds, I shall not have entirely mooned away my thirty days at sea—counting from Hamburg—thanks to this unwonted labor of the pen. But how surprised, and how delighted, my neighbors on the Orange River and in the Transvaal would be with our kinsman Schaumann, if they could read these cabin-scribblings of mine, always assuming they could lay hands on them. But there is as little prospect of the one as of the other, and my good friend, the president of the Boer Republic, has little time for this sort of thing, otherwise he might do me the favor of telling me what he thought of my manuscript.

It was a clear, starry night, and we were on our way home. Not to the Cape of Good Hope, but from the Brummersumm. Thank God that out of a dozen, or only half a dozen, Germans there is always one who knows a little more astronomy than the rest and can answer questions and name names and point with his stick, where the others, as they pass by in the awful splendor of the universe, feel lost and shake their heads and just say: Marvelous.

You can know your way about in many fields of knowledge and yet when the mood is right or the moment appropriate, you may have to let someone else tell you where Sirius is or Betelgeuse or Arcturus or Aldebaran. If you can spot Orion, you are way ahead of the rest. Most of us are very much in the dark when it comes to the constellations. They don't stand out in the sky all by themselves like my Southern Cross. It is a great deal if a Northerner can find the Great Bear. And even then people who ought to know better will often tell you that the Pole Star belongs to it rather than to the Little Bear.

So we were on our way home from the Brummersumm and were looking at the stars. It was on toward midnight when they are sometimes at their best and there is nothing to disturb your contemplations. To be walking a country lane at such a time with what is left of the friends of your youth—that is something indeed. No matter what you are talking about—politics, investments, industry, aesthetics—everyone, even the most expert of us, is free to break off in the middle of his best sentence and peer aloft and say: There is something in that too. Then, of course, he can take a pinch of snuff, if he takes snuff; I'm a smoker myself, and when I catch sight of the endless host of shining stars I like to start a fresh cigar, because that is a sort of light too, and here on earth you have to do what you can to ward things off, including "the stars in their hugeness," as Goethe put it.

Yes, and if on top of that you are a German of the older generation, you like to stick to what is closest at hand, the pleasant evening, the good company, and all that goes with it, even if for variety's sake you do wander off once in a while into the glitter and flicker above your head "as far as Sirius." It may be mundane, but we are perfectly entitled to do so. It is more important to know, at least to begin with, what sort of people you are living with and whom you have to deal with, or are going to have to deal with, than to find out whether the moon or Mars is inhabited, and by whom or by what.

On this particular evening the companions of the road were bound to mean more to me than anything that might be trotting about on the moon or Mars or Sirius or Betelgeuse or Venus or Jupiter. For the people I was walking beside were the same ones who in some far country would suddenly cross my tracks or confront me face to face, in waking moments and in dreaming, but especially in half-waking and half-dreaming—people you hadn't thought about for years and then had to think about with just that much more concentration.

For instance him, or him! I wonder whether the old boy is still alive and whether life is treating him as well as he deserves . . . And then—there—look at the stinker, the tattletale! Why do I think of him, with his trousers and sleeves too short, at this particular moment, here at this street corner by the harbor? Here among palms and sycamores and blackamoors in this tropical heat? But all the same it does you good, just because it is so hot and there are all those heathen blacks around, to remember that in cooler days you hobnobbed with Christian Teutonic compatriots back home and had your nose rubbed into just how heartwarming life can be among them. . . . And, good Lord, here comes Maier— Maier, just as if he had stepped out of the picture on a tea canister, with the heavenly porcelain pagoda of Nanking behind him. How did the dear old fathead come by that marvelous pigtail and that mandarin's button of the fourth class? And Lord bless me, Tubby Schaumann. And what is it now that makes me think of him, my fat friend Schaumann, the first boy in the fourth form, counting from the bottom? Tubby, Tubby—just imagine.

I hadn't come across them all again, either in town or at the Brummersumm. Death had taken one away and life had taken another. And as for the Brummersumm more particularly, the one was too badly married and the other too well for either of them ever to be in the mood for company and conviviality of an evening, and which, yes, sometimes lasted well into the night. There was one of us who had forsworn the Brummersumm and stayed with his wife for a very special reason, and his name, or rather his nickname, was Tubby.

He will have a good deal to say in these pages and there had been talk of him at some length in the old inn, and on the way home under the glittering stars and down the long avenue of poplars. But I had been trailing behind the others for some little time, not joining in the conversation, but just letting old memories have their way and saying to myself:

Tubby Schaumann! Tubby Schaumann and Red Bank Farm! Edward, can it be that you have saved the best piece of cake till the last? What dispensation is it that has kept the droll fellow, the fine lad out of your way till now? So Tubby Schaumann is actually living at Red Bank. Not all Africa and Europe together will stop me from setting out first thing in the morning for Red Bank to see my closest and fattest friend. Think of it. Tubby Schaumann really and truly living at Red Bank Farm.

As I told you, after years of absence I was once again a guest in my native town and at the Brummersumm Inn, or rather I had once again pulled up a chair there.

At this point I might luxuriate in a wealth of thoughts, sentiments, moods, observations—all very German, all from the bottom of the heart, and all very self-indulgent. But I won't do it; I'll stick to the essentials.

You see, I used to come out to the Brummersumm with my father when I was a boy. He kept his pipe there, and now and then I had to fetch him a new one. "A nice example the old gentleman set for his youngster," people will say. And they are right; they don't know how right they are. He set me a very nice example—and not in this respect only.

So I had been a regular visitor at the Brummersumm from childhood, which was one of the reasons why I got married. I wanted to share so many things I learned there with my own youngsters out in "burning Africa" just the way my worthy old father had shared them with me. Thank God, there is many a piece of cultural wisdom that originated in the Brummersumm that those rowdy young German-Dutch half-breeds of mine pass on to the Boers and Kaffirs and Hottentots. They usually say on such occasions: "I got that from my father and he got it from his, our grandfather back in Germany."

Yes, indeed, an authentic German philistine sitting over his beer in the inn. You may shrug your shoulders at him, but only, of course, because you are taking the wrong man for the right. Where in all the world is it easier than in the Brummersumm to hold your spear in position and let the silly, stupid, envious world impale itself on it? And where better in all the world can you give the hefty thrust that brings the wretched monster down and lays it at your feet?

What the philistine's wife thinks of the Brummersumm is another matter entirely. And what my mother thought of it is a very special matter indeed. It wasn't till I was appreciably older that I really understood the situation, but while the memories are mixed, the final impression is most satisfying. The good woman had made her peace with the Brummersumm and she would even remind my father sometimes that it was surely "time he was setting out." And strangely enough this would happen most often when there was sorrow, trouble, and vexation in the house and the atmosphere was bad and the burden all fell on her, poor woman. I can't think of anything that puts her in a better light, or the Brummersumm either.

On the evening in question, the evening of stars that opens these pages, I had revived old memories of all sorts. At the Brummersumm they were saying that I had come home from the land of the Kaffirs a very quiet man. As usual they were forgetting that you can have very little to say and yet be conducting the liveliest of conversations with one person or with many. Besides I had taken in most of what was said in my hearing that night, and one subject of conversation, casually touched on, had held me longer and given me more to think about than any others that came up at the old inn table.

I should explain that one of us is at present an official of the Imperial Post Office, and he told us or rather just threw it out in passing:

"It may interest some of you gentlemen to know that we heard today that Störzer is dead. Our oldest rural postman and the one who has covered most ground. I should be surprised if there was a single one of us here that hadn't crossed his tracks."

"Of course," they all said in unison. "Old Störzer. So he has laid his walking stick aside at last, has he?"

"Yes, and most honorably. He's been on the road for all of thirty-one years, and as soon as we heard of his death we set about calculating officially how much ground he had covered in the faithful execution of his duties without ever asking for a day's leave. How many times do you think, gentlemen, he might have walked all the way round the world?"

"I'd like to know," said the Brummersumm with one voice.

"Five times. Right round the world. Twenty-seven thousand and eighty-two German miles in fifty-four thousand, one hundred and sixty-four walking hours on duty. And, as I told you, the lucky fellow never missed a day's work in his thirty-one years—never had to miss a single day for illness. How many of you would have been glad to exchange legs with him and get rid of your chronic rheumatism, your more or less pronounced sciatica, and all the other attributes of a sedentary profession? Oh, if only he could have passed them on to someone."

"Yes, indeed, God knows," said several of the company with a sigh, and "So old Störzer is dead," they said again.

"So old Störzer is dead," I murmured too. "Gone to his rest after covering the equivalent of five times round the globe. Well, I would like to have seen him again and had a word with him before he took that last journey of all, the one that didn't belong to his earthly job." And an uncomfortable feeling came over me of having carelessly failed in a duty or an obligation. Did the man have to be in such a hurry this time? Couldn't he have waited, Edward, till you remembered him and paid him the friendly visit that you owed him on your visit home?

"You must remember him better than any of us, Edward," someone had said at the inn table shortly before.

"Yes, I remember him very well," I had replied; and Störzer is a reason, one of the reasons, why I have written these pages.

"Yes indeed, how well I remember him," I said to myself again half an hour or an hour later when I was back in the hotel where I was staying during my visit to my home town and was alone with myself and the impressions of home that I had gathered during the day. Of course, he was one of the people I knew best when I was young, Störzer was; and it was through my father that I got to know him and saw something of him. My father's advice was:

"Just look, boy, *you* take an example from him. He doesn't care how far he has to go or what the weather is like. And think of all the things he carries to people every day in that leather bag of his, wearing the same face day in and day out."

At the time I probably didn't fully understand the latter part of these remarks. Today I know that my dear departed father was probably leaving out the proper adjectives in front of the word "face," namely, stupid, indifferent, content with himself. But what real boy doesn't respect a man who is held up to him as a model because he doesn't mind either the road or the weather?

"I wonder where that boy has got to again," my old mother would ask in those happy days.

"That boy" was with Störzer, the man who could whistle, flute, chirp, or croak like every one of our native birds and some exotic ones too, the man who in the year of grace eighteen hundred and fifty was all "mobilized"[3] for war, the man who read—geography. The thing was crystal clear, however difficult it seemed to a boy's mother as she lifted the lid of the soup tureen and looked about her in vain. I should explain at this point that we belonged to the Post Office too (it wasn't Imperial then) and that my father in his last years had the title of Postmaster, and this no doubt had something to do with the friendly and intimate relations that developed between Störzer and me. We belonged together, as we say, and on my travels, I won't say round the world but through it, I have never heard the rare note of a post horn without thinking of my father and my mother, and of Störzer. Störzer, by the way, always got a cigar to smoke on the road if he met my father and me outside the town. So it was not surprising if, every time he met me alone, he asked, "Well, Edward, what about it, would you like to come, will they let you?"

He should have been the first, or at least one of the first, I went to see. But now I'd procrastinated again till it was too late. Even the Imperial Post Office had lost its claim on him, couldn't drag him out of his featherbed—or his straw bed—before daybreak to march off again in good weather or bad. And here was I, lodged with my friend Sichert, the landlord of The Three Wise Men, remembering Störzer the way you remember someone you looked up to when you were little and had gone with to places, with your mind brimming with all the romance and adventure the world has to offer.

There are times, you know, when all the life and all the liveliness around you becomes a distant hum and you only hear a single voice close at hand and very loud and clear.

"We'll have to give it up, Edward," I distinctly heard Störzer say with a sigh. He had wanted—on that particular day long ago—

to show me a cuckoo's egg in a hedge sparrow's nest, but it turned out that other naturalists had been there first and that someone— the devil, or, as we say, the cuckoo—had carried off the whole phenomenon from where it had lain hidden in a bush in the old quarry off to the right of the highway that was part of Störzer's route.

And I hear the same voice again, but coming from another of those distant days:

"You see, Edward, if I had been your mother, I mightn't have let you come with me this morning, summer holidays or no. All the folks who know nothing about it still think it's a really fine day. However, I'll say nothing of what I know about the weather in this area, but for me, the sun may be shining now, but it's clouding up too suspiciously over yonder and all round, and especially behind Maiholzen where the storms brew. If you would rather go back, Edward, before it is too late, you might be sparing your parents and your clothes too. I won't say any more, but the hour may come when they would rather have you at home."

It isn't always the same voice. There is another that chips in, but it hasn't broken yet, and has years to go before it will.

"There's been a big earthquake in South America, Störzer. My father read it to us out of the newspaper at breakfast this morning. It made rubble out of several places, one of them a town as big as ours. Gosh, if you could see a thing like that, Störzer."

"Yes, Edward, that's what a lot of them said back in the year eighteen-fifty during the general mobilization, when old men who had been there talked about the battle of Leipzig and Waterloo and the toil of the marches. Afterwards we were none of us sorry that it hadn't come to anything. The biggest braggart of us all soon got his fill just on the drill ground. And even Karl Drönemann, whom they made a mounted postillon in the army postal service, said it was small compensation for all you had gone through at the risk of your life to be able to talk about it afterward at home. It is just the same as with travel books. Just take our Levallyang,[4] how nice and cozy it is to read, because he wrote about it so nice and cozy at home . . . So the big earthquake was in South America this time? Oh, yes, geography is *the* science for postmen. About how many were killed, Edward?"

"Oh, a hundred thousand or so. They can't calculate it exactly."

"Hm, a few thousand more or less. One more or less. Yes, one more or less—one less. Edward, the Lord must know what he is doing. Don't *you* think so?"

"I don't know. But it must play the dickens with their letter and parcel delivery, my father says, and lots of things are sure to go back 'undeliverable.' Don't you think so too, Störzer?"

"One more or less in the world."

"Katerfeld, the tradesman—who has a wealthy brother out there, my mother says—came to see my father at breakfast and inquired about it."

"There, you see, Edward. One more or less. Yes, this fellow Katerfeld that went overseas. His first name was Sekkel. I know him well from when we were kids. It must have been in Chile, this earthquake of yours, because that is where he emigrated to and made millions. And that's what we all ought to do. He never married, because there was a girl here who wouldn't have him. You can think about that as you like, Edward, it's not so important. Look at that, so he got into the earthquake, did he? Well, if I'd been in Mr. Samuel Katerfeld's place, I'd have gone straight to your father, the postmaster, and inquired too. But, you are too young to understand that, Edward. So you want to come with me this morning, rain or shine. Well, let's start hoofing it and we can talk about Levallyang. That's the book for us. He'll drive the dismal notions out of our heads with the tale of his travels. His is the sort of life we all ought to lead among Hottentots, wild and tame ones alike. I sat up half the night again reading that book."

"Your bag is heavy today."

"Heavy . . . The things people write. Red Bank alone, I mean the man who lives there. If anyone at the post office would relieve me of Red Bank and all its mail, I'd go down on my knees and thank him for the deliverance. Today, I admit, it's just the newspaper. Perhaps you would run over with it again across the trench and deliver it for me. You will, won't you? Meanwhile I'll stay on this side and sort out the rest of the letters and the magazines and the fashion papers for all the farmers and pastors and factory inspectors they are going to."

What wouldn't I have done in those days to please Störzer the postman.

"Of course, I'll take the things over to Quakatz's, Fritz. I don't care how sour a face he pulls and I know that wildcat daughter of his would sooner scratch my face than look at it. You just sit yourself down under the tree near the trench and sort your stuff. I'll run over to Red Bank and take it by storm the way Tubby Schaumann means to take it. Then we shall be through before your thunderstorm comes up, Störzer."

"Lord, I hope it won't come up all that soon, Edward."

And sturdily uphill we go in the morning sun, undeterred by the weather threatening on the horizon.

Sitting in my room at The Three Wise Men I can hear my harmless old friend groan or rather sigh and say, "A heavy bag indeed." But, heart and soul with him as I was, what did I care about the letters he carried across the country for the farmers and the landowners and the industrialists? There were things so much more important crawling about and flying and running and whizzing and shining both on the highway and on the side roads. Yes, if the cuckoo and the hedge sparrow and the hedgehog and the hare and the rest of the company and the sun and the shade and the wind and the rain and the thunder and the lightning had all agreed to communicate with one another in writing and let Störzer deliver the letters, it might well have been more wonderful still. But it was good enough as it was, with the rye and the wheat and the cornflower and the poppy all around me managing without the help of pen, ink, and paper and coexisting busily and amicably within their isotheres and isotherms[5] without any advanced education at all!

Isotheres! Isotherms! If these learned words didn't go very well with the familiar names, the native names, for all that grew in the fields ("Consider the lilies," etc.), neither did they go very well with the rest of our geography at that time. But, for all that, what wonderful geographers and topographers and naturalists we were, Störzer and I. We would have been the right people for that friendly old scholar Karl Ritter[6] drawing his landscapes on the big blackboard behind his reading desk at Berlin University.

And at that age what flights you could make into the boundless world in the few hours it took us to get from one house or village to another!

At home, in Neuteutoburg, I know only too well that the world, or in this case the globe, is by no means immeasurable and that this lump of matter floating in the ether is not nearly as thick as it thinks it is. But if I have managed at least to travel as far as the Boers and Kaffirs, and made myself a tidy fortune, to whom do I owe it unless to Störzer the postman and his favorite book, Le Vaillant's *Travels into the Interior of Africa* translated from the French with notes by Johann Reinhold Forster? [7]

Sitting in The Three Wise Men how clearly I hear his voice, saying:

"Geography, Edward. Oh, geography. And a man like this Levallyang. Where would the likes of us be without geography and this model of a traveler and a man? Just think, the same round day after day, year after year. Knowing every village like the palm of your hand. Knowing everybody in every house, from the oldest grandmother to the youngest little brat just spawned, knowing them as well as you know your own kin in your own home. And at every house hearing somebody say: Here comes Störzer. And then: Störzer has brought the newspaper. Störzer is bringing a letter. Could you stand that for life, always on the same route, if you didn't have your thoughts and your dreams and your books, Edward? Wouldn't you get bored in the long run, without geography?"

"Not me, Störzer. We have geography at school and only yesterday I had an hour's detention because of it. Bithynia, Paphlagonia, and Pontus, I knew them. But who knows the names of all the ancient states of Asia Minor?"

"Sorry you had that trouble, Edward. But you would have been doing me a favor, while you were sitting there, if you had learned them all by heart, if only for me."

"For you, Fritz? Well, then: Mysia, Lydia, Karia, Lycia, Pisidia, Phrygia, Galatia, Lykaonia, Cilicia, Kappadocia, Armenia minor, that's all, because I've already told you Bithynia, Paphlagonia, and Pontus."

"Hang it, Edward, it's just as if you were listing us Germans in all our subdivisions. Only it sounds a bit nicer and more foreign-like. See now, what a pleasure it must be for you, to be able to rattle all that off and have it mean something, here on the main road with all the familiar places round you. And Red Bank Farm here, right under your nose."

"I like Campe's *Travels*[8] better. And I like you better, Störzer. Mysia, Lydia, Karia, you try to get all that into your head down there in that stuffy old hole and see if you don't long for Le Vaillant's Africa and his Hottentots, and his giraffes and lions and elephants. They kept Tubby Schaumann in with me on account of all that nonsense. But he doesn't give a hang for Africa. All he longs for every day is Red Bank Farm, as you know."

"Of course, I know. It's silly of him, that fat friend of yours. You know, Edward, when I read about the world and ask myself what a sloth looks like, I'm always reminded of him. Him and his Red Bank!"

Red Bank Farm. I had begun to find myself yawning over all these memories, this medley of forms and voices, and to feel like leaving Störzer to his endless sleep and going to bed myself, but these three words kept me awake a while longer and brought back my early life with the utmost vividness. Red Bank Farm!

When I remembered the two together, Red Bank and Tubby, in those days the fattest, laziest, and greediest of us all, a sort of smiling contentment crept over me.

"It is when I am in bed that I really have it in my grasp, Edward," he used to say. "When I dream, that's what I dream about, and the master of the place who won't let any schoolmasters or teachers or anybody over his trench isn't Farmer Quakatz, it's me. Me, I tell you, Edward."

And on this night, sleeping at The Three Wise Men in my home town, I dreamed about Red Bank too. And in my dream I saw the place again in all its fascination as I had seen it long ago when I was in third and fourth forms, this farm, this Red Bank, this glorious old earthwork of Prince Xaverius,[9] Andreas Quakatz's farm. From there, in the sixties of the eighteenth century, this Prince of Electoral Saxony had bombarded the town below, and the school too, our gymnasium, so vigorously that they both had to surrender to him at once, though he was by no means the greatest hero of the Seven Years' War. The Seven Years' War dated from well before the time when Schaumann and I were at school, but Red Bank was still in my dreams, as it was when we were boys and idealized it.

There it rose on its high ground, four-square and well preserved, with only an embanked driveway over the deep trench to connect it with the outside world. And with everything about it to make it mysteriously delightful to a boy's imagination: the cannon and mortars of Prince Xaver and the impenetrable thorn hedge that wicked farmer Andreas Quakatz had put around his property to shut off himself, his daughter Tina, his house, his stables, his barns, and everything else that was his, from a malicious world.

I can hear a dull roll and crash breaking into my dream of Red Bank; but it isn't the cannon of Electoral Saxony thundering against King Fritz of Prussia; it is that thunderstorm during which Störzer said: "It is catching up on us faster than I thought. There, Edward, be a good lad and run over with the mail to Quakatz's. Here is his newspaper and here are one, two, three letters. The correspondence that man keeps up, and oh, dear, Edward, always a few with official seals on them. There, that girl of his is peeping round the gatepost. Give her the letters. I'll be getting the rest sorted under the beech tree, before the storm breaks in earnest."

"What do you want of us, you stupid boy?" I hear a delicate voice say, pretending to be angry, and mingled with the yelping of half a dozen house and farm dogs of various breeds, all beside themselves with rage and ferocity. And they aren't content to yelp and show their teeth. They rush at my legs and jump at my throat. Old South African that I am, I had every right to wake up from my dream with a loud yell.

But I didn't wake up. I stood on the embankment in front of the two gateposts of Quakatz's farm at Red Bank and the little girl's voice shrieked in mocking laughter: "Keep off him. Come back here. The whole courthouse. Judge! Assessor! Solicitor! To heel, every one of you. Down Juryman Vahldiek, down Meier, down Brauneberg, down the whole jury!"

"There's your mail, your letters, and your newspaper, you nasty cat, you," I shouted, throwing it all into the apron the little redhead of Red Bank held open for me and retreating from this inhospitable establishment down the embanked road back to the open field and the beech tree and Störzer.

"Come on, Edward," said Störzer, "we'd better make tracks, so we get at least as far as Maiholzen without a wetting. Just look, how it is pouring over yonder. There's a nice summer day for you. Well, thank God, we have Red Bank and Quakatz behind us."

It was strange how that night at The Three Wise Men past and present were mingled in my sleeping and dozing and dreaming. There was a rolling and roaring as of a cloudburst and heavy thunder. There I lay in bed at The Three Wise Men, a husband and father and landowner and large-scale sheep-breeder of the Orange River and was, at the same time, a twelve-year-old boy running over the open fields with Störzer the postman in thunder and lightning and the pouring rain to reach Maiholzen, the village behind Red Bank, with life and limb, though not with dry clothes.

It wasn't till the waiter came with my shaving water that I learned that there really had been a heavy thunderstorm toward morning, and when the young man politely said he hoped I had slept pleasantly through it there was nothing to counter him with.

I had slept through the real thunderstorm of the night, or rather its din had so mingled with the rolling and roaring of the past that I couldn't tell what was dream and what was reality. But before the waiter knocked I had been listening for some time to something else that is often mentioned in the literature of dreams: the bells in the church towers of my home town. I had heard them strike six and half-past six and seven. And, lying there deliciously awake and stretching myself in bed with the bells ringing those hours, I had begun to think vividly of something else—a memory both sweet and harrowing. The hour, I mean, by which you had to be in school, seven in summer and eight in winter and not just me, but, horrid to relate, Schaumann too; Tubby, who "cared nothing for the whole tomfoolery or, at least, cared much less for it than all the rest of the class put together."

He was not remotely concerned with what "those fellows" (he meant his teachers) knew and foolishly wanted to teach him. He was all right as he was and—in short, it was a crime to have to "be there" at seven in summer and at eight in winter, only to submit contemptuously to their punishment, since "nothing else was any use."

Tubby Schaumann! It surely wasn't on account of the church bells (though he did make an attempt to study theology) but simply and solely on account of the clock on the tower, if he now rose up before me as vividly as Störzer—Schaumann, that other friend of my childhood days in field and wood, Schaumann who never ran in his life, except when the old vice-principal was chasing him with his hazel switch. Not around the world. But around the blackboard and the unsolved problems of mathematics.

Yes, in our day—thank God—we got the thrashing we deserved. At school we called him Tubby, but his real name was Heinrich Schaumann and he was the only child of parents so lean and shrivelled, so restless and wrenlike, that it seemed those townspeople were right who said he had come out of a cuckoo's egg and had been put into Registrar and Frau Schaumann's nest by some nefarious and shameful means. Be that as it may, they brought him up, thrust what they could down his beak, and he throve on it.

And just the way a pair of wrens take pleasure in their plump nestling, so Father and Mother Schaumann took pleasure in their fat boy and naturally wanted to enlarge him in another dimension and give him a career. Make him a pastor, of course, or a high official or a top physician, or something of the sort.

"The thing might suit me well enough," Heinrich would often say to me, "if it weren't for the damned labors you have to go through before you get there. That horrible Latin and then Greek, and then, to drive you completely crazy, Hebrew," he said with a sigh, rubbing his shoulders as often as not.

"And what about Red Bank Farm, Heinrich?"

"There's that too, Edward, though you are all very silly about it. Well, I don't care what you stupid people think and say about me. And anyway you can't mention the two in the same breath: school and Quakatz's Red Bank. I swear to God that if I could get possession of Red Bank, I wouldn't look at a parsonage for love or money. Why, I'd be willing to murder Kienbaum three times over."

"But Tubby!"

"Yes, Tubby, Greedy. Call me that if you like. I don't care.

When I get hold of a piece of cake, I wolf it down. You can bet on that. And as for Quakatz, I'll say it again: I don't care in the least what the whole world says about him. As far as I am concerned he can have murdered Kienbaum six times. That doesn't prevent him from holding Red Bank Farm and being the luckiest man in the world. And besides, there isn't a court of justice that has anything on him, and even if everyone is against him it doesn't prove a thing. Everyone is against me as well, and if you find Blechhammer, the learned Dr. Blechhammer, lying somewhere by the roadside tomorrow with his throat cut, there is nothing to stop you blaming it on me, saying I did it and finally paid off an old grudge. Quakatz at Red Bank is quite right if he would rather fortify Prince Xaver's ramparts with cannon than just with thorn-bushes to keep the world and everyone in it out. Oh, if I could rake them with gunshot from Red Bank—everybody, I mean—and then turn the dogs on them! You know, Edward, and you could prove it, that this time I was fit to go up. And they've kept me back again and not let me into Upper Fourth. You try going home after that and being happy with your parents and with life in general. No wonder a man turns hermit and puts himself behind his heavy artillery. There is nothing now for me but Red Bank and the thought of owning it. You go running round the countryside with Störzer and I lay siege to Red Bank Farm. Every man to his taste. All I think of is—washing my hands of school and everything and being up there—and then let that old beast Blechhammer come. Look at this, Edward. That little wildcat, Tina Quakatz, bit me in the hand yesterday, but it's all right with me. Why shouldn't you bite, if everyone is after you? Besides, I gave the little toad tit for tat and slapped her face. And when the old man came, he didn't blame either of us. Work it off, he said. It's better than stewing in your juice, he said. And nobody knows better than me how right he was. To have to sit on the bottom seat now and let Blechhammer say what he likes and not be able to answer back is ten thousand times worse than being charged with murdering Kienbaum when you haven't murdered him. Go ahead and stare at me, Edward. You are another of those who congratulate themselves every hour of the day that they aren't in Andreas Quakatz's shoes at Red Bank Farm, or in Heinrich Schaumann's either."

"You aren't fair to me at all, Heinrich."

"Oh, yes. I am. I just know you all, every one of you, inside and out."

I had shaved. I do it myself. Out there, or back there, in the land of the Kaffirs you might wait a long time for a barber, even if he mounted an ostrich and raced with his shaving tackle from kraal to kraal, or farm to farm, to serve his customers. The sun was up now and shining on my breakfast table. I could compliment the bed I had slept in at The Three Wise Men for letting me sleep there so very soundly. It wasn't my concern, how well ten thousand others might have slept in it before me.

It was a lovely morning, thanks to the thunderstorm of the night before. A morning so fresh and light in its beginnings that you could take it for granted another fine summer day was in the making.

"So old Störzer is dead," I said with a melancholy yet comfortable sigh, as I sat over my coffee reading the newspaper the waiter had brought me. What he said was: "The landlord is letting you see it first, because he thinks you will be more interested, after coming home from so far away. There was no hurry, he said, about taking it downstairs to the other gentlemen in the parlor."

These courteous words from the young waiter brought another bit of the old days back to life. It was a friendly gesture on the part of "mine host" at The Three Wise Men. But this time I wasn't very eager to read the latest news from the great world sitting in judgment on itself. I soon pushed the paper aside and said again: "Old Störzer dead. What a shame! It's your fault that you missed him, Edward. So I mustn't let anything stop me from going out to Red Bank today to see—Tubby Schaumann!" . . . It is amazing how vividly all this is coming back again, without my doing anything about it except keeping my eyes and ears open. Tubby Schaumann. A couple of weeks ago how little I remembered him, my crazy old friend, Heinrich Schaumann, who was so lazy and so fat and so decent and lovable, Heinrich Schaumann, alias Tubby.

And now I suddenly had him all back to life again, completely. Just the way I had Störzer back, poor Störzer. And it would have been very wrong of me, if I hadn't paid the former a visit without delay—now, while there was time for it. Hadn't I just discovered again in the case of the latter how easy it was to miss the last opportune moment?

I admit that at the time when we left school, he might have lived and died—Heinrich, I mean—ten thousand times without me having a minute or a second of my time to spare for him. I was too busy living and dying myself.

We went apart just at the time of life when you have least time for one another. And the casual attitude to letter writing today didn't help. Who writes letters any more in the age of postcards?

I can see the whole of the second half of the eighteenth century shaking its head, and a good third of the nineteenth too, and sitting at the breakfast table in the hotel at home, I say to myself: You might have written to one another at least once—you and your friend Heinrich.

Well, all things considered and speaking honestly, we had never been what you might call intimate in our personal relations. But school-friends, good school-friends—*that* we had been, Tubby and I. Which of us on occasion pulled the most hair out of the other's head or gave the bluest bruises or the worst black eyes doesn't matter now. What mattered now was to find out how time had treated the fine, fat lad, whether he had changed much, whether as a result of the change he was in a position, like Quakatz the farmer before him, to slam the gate of Red Bank Farm in the face of the whole world, including me, or whether, after putting the usual slightly embarrassed question as to whom he had the honor, etc., he would stretch out both hands to me and, falling into something like the way we talked at school, say: "For heaven's sake, is it you, Edward? My, it's nice that you remembered me."

In view of the fact that he lived "a good way out," I didn't think it necessary to observe the visiting hours customary in towns large, small, or middle-sized, and by about nine o'clock I was on my way to him.

It was a really choice morning. In the town the police had it to their credit that the streets were well swept, and outside in the open country Mother Nature had seen to it that everything was nicely washed. She had seen to it in person with soap and sponge, and thunder and lightning. Trees, bushes, grasses, and flowers were like freshly scrubbed children with the tears still in their eyes from the operation and you could see clearly enough that some of them had fought and kicked. But no matter, it was over now, and the result was good. The world shone in splendor, and the fresh gentle breeze that blew over it improved the morning all the more. Out there in the virginal Kaffir land among the Betchuans and the Boers the landscape could hardly look more youthful after an overnight thunderstorm than it did here in weary old Europe exhausted by countless centuries of usage.

"Everything just as it used to be, Edward," I sighed with sad contentment. But this wasn't quite the case.

When I came to look I remembered there used to be a pond, or rather a swamp, off to the right of Red Bank road, some four or five hundred square meters in size. It wasn't there.

It once teemed and thronged with the dark wonders of nature, and now they had converted it into a moderately fertile potato field, useful no doubt, but the place was prettier before and more "instructive" too. The least I owed to the frog pond, as we called it, was to look around for it with surprise and to be very sorry not to find it. Such a good acquaintance, such a good old friend! So full of sweet flag, reeds, cattails, frogs, snails, water beetles, with dragonflies whirring over it and butterflies hovering, and willows all around it, and smelling so nice. Yes, smelling nice, a sweetly familiar stench, especially on hot summer days when they had told us in the afternoon science class: "You will find everything that came in today's lesson, and very fully represented, in the frog pond."

"God knows, they could have left it as it was. And they should have," I grumbled as I made my way out to Red Bank. "They didn't have to have those few extra sacks of feed for themselves or their stock."

But they thought they did, and there was nothing you could do about it now. I just had to square myself with the loss. I didn't know, so it didn't concern me, that this "improvement," as they called it, had an elaborate lawsuit behind it that had lasted for years and had disrupted the lives of three or four families of market-gardeners in the town.

But there was another lawsuit that went back to my early days and was more serious: the ugly case of Quakatz in the Kienbaum affair.

Walking along the charming narrow path to Red Bank between the fields of waving grain, dewy from the rain, and shining in the sun, and slowly ripening for the harvest, it all came back to mind—the now so utterly forgotten stir and excitement over the murder of Kienbaum that swept the neighborhood when I was a boy. I began to remember the details—each more interesting than the one before it.

They had had him in jail no less than three times—Andreas Quakatz, the farmer of Red Bank—because new "evidence" had been forthcoming in the Kienbaum case. And three times they had had to let him go again, without chopping his head off, because these new indications and suspicions proved every time to be what they were—more or less frivolous reports, in some instances maliciously and vindictively contrived.

"Yes, Edward, who killed Cock Robin?" asked Heinrich Schaumann, alias Tubby, sorrowfully shaking his head and scratching himself behind those somewhat projecting ears. We had just left school and were standing together for the last time at that point on the road where you were high enough to get the first clear view—it is the same today—of the full extent of the Comte de Lusace's,[10] Prince Xaver of Saxony's, well-preserved earthwork. It is the same spot I had stopped at in my dreams and half-dreams the night before for Störzer to sort his letters under the old beech tree, just opposite the embankment—it's still there—that crosses the trench to the entrance gate of Quakatz's farm.

But the beech tree wasn't there any more. Like the frog pond it had been sacrificed to the interests of "increased production." Presumably it had cast too much shade over the plough land for this hungry generation or spread its roots too far underground. But, thank God, Red Bank Farm was still there, though it certainly wasn't in the interests of "improvements" that war, like an old mole, had burrowed and thrown it up out of the soil in the year seventeen hundred and sixty-one. And now I stood in front of it again and looked back at us two, Heinrich Schaumann, alias Tubby, and me, and what Tubby had to say then, from first-hand experience, about the case of Kienbaum *versus* Quakatz or Quakatz *versus* Kienbaum and about something not unconnected with it, Tina Quakatz.

He didn't look like an incipient theologian. He was already beginning to put on weight, and young theologians don't usually do this till later when they have a good living and can at their own well-stocked table make up for what they missed at the charity table when they were students. But he was a good lad, good to the core. And for his parents' sake he at least did what he could to "starve" his way into the best-fed job in the world. "What wouldn't you do to please your mom when she has set her mind on something and is shedding tears over it and an old man whose mind is almost insanely bent on getting his son into the first bread-and-butter profession that offers itself? You don't want to nip the aged couple's fairest hopes in the bud. They're a worthy pair and they are entitled to something in return for having brought you into this world of gnawed bones, and hard bread-crusts, and healthy, clear, refreshing, and, above all, inexpensive wellwater, Edward."

I need hardly say that these remarks, testifying to a dutiful and unspoiled mind, are also put down from memory. This was how he used to comfort himself at frequent intervals between the fifth form and matriculation. But on the day in question—the day we said goodbye to our childhood, if not to our youth, the day we both stood for the last time for many, many years under Störzer's beech tree, facing Red Bank Farm—he said something not at all like that.

What he said was: "There she is. In the midst of her warriors. Listen to the dogs and look at them, baying at us and baring their teeth. What grand dogs they are! If there is anything I enjoy in all the world, it's them. Just look how quickly they do as they are told. They know how to keep Tina Quakatz and Red Bank clear of people who don't belong there. Tell me, could that silly *monsieur* in the French Service, that Count von der Lausitz, Prince Xaver of Electoral Saxony, have manned the rampart over there better than Farmer Quakatz has done?"

"I don't suppose he could. I can see that it all goes together, Heinrich, the house, the farm, the trench—father, daughter, and bodyguard."

"It certainly does. God be thanked. And now I'm going to tell you something else, Edward, and I hope it won't offend you. It would have suited me better if you hadn't hung on to me today, on the way up here. We could have played the part of Damon and Pythias or David and Jonathan, or whatever other peerless friends you could mention, and said our good-byes on some other occasion, some other walk, when we weren't heading for Red Bank, but going in the opposite direction. But seeing that you are a good fellow and a real friend and there is nothing else for it, I don't mind if you stay. There is one thing, though, I want you to do for me: be as little in evidence as possible and keep your mouth shut. And then, back in town, don't make me more ridiculous with the people we know than you absolutely have to. Red Bank has got hold of me, and the poor girl there with her pack of dogs can't help it if she has made a fool of me too. It simply had to be; I have to take it. It's written in the book of Fate. Hello, Valentina."

"Hello, Mr. Schaumann."

Leaning there on the gatepost with her arms folded, she certainly didn't look as if she wanted to say a friendly hello to anyone. You couldn't help glancing to see whether she had a loaded shotgun beside her at the entrance to the farm or a sharp knife hidden in her right hand under her left arm ready to use in a flash. And she had something too of a wildcat about her that at a pinch didn't need to be armed at all, but only had to go at your face with her own genuine claws and to take hold with her own teeth in order to come out on top in any battle for herself and her father's hearth and home.

There she stood, neither big nor small, neither fat nor lean, neither pretty nor ugly, not like a town girl and not like a country girl, no longer a child and not yet a woman, Valentina Quakatz, the only daughter of the ill-famed farmer and murderer, Andreas Quakatz, keeping guard over his estate, all in that peaceful, sunlit landscape of green leaf and pale-yellow grain.

This time I didn't shout: "There's your mail—your letters, your newspaper—you nasty redheaded cat," in execution of Störzer's business at the entrance of Red Bank Farm. But she, young Miss Quakatz, silenced the dogs the way she did then, and did it almost with the same strange calls. The curs were slow, reluctant, to obey;

they went on growling softly and suspiciously watching our every move.

"Father isn't at home," said Valentina, and she added: "The hands are in the fields."

"Good," said Tubby, "then we have the place to ourselves, just the two of us, because I've made it quite clear to this fellow here that for the present he must consider himself no more than thin air. Of course, if he wasn't my best friend I would have made it even clearer to him how utterly superfluous he is here today. But he *is* my friend and therefore, so far as it suits me, yours too, Tina. And you are not such a fool, girl, as not to know that he knows as much about you and Red Bank as all the rest of our noble Christendom for five miles round. Lord, that alone is sufficient reason for jumping into theology—just to tell them—your noble fellowmen, I mean—what you thought of them from the pulpit. But now let's go into the house. To get the last noseful of the foul smell of Red Bank Farm to take with me into the better and purer air over yonder, outside the above-mentioned five-mile limit."

He was always ready, Heinrich was, to "say what he thought," to "throw words about," "to make speeches," in short to "preach." If it had come to that, he would never have been just the farmer at Red Bank; he would have been, let us say, a cisalpine pope, or a cardinal, or at the very least an archbishop.

"Where's the old man?" he said by way of a start.

"Up in court again," said the daughter and heiress of Red Bank grimly. "He's been having more trouble with the magistrate at Maiholzen. Shook his fist in his foolish face and told him again that he was a liar and slanderer in the old Kienbaum business. And so, of course, they've brought him up again."

Tubby showed now that he could whistle most melodiously. He vented his feelings in a long-drawn, lingering cadence and then expressed them in action, putting his arm round the girl's waist and turning to me and saying: "We couldn't have struck it better."

And then something happened that more than anything brings that distant day back to me in all its vivid reality: Valentina Quakatz resigned from sentry duty at the entrance gate of Red Bank Farm—resigned completely. Her angry twisted mouth began to tremble. She fought with her tears, but they were too strong for her. She sobbed, she cried aloud, and instead of clawing his face, she flung her arms around Tubby Schaumann's neck, clung to him, and said brokenly:

"Heinrich, you are so bad."

"Come, come, now."

"You're just as bad as all the rest."

"All right then, turn your dogs on me, you crazy wench. What do you say to that, Edward? Me as bad as all the rest?"

I said nothing. I stood there like a stupid fool with my mouth open, and watched. He kept her in his arms as a matter of course, patted her on the back, stroked her hair, lifted her face by the chin, and kissed her. I could see him awkwardly fishing in his back pocket for his handkerchief, getting it out at last, and wiping the girl's tears—a big grown stranger of a girl. It amazed me and I suddenly began to see Tubby with quite different eyes. I was so flushed and embarrassed that I wished myself at the uttermost ends of the earth, yet I didn't want anyone to take me by the arm and say: "Come along, Edward, this is no place for you."

Fortunately Tubby was far too busy with the girl to have more than a casual word now and then to spare for me.

"But darling, how can I help it? Do you think I'm going of my own free will? Don't I have to go? Haven't I committed myself, for my parents' sake, to fail my examination at least once? You know I'd much rather stay here for your sake. So be a good girl and stop your blubbering. Look at that dolt, Edward, watching us and thinking of the tale he'll tell about us when he gets home. There's my handkerchief again and now don't go on disgracing us both out here in public. Do you think Count von der Lausitz just threw up this rampart so that Heinrich Schaumann, whom they call Tubby, could show the soft side of himself to the philistines in that wretched hole down there? Don't you believe it. I'll bombard them again so that little Xaver-Palaver of Electoral Saxony will rejoice in his tomb, though all that's left of him is a heap of leather and old bones. Come along, Edward, since you are there. We'll go indoors. Because you see, Edward, it isn't always out of doors that you breathe most freely. That's an observation that I pass on to you for your own future use free, gratis. Naturally I don't want any silly jokes either here or in town when you're back among your folks and your friends and acquaintances. So we three have Red Bank to ourselves. Wonderful! Tina, tell the dogs what they have to do and make no bones about it."

Miss Valentina turned to her guard of quadrupeds. That is to say, she shook her fist at them and then shook it at the smiling summer landscape beyond the trench. The idea was that the beasts should keep an even better lookout than usual and let no one cross Count von der Lausitz's bulwark with impunity. And they understood and answered with a low, vicious half-whine, half-growl. And now we three were wonderfully and truly alone at Red Bank Farm.

Once you were past the gate and the dogs, the place was none too delightful to look at. Everything seemed neglected and run wild. Any work that was done was half-done, carelessly done, unwillingly. The garden was not well cared for; neither was the yard nor the house, nor probably the barn either. Implements and things lay about wherever they happened to have been left or dropped. Weeds and bushes grew unchecked. The drainage couldn't ask for anything better than it found here at Red Bank; it just had the run of the place. The hens were scratching away in the garden. Ducks and geese waddled all over the yard and in the house. You could see from the look of the animals that their master was often away and didn't keep an eye on them when he was at home. It was only too clear that the daughter of the house couldn't attend to everything and that the help took it very easy on that account. But as regards the latter, the help, there was another reason and a better one. When it came to help, men, maids, or boys, the farmer at Red Bank had to take what nobody else wanted. He had to take the dregs and the sweepings of the neighborhood.

It wasn't good for a decent person, a respectable girl, to work at Red Bank and try to do an honest job. There was no question of good pay or good treatment. Every penny that Farmer Quakatz let go of had the smell of blood on it. If you came from Red Bank Farm and tried to get a job somewhere else, you brought that smell with you in your clothes and they turned up their noses and let you know it and sent you on to the next place. And so it would remain, and there was nothing to be done about it, till Andreas

Quakatz finally confessed that he murdered Kienbaum or until the whole place at Red Bank was sold off by auction or, better still, was parceled out for the benefit of Maiholzen. Valentina Quakatz, the heiress of Red Bank, was helpless in the matter. The bitter feud included her and she had to endure it. It was Tubby who said (I hear him saying it while the long Atlantic waves carry me toward my new home on board *The Hagebucher* [11]):

"Well, Edward. Doesn't the place look charming?"

Their master being away again on matters of "libel and grievous insult," man and maid had pleased themselves about what work they did and were probably lying about somewhere under the trees, letting the world go by. There wasn't a sound to be heard except the chirping of the crickets or the chatter of angry sparrows on the roof or in the hedges. Tina wasn't even crying any more, either in that angry way of hers or choking it down bitterly. She led the way into the parlor without looking round to see if we were following. We did follow, though we were a little shy and self-conscious about it, and found her sitting at the table, her back against the wall, her arms on the black oak table and hands spread flat. Tubby and I stood in front of her, looking at her, in the dark low-ceilinged room, with our eyes still dazzled by the bright light outside. You could hear every fly buzz for a mile round. Oh, the flies at Red Bank Farm! *They* hadn't deserted Prince Xaver of Saxony's fortifications. Nor Quakatz's sitting room, whether or not he killed Kienbaum. There was nothing inside the four walls that they hadn't messed; especially the pictures on the walls: *The Ten Commandments, The Huntsman's Funeral,* and *The Man Who Fell Among Thieves* from the Gospel. They had been at the huntsman's funeral along with the other animals and had done all honor to his coffin. Similarly to the words: Thou shalt not commit murder. By the way, there were no new pictures on the wall for them to offer an opinion of. Even the latest events in world history had passed by this trench of the Seven Years' War without leaving a trace. No battle picture here of the charge at Düppel, from Neu-Ruppin, none of eighteen sixty-six, none of eighteen seventy.[12] No Kaiser Wilhelm, no Bismarck, no Moltke.[13] Why should the farmer at Red Bank bother with history? He had his Kienbaum. He had too heavy a burden of his own to bear, to concern himself much with the burdens of others, even if they were the great ones of the earth. For him, the world had hung Kienbaum on every wall he looked at in his own house; he didn't need the painter's art or a glass frame. He saw the man everywhere, even with his eyes shut, so clearly and tangibly that no painter, not even the best, could have equaled it.

I turned away from the garish illustrations of the *Ten Commandments* and looked uneasily, restlessly, at the girl who was staring at us, and then Heinrich said, "Now, Tina, stop that nonsense and don't stare the two best Latinists and Hellenists in this year's matriculation hoax out of the good opinion they have of themselves. Don't grin like that, Edward. Yes, you poor thing, the sweet years of childhood are gone forever; real life, responsibility—don't cry, Edward—is now beginning. If we were living in a more sensible age I would say: Sweetheart, jump up behind your knight-errant, grab him round the waist, and hold tight. In short, throw in your lot with me. But it can't be done, Edward. It isn't our fault that we aren't being promoted this time from the donkeys to the horses, but simply have to go away tomorrow by train. Tina, girl of my heart, don't look at me in that foolish way. I don't know what I shall bring home to my parents after my first semester, but I know what I shall bring you, I shall bring you the old Tubby again. As sure as the sky above us is blue and the earth is green, I won't let all the daily thrashings I took for the sake of Red Bank Farm be for nothing; I won't let it be for nothing that my only happy hours in this vale of misery were those I spent on guard with old man Quakatz and his little girl. If you would like that in writing, Miss Valentina, I'll give you it."

Something like a shiver went right through old Quakatz's daughter, but then she said, "I don't want anything in writing. If anything comes to this house in writing, my father prefers you to lay it on a manure fork and reach it to him. And then he takes hold of it as if it were a hot cinder. And you, you—oh, it would be better if nobody had a tongue to talk with, and lie with, and taunt with—not even you."

"Not even me?" asked Tubby, but with no hint of surprise, or offense, or anger in his voice. And then, half turning to me, he said, "Even in the present tragic circumstances you would do well to keep your head a little better, Tina. And you, Edward, can really learn something here that will help you later on in life. Not even you! A wonderful phrase. And look at the face she pulls when she says such a silly thing. This is what you get when you give a woman all the precious free afternoons you have in summer and winter, and the whole of your holidays too, from the time you were a child. Has this person any notion what thrashings etcetera I have endured from progenitors and pedagogues without a sound, and all for her sake?—Not even you! I tell you, girl, that if this sheepish fellow Edward weren't here, I'd show you again, and your crazy old man and the rest of Red Bank Farm, how much I love you, in a way there'd be no mistaking."

Another quiver ran across the shoulders under the gay peasant kerchief. The heiress of Red Bank was squinting up at Schaumann, the budding candidate for any job at all, like a half-tamed creature that has either been cowed or is beginning to learn. She started to beat the table with both fists, but she couldn't do it. She dropped her arms limply by her side and said with a sob:

"I didn't ask anyone to come and worry over me."

"You didn't," said Schaumann. "She is right there, Edward. I came of my own accord and befriended her. You know that, Edward."

I didn't know exactly how my friend meant it. All I knew was that in this instance in the opinion of both home and school there wasn't a crazier lad in all my boyhood than Schaumann, Tubby Schaumann. I ran around with Friedrich Störzer, the country postman, and Tubby sat down in front of Red Bank Farm, "like a cat at a mousehole," as he used to put it. He was good-natured, but far too lazy to go running around with anyone. He could eat his way through a mountain of rice pudding and on into never-never land and this was the general view of him, which I shared. That was all I knew, on the day we said good-bye, about his relation to Tina, Valentina Quakatz. It never occurred to me in my greenhorn simplicity that Quakatz's redheaded brat, that wild, shy thing, could play more than a very incidental role in his passion for Prince Xaver of Saxony's fortress. How should the world know, how should I know, that Tubby had it in him to be romantic in this business?

It was stuffy there and oppressive in that dark low room in the farmhouse. And Andreas Quakatz had worn a path in the dark floorboards from the kitchen door to the stove.

"That's where he has walked, even since I can remember," said his daughter, "and here I sit and hear him talking to himself, half the night long, till he sends me off to bed. You must know, Heinrich, why you started coming out to Red Bank and seeing me. But this friend of yours, Edward here, can't have any notion how I feel, now that you are going away. But if he wants to do me a favor, perhaps he will swear someday when I die that I left the Red Bank Farm to you, and everything in it. For there is no one but me that my father can leave it to, unless he leaves it to the dogs out there at the gate. Would you really be so kind, Edward, since you have come along here today, to testify later in court that, when the day comes that my father and I have nothing more to ask of this world, Red Bank Farm belongs to Heinrich Schaumann, and to no one else?"

How a man with Tubby Schaumann's physical constitution managed it so quickly I don't know, but he did. There he suddenly was, sitting at the dining table at Quakatz's farm beside the daughter and heiress with his arm around her neck, saying, "Now I've had enough of it. You can stand a certain amount of nonsense, but there's a limit, as Blechhammer says down there, Edward. Just take another look at Quakatz's castle from inside, my boy. Who knows, you may never see it this way again. Here is my dream—my house, my stronghold. Tomorrow the *universitas literarum* [14] and the open sea of life. Damned romantic and exciting for two boys leaving school. Wipe your eyes, you dear little goose of a milkmaid, and do please come on out of doors again. One breath in here is enough, and then you want to get out into the fresh air. *Vivant omnes virgines.* [15] Come *virgo.* [16] But if you start scratching and spitting I shall call you *virago.* [17] It's no use resisting, young woman. If they called me Tubby down there, there's a reason for it. I'll show them what's good for the heart and the digestion."

He took hold of the girl around the middle, lifted her out from behind the rude dining table, and sat her down again on Prince Xaver of Saxony's rampart. Valentina didn't try to stop him, and

I—followed them. "Like a sheep," Tubby would have said. I was taken aback, dazed, uncertain. If Tubby had now unfolded a pair of wings and slowly sailed off with the heiress of Red Bank, the daughter of the man that killed Kienbaum, and mounted higher and higher and higher in the blue spring air, all I could have done would have been to look passively on and say: "Would you believe it?"

There we stood on the high grassy rampart of Count von der Lausitz's old earthwork—we two freshmen and Valentina Quakatz—Heinrich and Tina arm in arm.

Suddenly that crazy Schaumann let out a jubilant yell, clapped me so hard on the back that my knees shook, and said in a voice that came from deep down inside him, "All in all, it worked out not too badly, that that hole down there wasn't completely wiped out in the year seventeen hundred and sixty-one by the Saxons and the French between them and wiped out us as a possibility as well. How nicely it lies, the place as a whole, and how well it has held out till now, thank the good Lord, despite the Seven Years' War. Yes, 'mead where as children we gamboled'—Edward, take another look at it and go away and learn something so that you can do honor to the place someday and preserve its good name. But you, Tina, don't need to bother about it. We know what we think of it, you and your dad and I, and from that point of view, our point of view, I may yet make myself one of its clergy, or one of its barristers. But in the first case I should want to be sure of a good solid pulpit for reading the law and the prophets to them." He sighed, held up his rough hand and looked at it, then, clenching it, stretched it toward the town in the valley as if to let them have a cautious, careful look at it, too.

"There they sit on their office stools, Edward, your old man and mine, never dreaming of the height from which Tubby Schaumann is contemplating them or, as you fellows say, 'looking down my nose at them.' "

"Evening sun, so golden fair," I hummed, as if to change the subject, but Tubby wasn't easy to switch, when once he was started.

"Of course, it's golden fair, especially when we are sitting on the Prince of Saxony's escarpment enjoying our hard-earned freedom and feeling that we are human beings at last. See how the sun flames in the windows of the school detention room and the provincial jail. Straight from a fairy tale. Edward, my friend, did you never, never crave to have your ogre of a father safely behind one of those barred windows and out of mischief the way I craved to have mine, especially each time we were promoted to ever-higher levels of German culture?"

And this was the man we had looked on as not only the fattest, laziest, and greediest among us, not only the most stupid, but as stupidity itself. Oh, what asses we were!

And who was it now who, far from switching him off his line of thought, quietly, deliberately confirmed him in it? Not the discriminating, well-behaved Edward, son of the postmaster, with his first-class matriculation certificate. It was Tina Quakatz of Red Bank Farm, who with her father had been banished, if not from the world, at least from all contact with their immediate neighborhood, which amounts to the same thing—all because people unfortunately could not prove that he had murdered Kienbaum.

Valentina Quakatz had also looked down from Prince Xaver's scarp, the hated rampart, at the town and the windows flashing in the sun; now she turned away and wiped her eyes with her hand and the tip of her apron.

"I've got an insect in my eye, or the glare has dazzled them and made them water. You must think I'm crying."

And then she clenched her fist and shook it at the glittering windows of the provincial jail. "But I'm not crying. I won't. Heinrich is right, it is silly, just to cry. The glare only makes me cry because so often and so long I've had to stand here, while he was inside, behind those barred windows down there, in prison, my father, whom I love. And because I had no one who . . ."

"Because she had no one but me, Edward. And because I have to go off again, while he is away. Well, you see, my dear Edward, what life is like, and how what pleasure there is in it just floats about on the surface like froth. I ask you now, put yourself in my place, and try, in spite of everyone, school, parents, and all the rest, to turn this half-frightened, savage little wildcat of a village puss into a nice, neat, clean, purring, cooing, sweet, and lovable little girl. Now take your apron away from your eyes and look at

me. Or my eyes will start to prickle too and I don't want that
with this clever, learned fellow, Edward, around. That's the way.
And now we'll just clench our teeth and set our jaws. I can't help
it if other people insist they have the right to make something out
of me that isn't in me. I give you my hand on it, Miss Quakatz:
I'm coming back and, until I do, I retain all the rights I have on
this spot of earth, and to hell with Kienbaum. Tell your father,
when he comes back, that I said this, Tina. And you, Edward, the
gentleman, be a good fellow and take one more look at the scenery and your native place—pity, they aren't ringing the bells for
you. That's the way, you bashful idiot, you."

I did look around—I was nervous, bothered, uncomfortable. I
looked at the landscape and the town in the valley. In short, I
looked away and while my ears rang and buzzed I heard behind
my back, on top of the old rampart of the Seven Years' War, a
quick succession of sounds that I can only reconcile satisfactorily
with the name of Tubby Schaumann. And, accompanying it, a
catch in the breath and a giggle and someone saying, "Oh, Heinrich, Heinrich."

I found, when I looked up from my writing, that nothing had
happened except that *the years had passed* and that the broad
ocean waves were rolling away under the ship, bearing it cheerfully, without too much rocking and vibration, toward the Cape
of Good Hope.

At first the place looked just as it used to look years ago. Only
today the light was different from that other time when we said
good-bye: it was about ten in the morning, a bright, clear day.

The same old trench and rampart, as good today in the second
half of the nineteenth century as they were in the eighteenth. There
it was, the same rectangular hedge enclosing the farm, the same
old treetops. But you used to be able to see the tiled roof of the
main house from the Maiholzen fields over and through the
branches, and now you couldn't. I realized that the hedge must
have grown and the treetops thickened over Quakatz's castle. It
was undoubtedly shadier in summer than it used to be at Red
Bank. To appreciate this fully, you needed to have crossed the

Line, as I had, and come back again or, at any rate, to have your home out there, where the average temperature is high, and shade is often deplorably lacking.

I stood and looked, with my hands folded in front of me. And as there was no hurry and no one in the wide expanse around me to disturb me, least of all the larks in the sky, I took a good look, before crossing Count von der Lausitz's trench.

I soon noticed something else. I didn't know how Red Bank Farm looked inside, but outside, wherever I turned, it seemed to me more neglected than ever.

It used to be that you could tell from the look of the driveway that, in spite of the feud, there was a peaceful farmhouse lodged behind that warlike excavation in the rich soil. You could see that men and beasts went in and out, loads of manure and harvest wagons, and that, even though Kienbaum's murder had its origins here, this was a place where human beings still attended to their wants and their comforts.

It didn't seem like this now. Not even a Roman road, where countless thousands had been slaughtered before, during, and after the migrations, could have looked more grassy and overgrown today than those old ruts and footprints on the embanked way leading over Prince Xaverius of Saxony's trench to the farm at Red Bank. There was only a narrow, narrow footpath going over now, no wheel ruts, hoof or paw prints, in the tall grass.

Thyme, bluebell, dandelion, and whatever else staked its claim to grow here, lifted its head serenely with no fear of being trampled on by hoof, claw, or boot sole.

"Curious," I said to myself, "it certainly looks as if the grass had sprung back up again behind *him*," and saying this I set my foot on the embanked road and entered the narrow path that led to Tubby Schaumann, as it used to lead to Andreas Quakatz. But there was yet another thing, a third thing, that was different from before. Where were the dogs?

Yes, where were the dogs of Red Bank Farm, the guardians of Quakatz's castle? Where was the watch, the watch that was known and feared far and wide in the land, baying its vigilance all through the quiet summer nights and winter nights, especially when the moon was full?

We have dogs on our farms in Kaffir land, and we need them. But I realized now that I had never run into such vicious dogs as those at Red Bank, and I had never missed the barking of vicious dogs, even thinking back on it, as I missed it here at the gate of this German farm.

The next few steps I made in the direction of Quakatz's castle made it clear to me that the watch had been relieved, but by no means abandoned. Others had taken over, and the reception I now got indicated that conditions were more peaceable than of old.

We all know those lovely, congenial old pictures in which a municipal soldier sits on a bench at the gate of a medieval town with the latest edict of the *senatus populusque* [18] at his back, his spectacles on his nose, his beer mug at his right hand and his flintlock at his left, knitting a stocking in idyllic contemplation and repose. I have such a picture myself, a Spitzweg,[19] out there at home, away off in Africa, hanging on the wall above my wife's sofa and sewing table (it sometimes appeals to me all the more, because under the table, my wife's table, we have a lion's skin to put our feet on), and I was pleased to find one here, here at home, at the gate of Red Bank Farm. But the present sentryman, on duty for the whilom Prince Xaverius of Saxony and for Farmer Quakatz who killed Kienbaum, wasn't knitting.

He was just purring. He wasn't sitting beside the gatepost, but on top of it, the right one. There he sat, the current watchman of Red Bank Farm, in all his dignity, in the morning sun, and looked quietly at me, and purred. But his purring didn't prevent him from stroking his moustache, and he even rubbed his martial fist over his ears (which in his battalion meant, by the way, that a visitor was coming) and wiped his nose and sneezed. I was quite close to him when he gave a jump, and then, coolly looking back to see if I was following, with slow and stately step he led the way into Quakatz's farm: Puss-in-Boots, the "white man," the spotlessly white tomcat, the house cat of the Comte de Lusace's fort.

He stopped again and wiggled first his right paw and then his left. There was some dew on the grass where the shade from the linden trees still lay. He looked at me once more and slowly went on again, as if he wanted to show me the way; he certainly didn't regard me as an enemy and he definitely wasn't going now to fetch the dogs and Tina Quakatz with a stone in her child's fist and Father Quakatz with whatever cudgel lay at hand, or perhaps the dung fork or the axe from the woodshed. Nothing could be more inviting than Puss-in-Boots, this new sergeant of the watch at Red Bank, nor did the sight of what he was leading me to beckon me to right-about-face and beat a hasty retreat.

Tubby Schaumann, as large as life.

Tubby Schaumann, the way he must have seen himself a thousand times in the sentimental, idealistic dreams of youth.

Oh, what a breakfast-table scene in front of that thatched hut, or more accurately, in front of this cozy German farmhouse, built to face the onslaughts of wind and weather. Anyway, there he was in front of the house, on a summer morning in Germany, between high-grown rosebushes, among lilacs, under shady trees with the sun shining on them, and with his wife and cat and dog (a sedate, intelligent old Pomeranian now), and the hens, the geese, the ducks, the sparrows, and so on, round about. And he wore one of those gray dressing gowns, or perhaps we should call it a housecoat, that you could stretch in as much as you wanted, and just right for the time of year. And one of those open waistcoats and a long, impressive parson's pipe and the pleasant parson's tobacco that goes with it floating up in blue rings in the quiet air!

"Tubby."

As I stood there like the Marquis of Carabas[20] of Puss-in-Boots, to complete my introduction into this genial atmosphere there was only one word that I could utter, and this was it.

"Tubby," I muttered, as I stood there waiting for someone to glance up from his comfort and take notice of me standing here once again at Red Bank Farm.

Naturally it was the woman who first noticed the disturbance, glanced quickly at the stranger, and nudged her husband:

"Oh, Heinrich. There's someone here, a gentleman."

I couldn't hear what he said, but I am convinced, indeed am absolutely sure that all he said was "Hm," reluctantly dropping his newspaper and turning his nose first to the watchdog, and then to the gate, and finally to the intruder on his morning's peace.

"Forgive me for disturbing you, old fellow. There was a time, years ago, when Edward was your friend, though he was no nobleman, but just came out of the post office at the foot of the hill," I said as I approached him and stepped into the delicious coolness around him, right out of burning Africa, as it were. The woman laid her knitting on the breakfast table, the man put his fleshy hands on the two arms of his garden chair, slowly wound his way to his feet, the stout bulk of him now emerging into view, and— leaped forward. He jumped. Like a fat frog jumps. But a jump nevertheless.

But it was again that nimble little wife of his who took the words out of his mouth.

"Why, Heinrich," cried Valentina Schaumann, née Quakatz, "it's really and truly your friend Edward."

"Hold my pipe a minute, Tina," said Tubby, and then he took hold of me by the upper arms and held me there for a while, not hugging me, but holding me at arm's length and looking me up and down. Then he asked, "Is it you? Is it really you? Can it be?" he added.

"It can indeed, Heinrich, old fellow. And I'm glad to see you and Red Bank or, let me say, you and your wife looking so well. You haven't . . ."

"Changed a bit. That damned cliché is more than I can stomach, especially on a hot day like this. The next thing you'll insult me by saying: Man, how fat you've got. In that respect you're all . . ."

"Schaumann, how good it is to find you your old self—your old self completely."

"Well, maybe I am, that is, if I stay in the shade. You don't want to die in the arms of your best school pal the moment you meet him. It's him, Tina, all right. He has actually been kind enough to remember us."

"Tubby."

"The word savors, I know, of younger days and higher spirits, but the fact remains. Why, my dear sir, didn't you come to see us before? We see enough of the newspapers up here at Quakatz's castle to have run over the guest lists and noticed how long you've been staying at the hotel down there, of course, bestowing your company on lots of other people. Well, it's very nice you've come."

Like anyone else, who has had his ear pinched and knows he

deserves it, I felt around for an excuse and produced the following: "A wise man always saves the best for the last. This, I remember very clearly, was a principle of yours in the days of our youth, Heinrich."

"I got over that long ago," replied Schaumann. "For some years now I've been taking the best when it came. I don't believe any longer that there will always be time or that once you've got something in your hands it's sure to stay there. Well, enough of compliments. You've at least had the luck this time. A nice juicy morsel you've saved up for yourself, what?"

"Come, come, Schaumann."

"And what are you doing standing around like a post, Pussy, little Quakatzy? He's pretty much proven himself to be our fellow man, brother, and friend; so you ought at least to offer him a seat and a cup of coffee, if it's still warm. Sit down for a couple of minutes, if you have them, Edward. And then, take a look at her. There she is, Tina, Tina Quakatz. What do you say, Edward? You've told me what you think of me, though you didn't know it, by looks and gapes and wigglings of hand and foot. Tell me honestly now, what do you think of her—in the flesh?"

It is beyond me to describe the movement of the hand, the look of the eye, and whatever else accompanied his introduction of Frau Valentina Schaumann. Or the tone of his voice when he called her Pussy.

And Quakatzy.

But I must make *some* attempt to describe her, a Quakatz, the daughter of Andreas Quakatz, the man that murdered Kienbaum, who in her husband's hands had developed into a "Pussy," and as I noticed later, a Pussikins, in affectionate prolongation of the word, and who now on this summer's morning asked me to take a seat at her breakfast table at Red Bank.

As a child I had never seen her as anything but thin. "Rattlebones," Schaumann called her. But, unlike him, she hadn't cultivated her physical propensities to the fullest in the course of years. She hadn't gone lean to the extent that he had gone fat. She hadn't shriveled up under his regimen, standing in the shadow—and a very considerable one it was—that he cast.

She had turned into a well-shaped, agreeable soul, with the touch of gray in her hair that you have to expect around forty. My first thought when I looked at her was whether she could still "sic" the dogs at "us kids" or anybody. And scrutinizing her closely for this, I was relieved to find not a trace left of the savage, half-furtive look that she had acquired as a child, in the "bloom of her youth," as a result of that dreadful feud. And as soon as she spoke her first smiling words to me, I knew without waiting for more that she had long since ceased to be the frightened little farm girl at Quakatz's that you pelted with bad words and stones and sods. There was absolutely no need, though Schaumann evidently thought there was, to prod my attention with such an artless re-mark as:

"Yes, Edward, culture is infectious, and I have always been a highly cultured man, though you chaps down there refused to ad-mit it. And then, Edward, there's the cookbook, a book that can also be studied with benefit to one or more of your fellow men."

"Anyone who didn't know that we have known one another very well for a long, long time would know it now," said Frau Valentina Schaumann with such a winning and delicate smile that you couldn't have found a better smile or remark in the salon of Madame Récamier,[21] nor of Madame de Stael,[22] nor of Frau Varnhagen von Ense,[23] whom they called Rahel in her day.

By now I had it clear that, for the first time on home soil, I had set a foot on enchanted ground, where I might hope to convert the disillusionment of my return into a real, a true, a veritable sense of being comfortably back home. After ten minutes' conver-sation, all of it devoted exclusively to our having met again and of no real significance, Frau Schaumann proposed leaving us and going into the house, and then gave an understanding nod to her husband's remark:

"Of course, Pussy, the stranger will spend the day in the Prom-ised Land. In the cool of the evening we might set him on the road back to town and to Africa again."

I hadn't intended to stay that long, but I was glad at the oppor-tunity of staying the day. And so I said to Frau Schaumann, "What are you running off for? Do stay. You need to have come from South Kaffraria and through the tropics for a visit home in order really to appreciate how nice it is to sit here in front of such a house on a morning like this."

"Do you hear that?" said Tubby. "Just as I've always said. But just you go about your ways. Our visitor will tell us later all about his own household, out there or down yonder. The right time for that is at dinner. Don't let him detain you now. You go and see to things. This wild fellow from Africa will be sure to have found his true Desdemona somewhere or other; all you will get now of his whims and ways will be the bits and pieces. Off you go to the kitchen, which is after all the main thing. I am sure he thinks so too."

He said this to her with a chuckle and a knowing look, drawing the edge of his hand across his throat, in perfect imitation of slicing the gullet from ear to ear.

"He's quite right, Edward. You men will have to excuse me for a few moments. Don't worry, Schaumann, I understand."

She slipped away, and if you had seen the way, the warm and friendly way, she nodded to me to let me know that she expected me to stay for dinner, you would never have thought that she was the daughter of an old murderer, the man that killed Kienbaum, that she had spent her life amid murderous thoughts.

But there was a word of reassurance in the cloud of smoke her husband puffed out after her, saying, "Take care, old girl. Africa spoils people. They say that elephant's foot roasted in the ashes is not to be sneered at. If our visitor went back home and simply *had* to tell them how much he had enjoyed himself with us two, that would give us a real reputation."

"What a truly delightful woman," I said.

"Isn't she?" said Tubby, and he added, "And well preserved, too, don't you think?"

And then we sat for a while, just comfortably musing, and only gradually became aware that there was a commotion at hand. The feathered tribe around the breakfast table at Red Bank Farm began to cock an ear, look about them, and put their beaks together, all in consequence of a noisy cackling and screeching in the yard behind the house. And not without reason, for across the low fence around the yard a solitary hen came scuttering, with wings spread and some of its tail feathers missing, to bring bad news.

"What's the matter with the creatures? Who's been killing Kienbaum this time?" asked Tubby, staring up at his pigeons, which suddenly rose from their cote and circled in alarm over our heads and over the green treetops of Red Bank, gradually turning into silvery points in the blue.

"They've gone plain crazy," he said. I, of course, pretended I had no notion that I was the cause of this upset and panic in the natural world, that it was on my account that Frau Valentina Schaumann at Red Bank had called into the kitchen, "Stine, we have a visitor today and if I'm not mistaken he's badly spoiled with living in foreign parts. What are we going to do? My husband has asked him to stay for dinner and we really haven't a thing in the house that we can set before anyone who has come from so far away."

"Oh, well, people always descend on you at the wrong time," is what Tubby's culinary understudy probably shouted back, and undoubtedly added, "But things are probably not as bad as all that for him—the visitor, I mean—and for us at Red Bank. Thank God, we always have the chickens and pigeon cote at hand."

I know from my mother's days what the next remark was: "At least we'll see to it, Stine, that they get a nice bouillon. They all like that, even the fussiest of them."

But on this day—and what a relief it was to her—she could add something more out of her larder, or better, out of the goodness of her heart. "And then, God be thanked, we have the ham in Burgundy. So Stine, quick, into the henhouse and the pigeon cote with you. The gentleman is staying till evening, he's an old friend of my husband's and I'm very glad, too, that he's come from so far away to see us again at Red Bank after all these years."

There may be a lot of people on board who would like to know just what sort of literary work the gentleman from the Boer Republic is doing, what it is he is writing that makes him harrumph and sigh and laugh in turn. But there isn't anyone in the whole company to whom I could really explain why a sensible man on a journey like this could concern himself in this detail with a ham long since eaten and digested, even if it was pickled in Burgundy. We have Germans, Dutchmen, Englishmen, Norwegians, Danes, and Swedes, the whole Germanic tribe, on board the *Leonhard Hagebucher;* but they would all take me for a fool rather than for a German with a bit of a talent and whim for aesthetics, if tonight

I were to go into the saloon and read them a few pages out of what I've been writing, of my logbook, my travel manuscript, my detective story. I recognize that, but I don't disclaim my manuscript; I'll stay with it as long as wind and waves allow. I have been often enough at sea to know which is the better way on a long voyage. It is a great mistake to think that something remarkable is about to happen every minute on the great waters or that the company of Germans and such on a journey is always ever so humorous or cordial or discriminating—or *interesting* . . .

The point is that we did find the excellent chicken broth and the fresh ham in Burgundy on the dining table. But we haven't got so far yet. We are still sitting with Schaumann at his *second* breakfast under the old lindens in front of Quakatz's castle at Red Bank, my friend Heinrich Schaumann and I, and indoors they are just pulling the dining table into the middle of the room for Frau Tina and the second help-girl to set it for the main encounter, the main gratification of man's daily need for nourishment.

"At last I meet a man who has aimed at a goal and reached it without being disappointed afterward," I said with a sigh, taking another cigar out of the proffered box.

"Just a little too much avoirdupois," growled Tubby. "A little trying on hot days, Edward. Especially with the running about on business I still have to do."

"Do you have to go running about still, my dear Heinrich? Haven't you finished with all the things out there that the rest of us have to run about after? Doesn't that all lie beyond outside these marvelous ramparts of Prince Xaver of Saxony's and of yours?"

"What you mean is that after all the plagues old man Quakatz suffered, all I have to do now is to make myself, this corpulent person of mine, into the embodiment of comfort at Red Bank Farm? I'll take your arm, Edward, if you don't mind. It'll be some little time before they call us to dinner. If you are agreeable, I'll let you have a close look at my fortress and farm—my house, my castle—and show you just what Tina and I have made of it. Umph! Slowly now. There's no hurry. Why shouldn't we take our time? What could a stay-at-home like me have to show to a globe-trotter like you that would call for all this rush? Gently, gently, my friend.

Let us go an easy, easy pace. And first of all we'll go the round again of the ramparts of Count von der Lausitz, of blessed, though not of glorious, memory."

"Blessed memory? That isn't exactly what they said down there in the town or anywhere in the neighborhood in the year of grace seventeen hundred and sixty-one."

"But it's what I say today. What do I care about the neighborhood and environs? Apart, I mean, from the view you get of it from Quakatz's castle."

I was so eager now to see what he had to show me that I really found it difficult to slow down my pace, after the gold fields of Kaffraria, to suit his pace at Red Bank. And now for the first time in my life I walked the whole length of Prince Xaver's quadrangular fortifications on the top of the ramparts. As a boy and a young man I had only seen them now and then from outside the trench, from the fields, from the glacis. And the years were beginning to tell. Today, however, things didn't move very fast. It wasn't merely on grounds of courtesy and affection that the friend of my youth hung on to my arm. Of course, he took his pipe with him and kept it going and pointed with it this way and that where he wanted to direct my attention, distracted as it was, he thought, by all my voyaging around the globe.

We strolled, or rather we waddled, again down his garden path between his red currant and gooseberry bushes, his Maltese Cross, his roses and lilies, his larkspur, his lady's slipper, up to the parapet of his fortress. As philosopher-historian of Red Bank Farm he grew in stature moment by moment. And in his well-fed solitude and the loving care of his wife he had turned into an unparalleled monologuist. He did ask questions, but he usually gave the answers himself, always much to the relief of his listener.

"Can you tell me, Edward," he began by asking, "where basically each man's destiny takes its origin?" And before I could answer (what answer could I have given?) he said, "Usually , if not always, from one source. I can remember from my baby-carriage days—you know, Edward, I've always been a little weak in the legs from the time I was tiny—I clearly remember that moment during a Sunday afternoon outing, when my guardian spirit first drew my attention to this. My father said to my mother: 'When we get behind Red Bank, thank God we'll have some shade. That youngster of yours ought to be walking on his own feet soon. Don't you think?'—'He is so weak on his feet,' my dear old mother said with a sigh, and I can hear her saying it still. Yes, Edward, I've always been a little weak in the head and weak on my feet, and that is my point. I've never been able to go any farther than into the shade of Red Bank. I really can't help it. This was my weakness or, if you like, my strength. This was where destiny took hold of me. I resisted, but I had to surrender, reluctantly. You, Edward, were carried off to burning Africa by Störzer and Mr. Le Vaillant, and my weak intelligence and still weaker feet have kept me in the cool shade of Quakatz's farm. Fate, you see, Edward, generally uses our weaknesses to make us aware of what is good for us."

The fellow was so impudently ungrateful as to fetch up a sigh from the pit of his stomach. Solely, of course, in order to rub in his self-satisfaction and make me more envious than before. But I didn't respond. I didn't give him the pleasure of hearing me return the sigh from still greater depths, and with more justification.

"Go steady, Edward," I said to myself. "Try to find out what else he knows better than you."

So I let him go on talking, while I quietly looked out of a shady corner of the old, and now so peaceful, fortress at the wide sunny landscape with its view of my native town, and of villages, woods, nearby hills, and distant mountains.

"There you have the whole battleground of Schaumann versus Quakatz before you," said Tubby Schaumann. "Take another look at the scene before you go off to your glorious Africa. It's a nice spot, after all, isn't it?"

"No doubt about it. A man doesn't need to have come from Libya or be heading back there to say that with some confidence."

"And then think of all that's happened here, Edward," said Tubby, prodding me with his elbow. "I'll say nothing about what happened long ago, but just take that beautiful Seven Years' War."

"But, my dear friend . . ."

"I've always had a deep, secret affection for that glorious Seven Years' War and for that splendid saber-rattler, old Fritz of Prussia."

"My dear Heinrich . . ."

"Yes, you may still have a faint memory of this enthusiasm of mine from our days of innocent childhood and scapegrace adolescence. Edward, if I weren't Tubby Schaumann, I'd like to be Frederick the Second of Prussia and no one else—nobody in all history but Fritz the Second. I don't know how you are for books out there in Kaffir land, but, I ask you, name anyone in the hurly-burly of history who is more appealing to the likes of us than him. So scraggy and desiccated, weak on his feet from the gout that he inherited from his father's Rhine wine, but never out of his boots. Always in his best form amid the yelling, howling, and roaring of the Furies and the cannon. With his cane, his nose full of snuff, his scabbard repaired by his own hands with sealing wax—razor-sharp, rude, biting, what you call snotty with the great ladies, Maria Theresa,[24] Elizabeth,[25] or Jeanne Antoinette[26]—a thing I can't wholly approve of on account of my great lady, Tina. But, on the other hand, his appetite. Perfect! Good when he was a child, when he was young, but beyond all praise when he got older. If ever I were to be prodigal with my words, it'd be here, on this point. That man could digest anything. Disappointments, provinces, his own bad luck or anybody else's, and, above all, the menu that he wrote out every day himself. Edward, if this man had been me, he'd have been master of Red Bank Farm, too. Edward, I tell you, if any man has helped make me master, proprietor, owner of Red Bank Farm and, therefore, of Tina Quakatz too, it is old Fritz of Prussia ever and always, you understand, in conjunction with his so worthy opponent on these fields—one who means more to me than I can say—His Electoral Highness, Prince Xaverius of Saxony."

This man, Heinrich Schaumann, whom they called Tubby, was talking such a jumble of contradictions that I had got past the point of sighing and saying, "I'd be interested to know what all this is leading to."

"Hadn't we better sit down?" said Heinrich. "I can see that you find me a little mixed up. It may get worse, but I can't help it. The only reason, by the way, why I put this seat here was to keep me from losing the historical ground under my feet, as even I am in danger of doing now and then. But if I'm boring you, I'll stop at once, O most interesting of Africans and best of all old friends."

"Please don't say such things, Tub—my dear friend."

"Go on and say Tubby, Edward. I still like to hear the dear old word. And I must first tell you about the old friends who jokingly attached it to me in better days. Then we can work our way round slowly to my dear departed father-in-law of Kienbaum fame. Well, then—this was the beginning of the story of Heinrich and Valentina, of Kienbaum, of Meister Andreas Quakatz, and of Red Bank Farm. Are you comfortable there, Edward?"

"Seldom been more so in my life. But don't be always interrupting yourself, you funny fellow. I honestly feel as if the sole reason I had for coming home was to hear what you have to say."

"There's a nice compliment. And another reason why I should begin with my old friends, you worthless, malicious, impudent rascals who, as far back as I can remember, did your best to make my young life miserable."

"Tubby, please . . ."

"Yes, Tubby. Was it my fault, if I was weak in the legs and strong in the belly and guts? Was I the creator of the strength and energy of my peristaltic movements and the frailness of my extremities and my general disposition toward idiocy? If I had had the choice I would ten thousand times rather have started as a jellyfish in the bitter salt sea than as Schaumann's boy, that fat, stupid Heinrich Schaumann. A nice way you all treated me. What a scandalous way to exercise your rights. You've got to admit it, Edward."

"Don't you allow any exceptions, Heinrich?"

"Not a one. Do you want me to make an exception of you, my best and dearest friend? Don't you think it for a moment. Just ask Tina, when we get to dinner, what she thinks about it. She used to see you at the castle walls in the old days along with the others. If you didn't howl with the wolves, you heehawed with the donkeys, and in any case, you went about with them and left Tubby Schaumann sitting on the doorstep at home or on the dullard's bench at school or at the edge of the field in front of Red Bank, left him there misunderstood as he was, like a piece of bread and butter dropped buttered side down. Oh, sure, you would look round to see where I was, if you had nothing, I won't say better, but more amusing, to do."

"Oh, Heinrich, you've no right to say that."

"But, Edward, if it weren't so, would I be sitting here now? And, besides, am I reproaching you for it? Didn't I let you all go, you and the others? Didn't I, so to speak, pick my piece of bread and butter out of the dust and gulp it down, with one part melancholy and three parts pride in my—solitude? Did I ever go whimpering behind your more volatile spirits and your more agile bodies, making myself more ridiculous than I already was?"

"No, certainly not. And to be honest as well, what more did we do, what more did I do, than leave you sitting where you sat?"

"There, you see. You see. And in the course of the day I hope to show you that even the lonely house-door step, the dunce's bench, in the classroom, the tearful seat by the meadow's edge can help a man to attain some sense of the world and give him a goal and a purpose in this earthly life. It doesn't always help you in running to be quick on the jump."

"God knows it doesn't," I said with a deep sigh, recalling all that I had accomplished in life, speaking as it were from farthest Africa.

"Not even an Indian at the stake with his enemies screaming and yelling their scornful triumph over him had anything over Tubby Schaumann in your merry circle. Those were nice dances of victory you performed in your superiority round the poor wretch, sweating there in his fat with hardly a word to say. And you were all so bright and clever. I 'ate my bread with tears' all right, in your good company. What else was there for me to do but stick to my appetite and myself, give you my blessing and turn my back on you?"

"Heinrich . . ."

"Well, well, just let it go. We have it behind us now and Tina is busy in the kitchen, where she should be, attending to your wants and mine. The sweet creature! Let us approach the subject a little more closely and so—long live Prince Xaver of Saxony, the Comte de Lusace, again, I say, health and prosperity to Prince Xaverius."

"Here's to him. But I haven't at the moment the faintest idea, Schaumann, what he has to do with you and me, or with any of the three of us. What you've just said to me you were entitled to say. But I don't see why I should put up with this Count von der Lausitz of yours, this Prince of Saxony that I know nothing whatsoever about. Tell me now, before your wife calls us to dinner, just what this queer Prince Xaver or Xaverius has to do with her or you or me on this wonderful windless sunny summer's morning with the green foliage around us and blue sky above."

The ship is pitching rather more today than yesterday.

"I know you've seen a lot of recent history, Edward, and had a hand in making it yourself in Africa, but you surely know, too, that there was—and still is—a cannonball stuck in the gable of the house at home that he, little Xaver, fired at us townsfolk in the Seven Years' War. Be quiet now and don't interrupt me; we're getting closer and closer to Tina and her kitchen stove at Red Bank. Ah, my father's pride, not Tina, but the cannonball. It was a curiosity of the town and my earliest thoughts are wound up with it. 'It came from Red Bank, my boy,' said my father, and now tell me, Edward, have you anything better back there in Pretoria, or however it's called, than a cannonball in the rafters or the house wall, if you want to open a boy's mind to things? A word like that strikes home and sticks in his head or his imagination like the cannonball in the gable. 'It dates from old Fritz's war, Heinrich,' said my father. 'You pay attention in school, they can tell you more about it there.' Well, I got spanked for a great many things at school, but not for the Seven Years' War. And I owe that to Prince Xaver's cannonball in the gable, the piece of shot that came from Red Bank. And in the course of time it helped me to make Red Bank mine and Tina Quakatz too. And afterward when we're sitting at table I want you to tell me that you like it here too."

"Haven't I told you that several times already?"

"No, at least not properly. For what do you know about us so far anyway? But, man alive, must you be always interrupting? Don't you have any notion at all what speeches lie suppressed, what tirades can be bottled up in a frustrated student of theology? There now, sit quiet and look at the pleasant landscape and the fields of home and let me blow off steam at last. Blow it off to a man who doesn't belong in that old hole down there, but who is going tomorrow to the farthest end of farthest Africa and won't be telling the story of Tubby Schaumann and Red Bank Farm to his wife in bed or his friends at the inn."

"I won't say another word till you ask me to, you or your wife."

"Very good, my dear boy, you'll be doing me a real service. So let's get back to the fateful cannonball in the house of Herr Schaumann, accountant. It wasn't the cannonball alone that did it. There was a musty old tome in the house that my mother had used for years to put under the fourth leg of a cupboard to keep it from wobbling. This carried me a stage further. Not the cupboard, the book. It was a local product telling the story of how Prince Xaver of Saxony besieged the cradle of our childhood, not perhaps telling it true, but making it a whole lot clearer to a child's mind. I pulled the book out from under the cupboard leg and that was the classic I liked to read. Much more than Cornelius Nepos.[27] And from there—don't get restless, we're coming closer and closer to Tina—I found my way to that living old tome, Schwartner. Of course, you remember old Schwartner, the registrar?"

Naturally I remembered him, but also quite naturally I merely shook my head.

"That's right. You're not to say a word," growled Tubby and went on getting his story off his chest with no interruption from me. "Old Schwartner in that dark old house under the somber chestnut trees opposite the church. Haunted, Edward, you remember. The house I mean, but the old gentleman was haunted too. When the old gentleman died, or rather when he had finally dried out for good and all, the doctors couldn't find a drop of fluid left, although he had more of what you call the humors in him than the rest of the town put together. And when they pulled down the old Schwartner house, after first cutting down the chestnuts, it happened more than once that the workmen threw down their axes, spades, and picks and took refuge in the church opposite, all in a sudden fright in broad noon daylight. I suppose you scholars put it down to old goat-footed Pan. But those lazy city workmen put it down to old goat-footed Schwartner. Well, I chummed up with the old fellow behind your backs, my fine, enlightened schoolfellows, and it was worth my while in more ways than you harum-scarums could ever have conceived. Don't get restless, Edward. I'm not taking you far off the subject. We're sticking to Red Bank Farm and getting closer and closer to Tina. I hope it won't be long before she calls us to dinner."

I might have said something at this point, but I controlled myself and didn't. Tubby pulled a little harder on his pipe and went on.

"So the cannonball in the gable at home was the first thing that worked on my childish imagination; old Schwartner was the first to work on my historical sense. And there are many learned men nowadays who say that the historical sense is the best thing we have. I don't share their view. Of course, if you could remember only the pleasant things!! . . . Well, anyway, old Schwartner had the historical sense and awoke what there was of it in me. If I managed to concentrate it on Red Bank Farm and nothing else, that indicates in my opinion that there was something in me that went beyond the historical sense. I don't remember clearly how I first got into his house. He probably found me staring at the cannonball in the house gable or at Red Bank itself and felt that I was a kindred spirit. In any case we soon got on a very friendly footing. If anyone wanted me and didn't find me at home he only had to look for me at Registrar Schwartner's and he would be pretty sure to find me. 'Learn all you can at school, Heinrich,' old Schwartner used to say, 'learn all you can at school, and especially history. Without history the cleverest of us is an ass, but if he has it, he is at the top of the heap and, academically speaking, can put the whole town, the whole community, in his pocket. Just look at me, a mere minor official, the only man who can tell them all where they stand.' Well, I didn't learn much general history from the old man's friendship, but I did learn the history of the Seven Years' War and Red Bank, no matter how things stand with all the rest. You see, Edward, old Schwartner's great-uncle or great-great-uncle was a town councilor and had spoken to Prince Xaverius in person. The Prince gave him a pinch of his snuff, but unfortunately he didn't let him off his share of the tribute money that he exacted after taking the town. He kept a lot of other things, the old registrar did, in that ghostly house as souvenirs of those troubled times, a spittoon in the corner behind his desk, plans and copperplates on the walls, chairs where his grandmother and his great-grandmother had sat with the Prussian commander, a table with a corner knocked off by the billeted soldiers, and, above all, accounts, account books, settlements! They had to shell out, I can tell you, Edward. God preserve your great-grandchildren in Africa from sweet souvenirs of that sort. Or at least give them the comfortable sense of history that old Schwartner had, no bitterness left in him about it, just his objective interest in what happened and the pleasure it gave him. He had a fairly large plan of the town dating from the end of the century hanging on the wall beside the sofa, and if he wasn't expounding that crazy old siege to me out in the fields he was lecturing to me about it on the sofa, and I had to follow him on the map with my finger, mostly, you understand, between the town and Red Bank. And now stand up and come over here, Edward."

And now, just as if there was nothing new or remarkable that I might have told him about Africa and my life there, he took me to the edge of his castle ramparts and pointed out the details of this utterly insignificant piece of history, thunder of cannon, trembling citizens, shrieking women and children, fire, and bloodshed: so-and-so stood here and so-and-so stood there. The *corps combiné* of the *Royal François et des Saxons* was twenty thousand strong. So many French, so many Saxons. "In the town there was a garrison of seven or eight hundred men, veterans and militia under old Major von Stummel. A descendant of his, a retired court assessor, is still living in the town. You wouldn't think to look at him that he was descended from a hero. They tell me he goes to the Brummersumm every afternoon and you probably met him there, Edward. I suppose he's one of the reasons why you never came to see your friend Tubby Schaumann and his Red Bank Farm till today. It wasn't nice of you, Edward."

He may have been right on the last point, but you will understand that, while everything about Schaumann and Red Bank interested me very much and appealed to me, there wasn't really anything in what he had told me that made me feel as if this was what I had come out to his Xaver, Quakatz, and Valentina castle to hear. But I had at least, as far as I could, made up for previous unfriendliness and negligence toward this fat friend of my youth, this dreadful bore.

Be that as it may, in one respect there was something wonderful to look forward to with confidence—Tubby Schaumann's dinner. The whiffs that reached us from the kitchen had got more and more appetizing and delicate till finally Frau Valentina Schaumann, née Quakatz, put her head round the bush behind where we were sitting and, with the sweetest and most inviting of smiles on her kindly face, asked if we would like to come now.

We would indeed.

Today, below the Line, I can't say that I didn't hear the dinner bell, but I didn't pay any attention to it. I stayed away from table and went on with my manuscript. The appetite of a Northerner is not usually any too good between the tropics of Cancer and Capricorn, and you are lucky enough in those fair regions if you can look back with pleasure or at least without displeasure on dinners you have enjoyed before and managed to keep down.

"Well, Tina, for once you have someone else whose arm you can take," said Heinrich, leaning his pipe against the garden seat and drawing his dressing gown around him. This was all he did by way of dressing for dinner, though his wife had appeared in a Sunday dress, very pretty and in good taste, quite dignified in fact. "The point is," he added pointedly, "I've got her trained and can rely on her more or less. She always offers me her arm without my asking, and I need it. But, as I said, today you may offer it to him. I can withdraw for once in favor of so rare and distinguished a visitor. So go first, the two of you, and I'll follow slowly in your tracks."

And so he did, and since we were really and truly on our way to dinner he neither sat down en route nor got on to the subject of the Seven Years' War and Prince Xaver of Saxony and the siege of our native town. He reached the house close behind us. Oddly enough, I was seeing it for the first time at close quarters on this particular day. Until now I had been smug enough sitting under the linden trees with the house behind me. Schaumann had made what he could out of this bloody battle-rampart, this infamous den of outlaws, of the man that murdered Kienbaum. I could give him credit for that and he was entitled to be proud of it without a doubt. You could see at a glance, if you remembered the place as it was when Quakatz had it, that he had driven out the evil spirits. But, without any boasting on his own doorstep, he said, "Well, come in, my dear lad. If, as the poet tells us, the man who cultivates his ideals should grow in stature, he ought by rights to be able to broaden his base proportionately with a good conscience all round and no fear of being sneered at. But just try to express such a modest wish in this wretched world we live in. I must add, by the way, that I haven't had to widen old Quakatz's house door yet. Well, Edward, I am delighted to be able to cross this threshold arm in arm with you." Saying this, he pushed his wife away from me and shoved her into the house ahead of us. And, sure enough, waddled along behind with me. But first he paused a moment and drew my attention to the inscription over his door. I could hardly trust my eyes; but there it stood, painted in large white letters on a black background for all to read:

> *And God spake unto Noah, saying:*
> *"Go forth of the ark."*

And when on reading these words I turned to my fat friend with a certain surprise, this easiest of armchair philosophers smiled a superior smile and said, "You probably think, of course, because you have wandered a bit farther over the globe than I, that I am quite literally stuck in the ark. No, Edward, my friend, this is indeed my motto: Go forth of the ark."

I could have said something in reply to this, but once again he didn't give me the chance and went on, "But, before we go in, what do you say to the little improvements I have made in Tina Quakatz's estate? Outside, I mean. Bright and friendly, isn't it? The best that brush and paint pot can do toward brightening up the place."

There was certainly no need to draw my attention specially. No one who knew that "murderer's den" at Red Bank in its former dreadful state of neglect could fail to be struck by the improvements.

"Look," said Schaumann, "I've already drawn your attention to Noah's Ark; now use your imagination and open another of your Christmas boxes. 'Town or village' is written on the lid of the one I mean. Go on, tip it over on the table and find me my model house for Christmas. And? Have you got it? The walls a nice sky-blue, the roof vermilion, door and windows as black as pitch, only the chimney nice and white. There are lots of pleasant mansions, houses, and huts in other colors in the box, but I chose a bright sky-blue for Tina's sake. That, I hope, at least won't remind people of Kienbaum's blood, but instead lead someone to say now and then: 'That old Schaumann at Red Bank is a crazy duck. I just hope his good wife keeps her eye on him.' "

The good wife in the vestibule turned round at these last words and said with a smile, "Heinrich, I ask you, do you have to act so crazily in front of this old friend of yours as you do in front of other people?"

"But I may be a little bit crazy, mayn't I, sweetheart?"

"What can I do to stop him? Can you tell me, Edward, knowing him after all these years as you do?" said Frau Valentina, laughing; and with that, arm in arm with Tubby Schaumann, I stood in the vestibule, pulled up short by another surprise.

"But, what in the world is that?" I cried, choosing as polite words as I knew how.

"A part of my geological museum," said Schaumann. "I'll show you the mammoth after dinner. That's the showpiece, the *pièce de résistance*."

I was dumbfounded.

"It's the hobby of my latter days," my fat friend continued. "A man must have something to sustain him, when he obeys the commandment of the Lord and goes forth of the ark. What is there to be surprised at? Not even Prince Xaver of Saxony is good for all eternity to satisfy a hermit's—or half-hermit's—need for a hobby to while away the hours, days, weeks, and years. But don't worry, Edward, this is my business, these bones are mine. They haven't been used in the soup, Tina sticks to fresher ones with more meat on them. I hope, in spite of my osteological museum, you will commend her cooking and tell them when you go back into the world that they don't just gnaw the bones at Red Bank. I'm surprised to see, by the way, that this dilettante's passion is not at all what you expected to find in me."

"It certainly isn't.'

"The appeal of opposites, Edward. Simply the appeal of oppo-

sites. *You* get as fat as me and see whether you won't look for
your opposite—in bare bones like these! Your doctor certainly
won't object. Mine, for example, thinks that all this crawling and
climbing and getting out of breath in the gravel pits and quarries
of the territory round Red Bank Farm is very good for my constitution. To hear him talk, you would think the Flood had been
arranged for my special benefit. I mean, just so that what is left,
the precious residue of it, should give me the exercise I so badly
need. And Tina has no objection to my folly, as she calls it, either,
and says just the same thing. 'That's what happens,' she has even
been known to add, 'when the fat farmer at Red Bank sells all his
arable land to the Maiholzen sugar works to grow beets on.' "

"Stop," I cried, "and let us sit down at table. Your wife is waiting and I urgently need to have a word with her about you."

"But not till after dinner," grinned Tubby. He "requested" this,
as we politely put it in such cases, adding, "You know from the
old days how little I like to be held up and interfered with on the
way to and in the course of dinner, don't you?"

I took a last glance at the fossils—all from the neighborhood of
Red Bank—stacked up on shelves and in open cupboards along
the walls of the old farmhouse hallway and, stepping once more
into Andreas Quakatz's living room, went to the table that was
now Tubby's dining table where Tina Quakatz so many years ago
had laid her head on her arms—in defiance, anger, fear, and despair—while I looked on.

"I'm so glad to see you here again, Edward," said Frau Valentina Schaumann.

I was really touched and shook hands with her over Tubby
Schaumann's wonderfully supplied dining table. But he was impatient; I was to unfold my table napkin and pick up my knife
and fork. No impatience of his, though, could stop me from taking a quick look around. There had been a lot of changes.

"Yes," he said, "you may take a look. Here you can clearly see
how she likes to turn the tables on me. My case of coproliths is
the only thing I have been able to smuggle in. There it is in the
corner and there she sits opposite you, waiting for you to compliment her on her good taste. She wanted to have the place thor-

oughly swept of all her early memories and she was entitled to that. There was nothing hanging on the walls or standing on the floor to gladden your eye, apart from the dining table. Still less was there anything of the sort lurking in the corners. But we didn't auction off the paternal and patriarchal household goods of Quakatz's farm. We committed them to the flames, partly in the kitchen fire, but most of them out there by the linden trees. We made a bonfire, on a fine sunny summer's day, between ten and eleven in the morning, and we sent the wretched old junk up into the blue sky. Oh, how we stood all those sweet, cloying sentimentalities about hearth and home on their heads! And with fire we purged Red Bank of its sickness! See, Edward, how to this day the child delights in what all the people called her incalculable, her boundless, brutality—this female arsonist. Does she look as if it would spoil her appetite to be reminded of that most idiosyncratic deed?"

She certainly didn't. Frau Valentina Schaumann smiled at me across her soup plate and said, "Do you notice how well he has brought me up? I have nothing against it if after dinner he tells you more fully how he set about it. And how to this day he still sits me down on my school bench. But, remember, dear, you first have to take your afternoon nap as usual; Edward is probably accustomed to one himself, coming as he does from scorching Africa."

"If Edward wants to have a nap, I'll have a few winks myself to please him. With the usual pangs of conscience on account of what the doctor said. If God has given you a paunch—etcetera. Well, may the Lord grant that we all die a quiet death on our sofas."

"Today and every day from today on, I insist that you go with your friend or me straight from table for a walk in the garden or on the ramparts," cried Frau Valentina. "Heinrich, I'm perfectly capable of lighting another fire by the linden trees and burning all our sofas under you."

"Oh, you sweet topsy-turvy Hindu widow *in spe*," grinned Tubby, and then for a space he fell to the job at hand—dinner, his dinner and nothing else. It was an excellent meal and he didn't say a word for a whole quarter of an hour. It was so cool and comfortable that we stayed indoors for coffee and cigars and Tina Quakatz sat with us and slipped to and fro, enjoying her husband's company and, I'm pleased to say, apparently that of the friend of his youth too; and to celebrate my visit, not one of us took that afternoon nap.

Just when the process of digestion was at its most satisfying Tubby leaned back in his armchair, folded his hands over his unbuttoned waistcoat, twiddled his thumbs, sighed deliciously, and asked, "And now, Edward, tell me, does all this remind you of a murderer's den? Would you be afraid of midnight and the departed Kienbaum and say 'No, thank you,' if we asked you to stay the night? Be honest now and tell us if there is the faintest odor of blood and corruption at Red Bank Farm."

I only hoped he was expecting me to jump up and protest with both hands and feet, roaring a thundered, threefold "No" in his ears. But I didn't give the fellow the pleasure, so macabre did I find his contentment. Instead I quietly said to him, "Even your antediluvian fossil bones outside don't smell to me of anything. Why, the finest lady need not hesitate to use those coproliths of yours in the cupboard as a paperweight, if no one asks and she doesn't tell anyone what they are. I would move with pleasure into the haunted chamber at Quakatz's farm, if circumstances allowed. I don't believe your wife would cut my throat in my sleep, but as for you—I would really like to get the truth out of you in the amiable light of afternoon, before the ghostly night comes. You curious couple, you inscrutable fellow—how did you between you, or how did you alone, settle the evil spirit, the evil guest, at Red Bank Farm?"

"I killed Kienbaum dead," said Schaumann. "That was all that was needed. The rogue—the poor devil, I mean—died hard, I admit, but I dispatched him. If any man killed Kienbaum, I'm the man."

"You? Heinrich, I . . ."

"Do you want to stay while I give him the details, Tina?" said Heinrich, turning to his wife, and she smiled and said, "You know that you don't need me for that, my dear. If your friend will permit me, I'd rather just listen in at odd moments to keep you from too much fantastic elaboration."

"Keep me from fantastic elaboration, Edward?"

"But I would suggest to you gentlemen that you should take the wretched old story with you and return to your seats under the trees. I am sure, Edward, you would rather hear about it out in the fresh air. I'll clear the table meanwhile and join you later."

"With your embroidery," said Heinrich Schaumann at the finale to her charming suggestion.

He put the box of cigars under his arm, and I offered my arm to him. His wife carried a burning candle for us into the quiet summer air and there we sat again under the linden trees, and I declined a further cup of coffee and—now I'm willing to ask anyone whether it isn't strange for me to be writing this way about so-called philistine life as it is lived out back home in the fatherland, to be writing about it on shipboard out on the so-called high seas, on my way back to the desolate, but fruitful, wide open spaces so far away . . .

"Yes, yes, Edward," said Schaumann, "go forth of the ark! Some are sent out into the world to found a kingdom or an empire, others to secure an estate at the Cape of Good Hope, and others again just to capture a little country girl, one whose native good spirits have been stifled and who has a poor devil of a papa who himself is tormented almost to madness—to capture her, I say, and to acquaint her with Henriette Davidi's cookbook and with Heinrich Schaumann's likewise dreadfully stifled desires for a little happiness and dignity."

"Go forth of the ark, Heinrich!"

"When we were at school, I dare say you all thought you had your ideals. I was sure of mine."

"That I know well enough. You've told me several times today: Red Bank Farm."

"No, nothing of the sort."

"I'd be curious to know what it was, then."

"Myself," said Tubby Schaumann, with imperturbable composure. But then he looked around over his shoulder toward the house to see whether anyone might be coming or listening. He put his hand over his mouth and whispered, "I can tell you, Edward, she is one in a thousand and all she needed was a sensible man, the ideal man, if you will, at the right moment to become what I have made of her. You surely see that, Edward, although I admit it was a real dilemma: in order to become her ideal man, it was absolutely necessary for me first to become my own."

"Go forth of the ark," I muttered, "just keep going forth." What else could I have muttered?

"You had all left me sitting alone again under the hedge and gone in search of your fun without me. And that morning in school Blechhammer had held me up again as a dire, scientific example of the bradypus. I cannot only quote him to this day, I can bring him to life on the stage with his: 'Look at him, all of you, Schaumann, the sloth. There he sits again on the dullard's bench, like the bradypus, the sloth. Has hair the color of withered leaves and with four molars. Crawls slowly up into another class—I mean, climbs up a tree and stays there till he has eaten the last leaf. Schubert's[28] *Treatise on Natural History,* page three hundred and fifty-eight: climbs up another tree, but so slowly that a hunter who has seen him in one spot in the morning still finds him quite close to it that evening. And you are supposed to give him a classical education and a taste for scholarship and an understanding of the ancients.' Now, Edward, you were one of those who hunted me, though not one of the very worst: how do you find me, after finding me in the morning in one place and finding me now quite close to it in the evening?"

What else could I say but, "You were going to talk about the thriving, verdant hedges of our youth, old Heinrich, my friend. But go on. Tell it your own way."

"All right. Yes, and I suppose you still have them too, green and healthy, and unclipped whenever possible, round your fields and gardens in Africa? Here they are gradually getting rid of them, the hedges. Down there, round about that miserable town we used to live in when we were young and foolish, they are happy to replace them all with their garden walls, house walls, and iron railings. You would think they couldn't bear to see anything green any longer. Even out here they are beginning to do away with them. Well, let them; for my part I have had the pleasure of lying under the hedgerows, sometimes in the sun, sometimes in the shade. I ought to have been born under a hedge anyway and not in one of those stuffy town bedrooms looking out on the courtyard. They should have hung my diapers on hedges and not round an over-heated stove. Sir Heinrich Hedge, Heinrich von der Hecke! That would have been the name for me, for the conqueror of Red Bank, and Tina Quakatz with it, dear Edward, now wouldn't it? Sir Heinrich von der Hecke, how much more dignified, noble, signif-icant that would sound than Schaumann, candidate in theology, son of the former Junior, later Senior Tax Inspector Schaumann and Frau Schaumann etcetera, etcetera, with all civic titles of re-spect. And especially when you consider that it was under a hedge so green and lovely and thriving so well in the sunlight, that I found my Tina, the young lady, the girl who was meant for me, my shy hedge sparrow, and captured her to keep for the duration of our bittersweet mortality. 'Go away, boy,' said the young lady, sticking out her tongue. 'This hedge is my father's and no one has any right to it but us.' 'Farmer's goose, silly Sally,' I said and that was the beginning of our acquaintance. Very much with your col-laboration, my dear Edward, for why did you leave me alone like that in the grass beneath the hazelnut tree in old Quakatz's king-dom? 'I'm not a farmer's goose, I'm not a silly Sally. I'm Tina Quakatz. Get off our boundary, you town boy. Those nuts are mine, this is our hedge and our boundary, they're always throwing mud at me. They hatched the plan again this afternoon in school and told me they would.' Whether that was intended to be a warning, I can't say; anyway it came too late. Because at that moment I got the pie in the face—nose, eyes, and some of it in my mouth, opened wide to let words out. But, for all my flabby feet, I was over the hedge in a second and had the rustic assassin by the collar and on his back, with the fist full of the dirt he had scraped up to throw. The very next moment I had the whole vil-lage gang on top of me, boys and girls and dogs, and Tina scratch-ing their faces and pulling their hair and the whole company of guard dogs from Red Bank Farm bounding over the embanked road to our aid. Delightful! I can still feel the knocks I got, back and front. And then suddenly we had Prince Xaver's trench and Farmer Quakatz's hedge between us and the enemy. Lord, how my nose bled, and them on the other side wiping the blood off their mouths with their jacket sleeves and shrieking and calling us names and throwing stones: 'Off with her head! Kienbaum! Kienbaum! Tina Quakatz. Off with her head!' Lord, and then the real fright that went right to the marrow of us all, not just me—there, on the other side of the trench, the incarnation of human wrath. There he stood—all of them flew like sparrows from a stone—there he stood behind me, close beside me for the first time in my life, the murderer of Red Bank, the outlaw of Red Bank, the farmer Andreas Quakatz, the man who killed Kienbaum. Ultimately it was all the fault of you fellows that I made his acquaintance this way and then gradually cultivated it. A man whom his contemporaries have left lying under the hedge seeks his own solitary pleasure and leaves them to theirs. Oh, when I think of my departed father-in-law that day. He seemed not to see me at all. He just looked over the hedge at the shrieking rabble who were still throwing anything that came to hand, his enemies and ours. And instead of saying a word about it he turned and went toward the house—Kienbaum's murderer. There was nothing he could do here for his own child and he had to let us deal with the situation by ourselves. But the single action he had taken had sufficed to scatter the young villagers from the field in panic. 'Come, to the well, you,' said Tina. 'What a sight you are. Your mother, if you have one, will kill you if she sees you like that.' Look Edward, there it is, the same old well, still giving good water. The shaft goes pretty deep through the fortifications of Count von der Lausitz down to the bowels of the earth. I doubt if you have any better water in Africa and if you want a drink from it just ask Tina afterward. She winds the bucket up today just as she used to do. But on that occasion she said, 'If it wasn't that we and the cattle have to drink out of it, I'd have had a few of them lying down there long ago,' and she shook her fist toward the village as she said it, and all the curs of Red Bank Farm barked in the same direction.—I washed the blood off and then we both drank out of one pail, kneeling down to it and putting our heads in together. It was a sort of blood brotherhood or sisterhood that we enacted in this way. When we had wiped our mouths, the lady of Quakatz's castle said, 'If you are afraid to go home alone in daylight, you can stay here till it is dark, townie. They are sure to be waiting for you in the village, I know them. They'll beat you up, and you might prefer to be beaten in the evening by your father or your mother for staying out late.' You fellows never counted me a part of your heroic band, Edward. You bright-greaved Achaeans would never have put the best piece of the pork roast in my hands in token of honors won. Of course, you had no idea how much more heroism, under certain circumstances, there was in me than in you. If I wanted my pork chop from the spit sprinkled with floury brown crust I had to do my boasting without your knowing anything about it and say, 'I'm not afraid of anything in the world, and certainly not of that Maiholzen gang. I go any time of the day I like, they can't stop me; but now that you've said it, why, I'll stay.' Registrar Schwartner and Prince Xaver of Saxony had nothing to do at this moment with the eerie, sweet feeling that I was at last standing inside the notorious and myserious Red Bank Farm. 'Father is back in the house and won't bother us,' said my present wife. 'You've been good to me, townie, so you don't need to be afraid of me this time. I shan't throw you in the well. Let's climb up into the pear tree, or would you like to see my rabbits first and my goats? We have some puppies too. But father is only letting one of them stay with the mother this time; we have dogs enough on the ramparts. If father hadn't forbidden me to take them with me when I go along the hedge in that field over there, if I were free to set them loose, there'd be nobody in Maiholzen without a limp and torn skirts, aprons, and trousers. Look how they're watching you, waiting for me to say: At him! At him!' They certainly were. They were all keeping a vicious eye on me and growling at my heels. Well, I gradually got to know them better, Edward. Here, Prince, here, boy. See now, he's one of the old guard, or at least descended from it. He ought really to have been put out of his misery by a bullet or some prussic acid long ago, if I had the heart to do it. My wife, of course, won't hear a word of such merciful violence, and even our tomcat there would be sorry for it, I'm sure. Well, I hope one morning we'll find him in the corner, gathered to his forefathers on the list of those who have made their way out of this harsh world and have crossed the bar.''

"Is it possible that I made his acquaintance that time when we were saying good-bye before going to the university, Heinrich?"

"Scarcely. No sensible dog lives as long as that. An intelligent man might."

"Excuse me for interrupting you. Go on, Tubby."

"For the son-in-law of the man that murdered Kienbaum I don't tell a tale badly at all, do I? Yes, it was really a dickens of a household that slowly took one in as the only family friend. I can assure you, old man, that it is only very rarely that a father-in-law gradually takes a son-in-law to his heart in the curious way in which Father Quakatz did me, his fat and faithful Heinrich. And then there was that hedge sparrow whose tail I put salt on in the heat of battle, or rather that butterfly that I clapped my school cap on, though my nose was bleeding and my back was black and blue. You don't catch one of that sort every day, I can tell you. Lord, what a sight the wench was in those days, what a baggage, my mother would have said, what a baggage washed by the rain and dried in the sun and tousled by the wind, what a helpless motherless baggage who patched her own clothes and pieced her costume together herself using only the fashion journal of Red Bank. And with that rank order of blood, corruption, and un-avenged murder about her, that Kienbaum smell. Do you know what she said to me, what Frau Schaumann said, while she was throw-ing pears down to me out of the pear tree? She said: 'He's in the house now, my father is, and if he doesn't see you, that's fine with me. They all tell me in the village, and down in the town too, that he killed Kienbaum and I don't believe it. I'll stake my life on it to every one of you that he didn't do it; but what I do know is that he is fit to poison the whole world, including you, townie. Of that I'm sure. He says that the reason why he lets the mice run free everywhere, house mice, fieldmice, or any sort, and do what damage they can is because he can't get at you.' What else could I say to that but, 'Tina Quakatz, just you see to it then that he counts me among the mice in his natural history; because I'm coming out to Red Bank again tomorrow, unless they keep me in at school.' 'They kept my father in jail, but they've had to let him out every time. Try as they may, they can't get anything on him. No one can prove that he killed Kienbaum.' "

At this moment Frau Valentina came out of the house again, bringing her work basket with her this time, and sat down with us, pushing her chair close to her husband's.

"Not too close, my girl," sighed Tubby. 'What a summer it is for growth. Good God, look at the people out in the fields without any shade, or none they are free to lie down in. Edward and I have just got to the point where we're under the shade of Red Bank and I'm telling him how you washed my face, or rather my bloody nose that time, and what a hero I was and how our dear departed father would have liked to turn the mice loose and poison all humanity."

"Don't let him talk too much nonsense," Frau Schaumann said amiably, calmly threading her needle. "There are times even now when he's ever so quiet and capable of anything, just as when he was a silly little boy. Well, but then you know him, don't you, Edward?"

"No sooner does a woman come on the scene than the carping and nagging begin," said Heinrich, laying his hand on his wife's head while exposing his broad comfortable stomach to full view. "The poor little thing! If she hadn't found me with all my follies! Well, Edward, where had we got to?"

"The pear tree. I suppose that one there."

We all looked and Frau Valentina gave an emphatic nod.

"Right," said her husband. "She was sitting up in the tree and I was sitting down below. She picked and I ate. Edward, my physiological proclivities have always prevented you from seeing my spiritual ones properly. You cunning dogs, you lightweights, you young monkeys at gymnasium had no idea what can go on in the head of a bradypus. With this urchin, this lassie here, I was all straight. She was my girl now, my protégée, and I was her patron saint, her Saint Heinrich of the Hedge; that was obvious. . ."

"My dear . . ."

"Same to you; and just as obviously, or rather logically—don't be always interrupting me, old girl—the old man came next. And, of course, that went all right too. You fellows thought I was stupid and greedy; he probably took me for greedy too, but also, along with my general harmlessness, for a light shining in some portion of the darkness that had settled on his life, his wretched life, Tina."

The last few words were said in such a way as to make his wife move her chair closer to him again. She put her hand on his and he put his arm round her and said, "Tina, my dear Tina Quakatz."

Then he turned back to me and I knew now how to account for his change of tone.

"It was like this. The very next day after the fight at the hedge I was back again as a matter of course in Registrar Schwartner's magic kingdom, and this time I was up the tree, a little apple tree, that one there. And Tina was standing below this time, holding out her apron, and again the old man suddenly appeared from nowhere and glanced up to me, saying nothing, and it looked as if a storm was brewing. 'Father, he only wants to study our fortifications,' said Tina, a little hesitantly. 'He's brought his history books about the siege and they bombarded his house from here.' 'You just come down from there,' said old man Quakatz. And I showed them how fast a bradypus, a sloth, can get down a tree. There I stood in front of the man that murdered Kienbaum. And if I wasn't exactly expecting to be struck dead on the spot, like Tina I was certainly thinking the old man would at least point across the trench at the open fields and say firmly, 'Clear out!' But that isn't what happened. He just said, 'All right,' meaning my studying the place. He can't have meant anything else. Then we thought he would swing around in his usual way and go. But that isn't what happened either. He stayed and said, 'You go to the gymnasium?'—'Ye-yes, Mr. Quakatz.' 'Can you read that stuff, Latin, I mean?' 'Ye-yes,' I stuttered, not meaning any harm. 'Divide up your apples and then come into the house. I want you to translate something for me out of the Latin.'—So there I was, caught. I hadn't intended it that way when I said I could read Latin. And now, wife, I call on Edward, the learned African, to tell you how completely your papa misunderstood me. But if you're trapped, you're trapped, and after a dreadful, dilatory, apple-chewing quarter of an hour outside, I then found myself trapped all the more inside, sitting with the outlaw of Red Bank in his parlor, our present dining room, Edward, that stuffy and cheerless room you saw, the day we said good-bye as youngsters. As I had waited too long for the old man's liking, he had come back into the garden, grabbed me by the upper arm, led me into his murderer's den, clapped me down at the table on the bench under the penny print of Cain and Abel, and said, 'What are you shaking for, boy? I won't cut your throat.'—Then he went to a cupboard—I have now replaced it with my case of coproliths—took out a fat pigskin volume, spread it in front of me on the table after turning the pages for a while, sat down beside me as if I were a grown man and a lawyer, placed his hard bony index finger on a passage and said, 'Here, you Latinist. Make this clear to me in German as best you can, word for word. It's the *Corpus Juris*,[30] the *Corpus Juris, the Corpus Juris,* and I want to have it in German from some one who doesn't know anything about the *Corpus Juris, the Corpus Juris.*' The passage was heavily underlined with red pencil and the page had been dog-eared, all suggesting that the trembling, excited thumb and forefinger holding it had done so frequently before this. But I sat in front of the book tearfully rubbing my eyes with my knuckles: we hadn't got so far in school that we could explain the lawyer's book of books to the farmer Andreas Quakatz. And with schoolboy evasion I finally stuttered, 'Mr. Quakatz, I need my dictionary just to know the words and I have it at home.'—'Then get it and bring it out with you tomorrow. I'm a fool to talk to you this way. But that's the way the world would have me, and you are just as good as anyone else, if I want to talk to someone about my case. I've had enough, I don't want any more scholars, lawyers, bigwigs helping me. You're clever enough for me to talk to as if you were a sensible man. That's what our ancestors did in the old days, they stuck to fools and children. Lad, my Tina says you came out to study Red Bank. Study it and find out who is right, the world or the farmer at Red Bank. You protected my lass out of a sense of justice—I was watching from behind the hedge on the ramparts—now I'll see whether what is written is true: that truth has its abode in the mouths of babes and sucklings. If you can find out who killed Kienbaum, I'll give Red Bank Farm to you and Registrar Schwartner along with all your histories of the Seven Years' War and the

Thirty Years' War and I'll take the road with my child, a white staff in my hand. The girl tells me they are all against you, too. So try it, find out who killed Kienbaum and I'll make Red Bank over to you and your heirs.'—Yes, yes, Valentina Schaumann, née Quakatz, that's the way he disposed of any claims on the world you might have had. But if an incalculable, gluttonous, limp-footed bradypus was capable of helping you to what was yours, I was the one, Heinrich Schaumann, alias Tubby. But, to begin with, I whimpered to the farmer of Red Bank: 'Herr Quakatz, I don't know whether I can. They've kept me back in the fourth form again.'—'Try,' said my future father-in-law, and his daughter prodded me with her elbow, as much as to say, 'Do it to please me,' and when we were out in the garden again, she whispered to me, 'Don't be so stupid, he doesn't know himself what he wants with that old book. It's just because he hasn't anyone, not a soul, no one he can talk to, apart from the lawyers that he's sick of. And tomorrow he probably won't mention it to you at all: he just took that notion because he figured you were a scholar. Bring along the fattest book you have. He doesn't mind having you on the farm now, and you can keep your eyes open and see what you can figure out for us.'—

"Oh, well, my dear, you can tell Edward really much better than I can, how I started coming out to Red Bank Farm from time to time, till at last I stayed there for good. One thing is sure: I didn't translate the *Corpus Juris* into German for the murderous farmer of Red Bank. But another thing is sure as well, sweetheart, my lamb, you dear old thing, and you my African friend: just incidentally, and practically without my doing anything about it, I did find out the murderer, I did find out who it was that murdered Kienbaum."

We have got through so far without a storm or a waterspout. But yesterday noon the cry suddenly went up on the *Hagebucher,* "Fire on board," and only the cook kept his composure; because he was the only one who knew at once where the smell of smoke came from. He alone knew about the old woolen stocking that had got in among the coals and into his cooking stove. The worthless blackamoor had worn it in northern Hamburg; but now beneath the equator he had seen fit to dispose of what lovely remnants were left of it.

And just as if someone at the house had shouted, "Fire, fire at Red Bank Farm," I sprang to my feet and Frau Valentina stood bolt upright at the table and flung down her knitting.

"Can it be?" I stammered. "Frau Valentina—"

She stood there pale and speechless and stared round-eyed at her husband.

"It certainly can," he said. "It's the old story; even the stupidest of us can get somewhere, it he sets his silly mind to it and stays with it. Yes, folks, I now know who killed Kienbaum."

"But think of your wife, man. Just look at her. Has she to this day known no more about it than anyone else?"

"This is the very first she's heard about it as far as I know. You only need to look at her to see. But sit down again, Tina, do. My dear old wife, be steady now. Remember our agreement. When we're discussing something, it's only after my pipe has gone out that you get your turn to cry 'Murder,' to stamp your feet and throw your arms about and treat the world to a display of tears or insults. Please, good people, oblige me and calmly take your seats."

Whatever they had agreed on about his pipe, it was very near going out at this moment. But he got a good fire started again with a few pulls, puffed a blue cloud of smoke into the sweet summer air and—well, we hadn't called him Tubby for nothing. Since his wife did as he asked and sat down, there was nothing for it but for me to follow suit.

"Heinrich," whispered his wife anxiously, imploringly. I involuntarily growled, "Come forth of the ark, you ogre," but Tubby said in fits and starts as he sucked away at his briar, "But—people—please—If you want to hear it, then let me finish the story of how I conquered Quakatz's castle in peace. Don't keep interrupting me. In every generation of humanity there's this everlasting excitability, till they lie down dead and the next one arises! If we are to have done with this business by suppertime, don't be breaking in on me every second word."

And indeed the fellow referred to supper as if it were our main business. There was nothing for it but to let him crawl slothlike into his tree. But even for someone who thought he had kept a cool head and seen a thing or two on all his journeyings up and down the globe, this coldbloodedness began to have something uncanny about it.

"Sweetheart, give me another cup of coffee and give Edward one, too. You're not getting worked up, are you, child? What a wonderful day it is here in the shade with all that blaze of heat round us. There—another piece of sugar."

The poor woman did as he asked, but as if she were sleepwalking or hypnotized. She never looked at the cups or the coffeepot— she kept her eyes fixed on her husband as if she didn't know whether from now on she should live in mortal fear of him or go on loving him.

"Please, Heinrich . . . "

"Don't do that. You know, girl, that that's unnecessary. Don't I know all your wishes before you say them? I tell you, Edward, I know them without even looking in her eyes the way your normal good husband has to do. You shall know everything, Tina. It won't hurt anyone any more, it won't give anyone any malicious pleasure, either, if we pick up that stuffy old forgotten atrocity with a pair of tongs, drag it out into the daylight, and then carefully turn it over in the sun with the tips of our boots. Besides, it's up to you: do you want me to go on as I've begun or do you want me to dispose of it quickly in three short words?"

"Go on, man," I couldn't help shouting, and his wife said, more than ever as if hypnotized: "I give in; it's probably best for you to do it your own way."

"Then we'll stay for a while in our idyll and let Kienbaum alone as long as possible," said Schaumann. "What's the good of these blank faces? Am I pulling one too? Isn't the sorry case of the farmer at Red Bank warning and example enough? We could all learn from his misery, I think, to keep calm and quietly take the world as it comes. Of course, you have to be made that way from the start. Not everyone has to have the stuff in him to set the new German Empire on its feet and say: Now the rest of you, etc., etc. . . . Yes, my dear Edward, let each of us get out of that zoo of an ark in his own way. Take for example Heinrich Schaumann, alias Tubby. He at any rate did not live entirely according to his nature, he did or didn't do what he was told to do or not do; should it be considered his fault later on, if somehow something sensible results? Not at all. I take no responsibility whatsoever. Since I am not allowed to live in a nice, neat, comfortable world, what do I care whether the one I do live in is sensible or intelligent? Plato, Aristotle, our dear old Kant . . ."

"For heaven's sake, stop, you're driving me crazy," I cried, putting my hands over my ears, and Schaumann laughed and said, "There, you see, Edward, how the man who is on top of things after waiting quietly for years gets his revenge for the mocks and rebuffs he patiently endured. This is the satisfaction I have been waiting for in the cool shade while you and your Le Vaillant were out hunting elephants, rhinoceroses, and giraffes in burning Africa or sweating yourselves to death in some other useless way. So let us stay a while in our idyll, before we go on to Kienbaum and how he met his end. You may judge for yourself afterward whether you regard his, your, or my story as the more important. Go easy, Tina, and trust your husband today as you have done before. You are an important part of this, but you know, don't you, that your husband always takes your part."

And so, since we had no choice, we let Kienbaum go unavenged, we let him rot for the time being and stayed with our idyll.

"I believe I have already asked you several times to take a look at my wife; but now I ask you again: just take another look at her, sitting there, so pretty. Would you believe it today that she sat there once like a maiden transformed into a wildcat who was waiting for her knight-errant to come and deliver her? You don't need to check up on me. My knightliness had something so large and impressive about it that you fellows at school couldn't miss it in those early years, and you made me pay for it plenty. But you fools underrated me even then. Tell him yourself, old girl, how many dozen novelette heroes I had in me and put on display after you first said, 'Listen, Father likes you, so you just keep on coming.' No, it's better if you don't tell him; if you do, he'll quickly make it an opportunity to play himself off against me as a Pylades who wasn't given his due and pretend he always understood me.

Let us stay with your old man, Tina. 'Of course I'll come again tomorrow and not just for your pears. Your old man is swell, and if he's killed anyone, the fellow deserved it six times over. That's all nonsense about his fat law book and my Latin; but there is no nonsense about the cannonball fired from Red Bank that hit our house. And if I tell old Schwartner that your father let me into Red Bank, he'll give me twopence and there'll be cake for us and not just apples and pears. I'll be back tomorrow.'

"And tomorrow there I was, since neither father nor mother nor teacher barred my way. And now, Tina, who had better grounds to hip-hip-hurray? Prince Xaverius of Saxony lording it over the town from Red Bank, or me lording it over Red Bank from the town?"

"You," said Frau Valentina, and added, turning to me, "It's no use; we must let him have his way."

So we let him have it and away he waddled down it, in the certain knowledge that he had us in the palm of his hand.

First he refilled his pipe and sighed and said, "Since the world washed its hands of the man at Red Bank because it couldn't squeeze him dry, he did what he had every right to do, and tried to get along without it as best he could. He managed badly, not being as equal to the task as I with my temperament would have been. He wasn't nearly fat enough for the job, was far too vivacious and sociable. It happens all too often that the knotty problems and the hard nuts go to the wrong man. Would it have bothered me, old roly-poly, to have to vegetate my way through the world under the suspicion of having murdered Kienbaum? Not in the least. The affair might have shed a certain glory on me, because people would most certainly have said, 'There, you see, you wouldn't really have thought the lazy dog was capable of it, and he hasn't got the intelligence either.' But Papa Quakatz? What else could he do if he wanted to keep his reason but turn his mind and his thoughts to all sorts of things that no farmer before him at Red Bank had ever hit on? It may have been purely an accident that I, Heinrich Schaumann, alias Tubby, was able to help him, but the effect was the same as if it were the hand of fate. To begin with, there was the history of his fortress; and I said to him, 'Herr

Quakatz, it was from here that the Prince of Saxony slaughtered a whole lot of people down in the town.'

" 'Yes, boy, that was when the Swedes were here.'

" 'No, Mr. Quakatz, it isn't as long ago as that. It was in the Seven Years' War.'

" 'Can you give me any of their names, boy?'

" 'No, but I can get them from Schwartner, the registrar, and copy them down for you. He has them all in writing.'

" 'Then just bring the list out with you, my fat friend. But don't tell him I wanted it. If you do, they might start thinking things again.'

"And one day soon after found us sitting with our heads together, not over the *Corpus Juris,* but over what I had copied out of old Schwartner's collection, and the farmer of Red Bank was trying to figure out what people today were the assignees of those who were killed in seventeen hundred and sixty-one and possibly entitled to bring a suit against the assignees of the Count von der Lausitz. It wasn't clear to me then what comfort there was in this for your father, Tina. Today I think I know. We shifted over then from the bones of recent history to the bones of the truly primal past; and it was a great day for me, my dear Edward, when Farmer Quakatz first led me to a locked stable and pointed to a queer-looking heap and asked, 'What is that, boy?' Yes, and what was it? It was the fairly complete skeleton of a mammoth and—'I came across it in the gravel pit behind the farmyard,' said the farmer, 'there may be more of it there; because this Red Bank is probably a deposit dating from the Flood. Dating from the Flood, my boy. You can't know how the farmer at Red Bank feels when he reads in the Bible about the Flood; but if you have anything in your books about these bones and things, bring it out with you but don't tell anyone what a fossilized dragon Kienbaum's murderer has found in his gravel pit and how glad he is to have it.'—I didn't tell a soul at the time what an interesting discovery Tina's father had made; but today if the postman comes out to Red Bank—it isn't our old friend Störzer now—along with the newspaper he generally brings Herr Schaumann something from some geological or related society. The notion that one might be discovered as one of the more remarkable fossils in a later stratum is so stimulating for a man of reason and sentiment that it is bound to lead him into the study of petrifaction and paleontology, particularly if he has the time for it. And you would only need to step over again to the edge of the rampart, Edward, and look at the surroundings with this aspect in mind, to find they had suddenly become extremely interesting in a quite novel way. Between the Triassic and the Cretaceous nothing but water, and the nearest island that blue hill over to the south. If the flood receded a little in the Eocene and in the Miocene, it became what we call dry land, and if in the Pliocene the dust blew now and then at Red Bank—why, that was all the same to the farmer. All he cared about was who knew anything or could know anything about his relation to Kienbaum. But as the years have passed, it hasn't been all the same to me, the present farmer at Red Bank. You see, the doctor said to Tina, 'With a physique like his nothing could be better for him than this hobby of his and all this crawling about in gravel and marl pits. The more he sweats in his hunt for bones, the better it will be for both of you.' And, my dear Edward, if ever a wife encouraged a crazy hobby in her husband, Valentina Quakatz did after what the doctor said to her. Edward, in the Tertiary Age they say it was as hot here as it is in the hottest part of your Africa, and if I had come here then, I couldn't have done anything about it and wouldn't have wanted to. But think, it wasn't till the Ice Age, the Ice Age, that mankind migrated from Asia to Red Bank with the first of the mammals—so why shouldn't a late descendant sweat now in the summertime when he pokes around studiously and reverently for the earliest traces of his ancestors in the soil that Prince Xaver of Saxony threw up."

No chance of doing any more writing today. The ship is tossing too much. A large swell. No getting near the captain. Crew all very busy and—understandably—very rude. The Negro steward drunk. Passengers—devil take their yelling. You can hardly hear the storm for them and the men at work. "Heigh, my hearts! Cheerly, cheerly, my hearts! Yare, yare!" Go and see Shakespeare's *Tempest*, but, if you can, see it from a seat in the stalls, anywhere it's comfortable.

The bad weather went on for two days and two nights. "The giants under the waters were alarmed" and "those that abode with them too." Who wouldn't have got out of that ark if he could? Truly, the Lord has shown me great marvels upon the deep, making it all the pleasanter to live in one's memories great and small and to be Heinrich Schaumann's or Tubby's guest and hear my fat friend say to his wife:

"But what concern is it, really, of Edward and you, my dear, this hobby of your father's and mine, and the study of petrifactions anyway? What concern is it of yours how long the ocean spread over Red Bank before the possibility arose of Kienbaum being murdered in its vicinity? Isn't it much more entertaining to talk about how the Lord made grass, bushes, and trees to grow again after the Flood was over, and how he stuck flowers on them like Christmas candles and hung all sorts of fruit on them, sweet to behold and pleasant to taste? Edward, how many times have I to tell you that you don't bear the noble name of Tubby without having earned it? And, while we are on this point, what a life and what a table here at Red Bank. Oh, Tina, Valentina, to think of you and me sitting under the bushes, chewing and smacking our lips, while the others were toiling to fly their paper kites in the blue sky over the autumn fields."

"Oh, Heinrich," the poor woman interrupted him. "Heinrich, dear, I implore you, don't for heaven's sake make yourself out to be worse than . . ."

"Greedier, you mean . . ."

"All right, greedier, but please, please, don't make yourself out to be more horrid than you are, especially at this dreadful moment when I'm trembling all over at what you said about Kienbaum. Was it only for the apples and the gooseberries that you came out from the town to see me, to see us?"

"Most certainly not, sweetheart. The larder and the dairy had their charms, too. Now just take the fresh butter and that country bread. And then your cheese. The only use I could see in all the books, ancient and modern, that had been written and printed was to supply the necessary wrapping paper. You see, Edward, I didn't just stuff my belly, but my pockets too."

"There's no doing anything with him," said his wife, turning to me with a sigh. "I really hadn't known him very long before I gave up trying to improve him, and I only try once in a while now for form's sake when we have strangers here or a visit from a dear friend. But in all seriousness—in deepest, deepest seriousness—let me say a word myself about what passed between us then, unless you would first like—yourself . . . to tell us . . ."

"No, I don't want to do that. If there is anything today that there is no hurry about, it's that, thank God. You can't hang or behead him now, sweetheart. It's too late for that. The only man who can get at Kienbaum's murderer now is the judge of the dead, and, for that matter, who knows whether it isn't he who has brought us together here today as his jurymen and assessors?"

"Oh, Heinrich, the ghost that haunted my poor father day and night . . ."

"Let it be for a minute, child. Look up into the lovely blue sky over our heads. Look into Edward's lean kaffir-face, a little strained and embarrassed, but kindly, and so stay a little bit longer in our idyll. Tell him your version of our love affair, if you like. I give you my word for it: as far as that other business is concerned, it really doesn't matter whether you learn the details of it a few minutes earlier or later. We helped your father, our father, to die in peace, and from now on the only way people will be able to get at the man who murdered Kienbaum will be with their dirty tongues. And then perhaps only if you two—you and Edward—prove unable to keep it to yourselves tomorrow."

The woman shook her head once more at her husband's better knowledge and understanding, then she laid her folded hands on the table and stayed in the idyll that was hers and his, and in spite of the melancholy and the tense excitement of the situation, she told her story in such a charming and heartwarming way while waiting for Schaumann to reveal the secret of Red Bank.

"I can't tell you how glad I was when the boy started coming out to see us," she said. "I can't think of anyone I ever knew who had a childhood like mine. Poor people have much to bear, in town or in the country, but here at Red Bank we weren't poor at all, and yet if I'd been born in a ditch and fallen out of my mother's basket and onto public charity I should have been better off than I was as the only child, a daughter and a well-to-do one, of the farmer at Red Bank. If after all I went through at school and in the fields and pastures I didn't end up murdering a hundred people to my poor father's one, you can't call it anything but one great miracle. The things I have had to hear, feel, and see from the time I first began to find my way in this world, no book could ever tell."

"Hum," growled Schaumann, "just now it might make more useful reading than a lot of other things."

"Oh no, Heinrich! It was too horrid."

"That's why," grunted Schaumann, but his wife cried:

"I let you have your say, now let me have mine after asking me for it. And Herr . . ."

"Edward."

"Well then, if our dear friend Edward will be so good as to bear with this little tale of our lives here in this secluded spot."

"Secluded," grinned Schaumann. "No doubt for him that African desert of his sometimes gets livelier than he wants. If I want to think of an eternal Sabbath rest somewhere, I picture just the part of the world he has sought out for himself, our dear friend— Edward."

I controlled myself and didn't box the fat fellow's ears despite his knowing smile at the life I had led and at all I had achieved in remote parts. I just took his wife's hand and said: "Let it be, my dear friend, my dear Frau Valentina, and tell me about yourself and your father and Red Bank Farm for me to take it with me into *my* secluded spot."

"Yes, the three of us is all I know anything about. I've never been on a desert island, but the way I imagine it, it was like being on a desert island for us."

"Not with the blue Caribbean Sea round you, though, but a sort of soup, all sticky, and smoky and yellowish-gray with green flecks of mold on it and smelling of pitch and sulphur and worse," grunted the incorrigible fellow.

"If you were set down in the world, Edward, a hunted creature and a deserted child, could you imagine a better place to be in than this forsaken old castle of ours?"

"I certainly couldn't."

"Wasn't it a pity that when I was so young I had to train the dogs to share our hatred of people? But wasn't it good that when school was over I could sit here in safety on the ramparts and have the village and the town and the evil looks and the unkind words and the peering and whispering of even the best and most sensible of them—have all that down below me? Oh, God, I ought to be ashamed to this very day to think how often, virtually every day, when I had reached the last rampart I was driven to having to stick out my tongue, to throw stones and sic these poor, faithful dogs on people. Heinrich has just been telling you how my poor father stood behind him without saying a word. Good God, that's the way he always stood behind me, from the time I first began to be aware and understand things. It was a long time before I was able to see why he was so angry at people and on friendly terms with no one, except now and then a lawyer who simply repeated what he wanted to hear. It is hard for a child to find out from children that you are going to be alone on God's good earth. And although I wept and said, no, shrieked a thousand times over, 'Liar!' they went on making the same signs behind the teacher's back, like putting a rope round your neck or felling an ox. Sometimes Father would stroke my hair after we had sat without speaking on a winter evening, me in one corner and him in another, and he would say, 'I can't help it, you poor little thing, off to bed with you and sleep; I'll come and see if you've dropped off and no longer have to think about me,' and that was a comfort to me and brought a lump to my throat. Sometimes I crept out of bed again late in the night and tiptoed to the door in my bare feet and saw him sitting there wide awake. Oh, Edward, there can't be many people who have slept as little as my poor father. And then the help, the farmhands and the girls. Oh, how often what a near thing it was that I might have turned really bad, turned perhaps into a real killer and murderer. They brought back all the street ballads and everything else of that sort that they picked up at the fair and they sang them to me and whistled them to me, but if they talked to one another about it and only peered over my way as they did it, then that was worse still. On every green meadow, where other children are allowed to gather flowers and make dandelion chains, they built a gallows for me. And among all the strawberries and blueberries and raspberries in the wood they built me a scaffold. The shepherd and the ploughman out in the field, the women and the girls hoeing the turnips and grubbing the potatoes, they all had their tales to tell for me to take home to the ramparts of my father's farm, and I would even take them to bed with me, hiding under the covers that I often pulled over my head, my heart quivering with dread, even in the heat of summer and at the risk of suffocating. Oh, how many a night I have gone to bed with my clothes on because I was too frightened to take my dress and shoes off, and not only on a stormy winter night, on summer nights too with the moon shining."

"You poor child," I murmured spontaneously.

"Yes, you poor child, Edward," grunted Tubby. "I, poor child, when I was little I could pull as long a face as I liked: it made no appreciable impression on anyone. 'That youngster is getting mopier from day to day,' was the only remark I would hear."

But as he said this, the fat fellow's eyes began to shine strangely and he rapped me on the knee and asked, "Wasn't it time I took things in hand? Wasn't it the best thing we could do, to pool our misery and put our grief in one pot by the fire? And isn't the result satisfactory? Haven't I fed her well, the wildcat of Quakatz's castle, and made her pretty and chubby and nice and sat her down comfortably in the comfortable sofa-corner with the customary and ever-so-cosy knitting in her hand? Well, you ought to see the pussycat now purring and mewing and whirring there by winter storms and summer moonlight."

"It's my turn, Heinrich," the dear woman said with a smile.

"It's yours. It's always yours. You always have the last word and can keep it. All I want to say is that we no longer read either of those cursed books, not the big lawbook nor the little dictionary, of an evening, Tina. You see, Edward, if she disturbs my reflections and my paleontological studies now, it is only with Frau Davidi's cookbook in her hand, coming up to me savoring some new triumph, the tip of her tongue moving along her lips, and saying, 'What do you think, old boy, shall we try this recipe?' And naturally the only answer I can give to this bothersome question is: Nothing ventured, nothing gained. Go forth of the ark."

Frau Valentina was shrewd enough to ignore her gourmet and his famous cookbook and, turning to me, went on with her story, just as she was entitled to do. And, thank heaven, she did it as if she were indeed sitting in her sofa corner, but with a moist shine in her eyes and a rise and catch in her voice much like a child that, overcoming some recent care, now joins in the laughter around her.

"Yes, it was bad. And it was high time both for my father and me that we found someone to keep us company—someone the dogs would let in by the embankment over the trench without jumping at his throat and yelping and howling the tale of our domestic bliss in his ears. I couldn't have known beforehand that the townie would be any use to my father. To begin with he had merely sided with me against the village kids and got a bloody nose for his pains. And it was really for my own sake that I brought him with me through the dogs to the farm and led him to the well where he could wash his face a little. But it turned out to be a blessing for both father and daughter and for Red Bank Farm too that by the mercy of God there was more to him than we know. Didn't it, Heinrich?"

This last remark was a mistake. Because it set her pudgy lord and master going again. Fortunately he had been daydreaming and watching the puffs of tobacco smoke soar up towards the treetops, and all he muttered was, "You're right, old girl, as always. What was it now—what did you just say? Oh, yes, of course. Well, Edward, are you beginning to see that the three of us, Papa Quakatz, his Tina, and Tubby Schaumann from the town here, had no need of any fourth person in our company?"

"We certainly hadn't," cried Frau Valentina Schaumann, without waiting for my answer. "If God sent us just one person, that was all we asked for. But it had to be someone who either hated or was indifferent to everything else: everything but us at Red Bank Farm. He had to like everything that Farmer Quakatz and his little girl were able to offer him, neither fearing the whiff of murder and of the knacker's yard that clung to it, nor shrinking from it in disgust. And, Edward, it turned out that that was what came of the townie's lying under the hedge over yonder on the town side of our property and protecting me against the village lads. And what came of his having just Latin enough to look up words for my father in his big dictionary and translate documents and papers for him at a time when he didn't trust lawyers any more. Edward, please don't listen to what he says now. It may be that he learned more at school before he came out here with you as he was going off to the university and wanted to say good-bye. I'm no judge of that, but for Red Bank Farm in those days he knew all he needed to know. He not only calmed the dogs, he calmed my poor father and gave him better days."

"Just listen to her, Edward. Yes, yes, but she's right. Truly the clever ones haven't brought the world nearly as much comfort or made nearly as many people happy as the simpletons."

"Quite right, Heinrich. At least my poor father thought so too. 'Tina,' he said, 'I've no objection to that quiet fat boy coming out here. If you can get on with him, it's all right with me. He doesn't bother me and it gives us someone in the sitting room who isn't like all the others.' "

"Your dear departed father was saying something there, Frau Valentina Tubby," grinned Heinrich Schaumann in his incorrigible way.

"It is simply what a man said who had to hold head and heart with both hands for years and years and years for fear they would burst with rage and fear and fury and shame. And, Edward, if there was a man who wasn't one of the others, it was this husband of mine. Not so much because he had anything special about him, but rather just because he hadn't and didn't find anything special in us, in our anxiety and banishment, but simply associated with us as if we were ordinary people like anyone else."

Naturally Frau Valentina hadn't the slightest notion what a wonderful tribute and testimony she was paying my friend and that she was relegating me to the ranks of the quite ordinary, the quite common individuals found by every roadside, to those who boldly go out into the world, to Africa or somewhere, to have their trivial adventures. The fattest of my friends just grinned once more, but understood it all, I'm sure.

The woman went on:

"He would sit in the room with my father or lie with me out under a tree on the ramparts thrown up against mankind. Yes, Edward, against mankind because they threw stones at him too from across the trench; but not for long. Your young colleagues and schoolfellows didn't fully know what my husband was like in those days . . ."

"Good girl," laughed Schaumann.

"Oh, well, I suppose I didn't put it the right way. Well then, they didn't completely know what you had in you, Heinrich, and what you were capable of doing or saying when you were hit on the head by a sod really meant for Kienbaum's murderer. Oh, Edward, your friend could call himself master of Red Bank Farm, even as the first long summer holidays came round. He had wrested it from an evil enemy, for both of us; and then, when I didn't have to be as afraid of others at night, I would often lie there in a rage and ask myself why I should put up with it from him. For you see, Edward, he didn't really treat me at all as nicely as a knight-errant should. 'Silly goose' was the politest title he honored me with. And woe was me if I let him know that I still had a stock of nicknames on hand learned in my fights and dealings with the other children. And if I tried to defend myself with tears, it was worse. At the most he would say, 'She has the best place in all Germany and she's sulking. Girl, just you sit for a moment on my . . .' "

"Podex," suggested Heinrich.

"Seat in the classroom," Tina went on, preferring the gentler expression. "In that respect, no doubt, things didn't always go very well with him at home and at school. Well, at Red Bank Farm he sat as safe and secure as I, despite all his sins and shortcomings. At Quakatz the Murderer's farm no one made him suffer on that account. Quite the reverse. Perhaps the reason why he was right for me, and suitable company for my father, was that he often had something on his conscience too and would come out to see us with the tear marks on his cheeks and would rail and curse from the ramparts at the town and school below with no one to stop him. He must have been lazy to the core in those days, Edward."

"In point of laziness, Edward, she has no quarrel with the congenial conditions under which I live at present. Though my collection of fossils and the learned correspondence connected with it do impress her somewhat. You can stand up to your wife, you see, when you are a member of half-a-dozen paleontological societies. And there is something yet in store for her. My treatise on the mammoth and its relations to Red Bank, Prince Xaver of Saxony, and Andreas Quakatz, the farmer, with an appendix on the megatherium, shall most certainly be dedicated to her. Who knows, the giant sloth may yet clap the crown of immortality on her cap or, should I say, her pretty locks."

"God preserve me," laughed Frau Valentina, but she went on: "Oh, Lord, look where he leads us, Edward, with the way he manages things. He knows who killed Kienbaum and here I sit and talk all sorts of stuff and nonsense, just because he wants it so. Oh, my poor, poor father. And when he, my husband I mean, had rubbed at the dust and the moisture around his eyes with his sleeve . . ."

"Muck and tears, you mean, my dear."

"Yes, and with your coat sleeve. And when he then, as he sometimes did, reached behind and rubbed himself between the shoulder blades, my poor father would say . . .

" 'Go and cut him a nice piece of bread and butter and give him a nice piece of sausage with it. He's had his troubles too and knows in his young years what to expect of the world.' "

"So I did as he told me, and then we moved on to the cheeses, the gooseberries, the apples, pears, and plums, and whatever else the season offered as comfort for him and for me. Yes, Edward, in this respect the Prince of Saxony's Red Bank was the very place for him. Oh, and the things he knew about it from that Herr Schwartner. I can still see them sitting there, him and my father, expatiating on the history of the Seven Years' War and saying what a pity it was they didn't smash the wretched town down there to pieces."

"She got the word 'expatiate' from me, Edward," smirked Tubby; but his wife smiled and sighed and continued:

"Even in those days I thought him the wisest and most learned of men. But you couldn't expect me to let on right away. He was still too foolish for that, and I had grown up too much up in arms and rebellion against everything. But, without my letting on, he gave me an understanding for so many things and a taste for so many things . . ."

"She got the word 'taste' from me, Edward."

"And my father and he came to the conclusion that no one cares a hoot any more for the Prince of Saxony and his horrible war and that the day would come when no one would care a hoot for Blechhammer and the rest of us and—and—Kienbaum. Not a dog would bark at our heels, and no one turn his nose up. All that mattered on earth, they decided, was a good conscience and an inner self-content . . ."

"She got the expression 'inner self-content' from me."

"Of course. I got everything from you," cried Frau Valentina, now really becoming a bit jittery and excited and irritable. "Well, it's a comfort that you let me claim my good conscience as something of my own. And if you say that I got my inner self-content from you, I at least had some of it in me to begin with, and all you did was to . . ."

"Make you realize it. She's right there, Edward. I tell you, Edward, you have no idea what all she had bottled up ever so tightly inside her, waiting for me to come along with the corkscrew. Oh, my girl, my dearest dear old girl, why else should we have suited one another so well? Oh, Tina, Tina, you and me—'fair fragments of the godhead'—didn't we belong together from the beginning and shan't we stick together to the very end? You from the farthest end of Africa, you Edward, what do you say to this?"

Years ago I had looked away. This time I looked closely and saw the two of them put their arms around one another's necks and hug one another and give one another a loud kiss. They weren't at all embarrassed in front of me this time, but Heinrich's head, it must be admitted, shone bald and there was here and there an early gray thread in Valentina's hair. But it was nice nevertheless, and it didn't spoil it at all that Schaumann was a little fat and that his brave little wife was not in the least like the Aphrodite of Melos.

"I can tell you, Edward," said Valentina, unabashedly straightening her cap, "when I look back as an adult, as an old woman, at the way I lived as Quakatz's girl at Red Bank Farm and ask myself how it all came about and how by making Heinrich and me acquainted, Providence managed to give me peace and to make a human being out of a wild animal, why then, I'll not let anyone deprive me of my belief in the God I learned about in the Bible and the hymnal; not even my husband there with his bones and fossils and his letters and publications from his learned societies. And if he has ceased altogether to believe in miracles and a higher power, he's got to agree to half a miracle, with all his superior knowledge. For a boy like him to have such a wonderful influence on a woman like me, to say nothing of my poor old father, that isn't just half a miracle, it's a whole one, it's a double one, a double one three times over. I suppose you read what he wrote over the front door: Go forth of the ark. That's all nonsense; because it has no bearing on us. I've read about it in Genesis; it just applies to Noah's Ark and old Noah and perhaps his family and his animals. It wasn't one of Heinrich's mottoes then. Perhaps you remember what his maxim of consolation was in those days, Edward?"

Unfortunately I couldn't remember and Tubby merely looked at me with an expectant grin and didn't help me out. When I was expected to help *him* out—at school—he had a different look on his face.

"Well, Edward." That was his only concession today.

" 'Lick the plate clean and you'll lick the world' is what he always used to say then," said Frau Valentina, in a tone of voice that left a doubt whether she quite approved of it now. But Schaumann, nicknamed Tubby, took over again and said with a sad but delicious sigh:

"As far as I am concerned, you can set it in gold letters on my tombstone. Of course I'll not stand in the way of anyone who thinks he can hit on something better."

"Heavens," sighed his wife, "in those days he usually added: 'There's no other way to get you through life, Tina.' "

"Don't you think yourself that all the other mottoes are a bit of a hoax, Edward? Or have you at this point some really new wisdom to contribute from that noble Zulu king, Uncle Cetschwayo? If you have, out with it: what did you inscribe on his hero's grave after that proud old Kaffir king had licked his plate and licked you Englishmen, Dutchmen, and Germans? But excuse me, sweetheart—Madame Tubby, I mean—we're supposed to be in the midst of your idyll, and not that of our dear visitor from Africa."

Frau Valentina threw a glance at me which could only mean: What can you do against the will of God and the tsar of all the Russias? You couldn't tell a story with him listening. She gave up and resumed her knitting and let him get back to his oratory and, as she put it, his better understanding of things. She probably hoped by this means to find out a little sooner who had killed Kienbaum and had had her father's misery on his conscience into the bargain. This may have been partly why she acted as if she were just quietly going on with her knitting.

"So I simply said to her, if the world had been more than usually cattish with her or, as sometimes happened, she tried to be cattish with the world and went at it spitting with claws spread wide—notice the alliteration, Edward, so easy and unforced—I said to her: 'Don't eat me, sweetheart, but lick your plate, girl, and you'll lick the world, and, by God, I'll help you to do it.' With this warmhearted advice I took her by the scruff of the neck and drew her—*peu à peu*—out of herself and gradually found that I had landed the whole of Red Bank, Papa Quakatz included. We licked our plates and we licked the world, poor creatures that we were. For the many things that I had to keep to myself down there in the town and in that school of yours I had all the outlet in the world up here. And this is where I developed the lyrical and epical qualities buried within my genial corpulence, as you used to call it down there. Of course, my sense of the dramatic I gladly left lying dormant there in what you termed my paunch. That calls for too many capers and stunts and flowers of speech, and, thank God, it is always permissible here and there, *ore rotundo*,[30] to tuck your serviette—to eschew the French for the fashionable Germanic, or, ought I to call it napkin now—under your chin and fold your hands over your sesquipedalia and twiddle your thumbs. Would I be sitting here with Tina, Tina Quakatz, today, if I'd gone after Red Bank Farm dramatically? Certainly not, my dear Edward. Here stood this bellicose fortification of Count von der Lausitz, this monumental exclamation mark reared up in the landscape to follow on the words: Children, love one another, and the only way to get it was lyrically and epically. And I saw to that, didn't I, Tina Quakatz? I can only say what I've said before, Edward. You all misunderstood me. To be frank, the treasures in my bosom were far too deeply hidden for you silly youngsters. What was needed to fish them out was a cunning little girl. As for you, Edward, all you did was run around with your friend Störzer, preparing yourself with the help of old Le Vaillant's tale of wild asses, giraffes, elephants, rhinoceroses, and nice Namaqua girls, and the story of Swanepöl, that bravest of brave Hottentots—for your Eldorado among the Kaffirs. In due time you presumably came across that worthy Boer, Klaas Baster, taking him to your heart grown sentimental about Africa; but the worthy Heinrich Schaumann you didn't find in those days; along with the others you called him Tubby and left him lying under the hedge. Excuse, then, the digression. Meanwhile, at the house Farmer Quakatz and his savage, tousled little kitten, *there* the magic harp resounded. The spirits of Red Bank took it up and drew from it tones that sounded like 'utter idiocy'—your friendly name for it—to you tame European asses, monkeys, and rhinoceroses, who were out of your cultural cages in the royal gymnasium zoo every afternoon at four. Oh, Edward, if today, now, after all this time, I could experience the joy of taking a theatrical interest in my own person! But there's nothing doing there, not even now that you've come back. I can't manage it, and so without moving an arm or a leg I go on sitting where I sat me down, at Red Bank Farm. Don't pull faces, Tina; I'm not getting off the point. You know, however foolishly I talk, I'll always stick with you. So don't worry. There isn't a child that clings as convulsively to its mother's skirts as I cling to your apron strings and especially—Edward dined with us today and will be able to back me up—to your kitchen apron. Yes, my dear Edward, there isn't a corner of the house, a patch in the garden, a bit of wall, a bench, a tree, or a bush, and, above all, not a creature at Red Bank that didn't gradually begin to shine a bit from the luster shed by Robinson Crusoe, Ferdinand Freiligrath,[31] the Brothers Grimm, Hans Christian Andersen, and old Musäus.[32] I was fat and lazy, but I was a poet of the first rank, no matter what you say, and that long before I sat down at the table of the Wise Man from Frankfurt.[33] All that meant nothing to me yet; I got it all under the hedge, from personal experience, with the warm sunshine of life on my belly. Each drew the other into his worlds, or rather world: Tina me, and me Tina. But the day when Papa Quakatz stood behind me and asked for the first time, 'How did that tale go, boy?' then I had my hold on him as well. Do you remember, Valentina? It was the story of the two invincible fat millers that caught his interest. Yes, what with the Kienbaum murder, the world had got him to the point where he would have liked to be like one of them, to arm himself like one of them. A doublet of lime and sand lined with molten pitch to bind it, covered back and front with old cheese graters and pot lids, three or four shirts underneath, and nine woolen coats on top of them; for attack and defense two spears, a crossbow, a two-headed sword as long as a man, and, for long-distance shots, a bow and a quiverful of arrows."

"Yes," sighed Valentina, "and finally a hut in the desert on the far side of the world. Yes, and if he hadn't died, he'd be living happily ever after, as the fairy tales say. My poor, poor, dear father. I'm sure he couldn't have borne it, to have you keep us waiting so long to find out who really killed Kienbaum, in whose place he had to suffer all his life long."

At this moment the poor woman was called away, and Tubby seized the opportunity to whisper to me, "I hope she'll leave us alone for five minutes. To be quite frank with you in confidence, I prefer to talk about her father when she's not there. She doesn't quite like it when I honestly touch on what I really think of him while she's within hearing."

Fine weather at sea! How could I have spun my yarn the way I have had it been otherwise. Halcyon days have escorted us over the ocean during the last week. Consequently a pleasant mood on board and a quiet time for "the queer gentleman in the saloon, who has been busy with his accounts uninterruptedly ever since Hamburg and probably won't be finished with them till Judgment Day."

But the passengers and crew have reason to be amazed and smile and shake their heads and put them together and whisper. There that curious man sits on the good ship *Hagebucher* and it is indeed most curious of him to try repeatedly, on the high sea of all places, to bail out the whole of life with a thimble.

But what would these ladies and gentlemen say, who have now and then gone so far as to give me a friendly pat on the shoulder and try to get a peek at the "queer stuff" I am writing, if they succeeded in the attempt?

Probably nothing more than, "Well, he could have done that more comfortably at home."

But they would be wrong. I won't be able to do it more comfortably at home, and that is just why I've written it down on the ship, in order to have it ready later if I ever got a quiet moment in the bustle of life.—

Bringing his chair a little nearer and glancing cautiously in the direction of the house, Schaumann said, "*Evasit*—she pattered off. Yes, Edward, there he was, a cringing, sour-faced, horrible fellow, in short not a nice person, with his heavy lower lip sucking his upper and with Malayan rolls of fat behind his ears. And if ever the world was entitled to say that murder was the least of the crimes it would think him capable of, then that was the case of my departed father-in-law, God rest his soul. At bottom he was a horrible fellow, that none of your worst, your nastiest Kaffirs could hold a candle to. A suspicious, grudging peasant of the lowest type, keeping watch over his goods and chattels. Whether or not he, old man Quakatz, killed Kienbaum, you'll learn later. But that I didn't kill him three or thirty times over was no small matter, I assure you. It required a nature, or perhaps I should say a temperament, like mine to get at the core of such an unsuccessful image of the Godhead. You know the old nursery rhyme, Edward:

> Oh, apples, almonds, and rice
> The monkey finds quite nice.

But you must remember that he likes nuts too and breaks them to get at the sweet kernel. Well, it was to get at the sweet kernel that I cracked Farmer Quakatz of Red Bank—with Red Bank. But not, I admit, without turning the hard nut from one side of my mouth to the other for quite a while and putting all the force of my jaws and molars into it. We'll leave aside meanwhile the question whether he deserved to be hanged over Kienbaum. But there are many other reasons why, if he didn't deserve to be hanged, he deserved to be thrashed. Especially on account of Tina. She always manages to leave the room when the matter comes up. You can't knock the filial piety out of these damned women, try as you may. And, incidentally, no matter how much it can annoy us sometimes, we very seldom ask ourselves or anyone else what such piety is good for. Good—what I mean is, Lord knows, the world was cruel to the girl at Red Bank Farm, but not as cruel as the farmer at Red Bank, her own father. Not by a long shot. School was rotten, and my parents weren't exactly of the most amiable variety, but they never intimidated me the way old Quakatz managed to intimidate that kid of his. He set himself against her, using whatever means he could find down in the bottommost drawer of his soul's cupboard. As far as I am concerned he might have killed Kienbaum a thousand times and denied it before his fellow men, right on until Judgment Day; he didn't need to work off his spleen on his own flesh and blood like that. Don't deny it, Edward, there have been times when you thought me not only lazy, but cowardly, but you were wrong, really. You poor jackrabbits, all your heroics amounting to nothing more than torn trousers now and then, a good thrashing, or a few hours detention. What if you'd had to conquer Red Bank Farm? That would have been something to set you wishing you had a new Plutarch. And then take schoolmaster Blechhammer. He would poke and poke around in my head with his pointer, searching for the owl of Minerva, only to convince himself all over again that there was an owl in there, but it wasn't hers. God give the worthy fellow all he ever promised him and set him down in the company of his best-winged angels. But was he, was that noisy old Ciceronian Cochin-China rooster capable of appreciating my purpose in life? Certainly not. I say this with all the emotion memory can supply. But I digress. This warm weather so agreeably opens all the pores of both mind and body. Now where was I in the main argument? Of course, I was still on the subject of Papa Quakatz. Lord in heaven, the places Tina and I found where we could hide from him! The nooks and crannies where we took refuge under the protection of Saint Xaverius, *comes Lusatiae,* from his unreason, after I had tried to talk reason to him and even occasionally succeeded! In the pigeon cote, the pigsty, the hayloft, the wardrobe, behind the bed, and under it. Where didn't he hunt for his daughter, cudgel or whip in hand? You young heroes used to enact your Fenimore Cooper Indian stories stupidly and unimaginatively enough out in the open fields in those days, but I protected Cora and concealed Alice in real life and in the flesh, not in a rocky cavern perhaps, but behind the kitchen cupboard, and it was with dread and rapture in my heart that I heard that raging old lunatic Mingo hunt for us and heard his snuffling breath and his war whoop. And when on such occasions Tina whispered, 'I've put the brandy bottle on the kitchen table,' I know now to value her that much more as a Miss Cora than as a Miss Alice. But I didn't know it then and thought I was more of a noble Leather Stocking, so wise in the ways of the forest, than I was. The main thing was, of course, that the old man found the bottle. As soon as we heard him say 'Ahhh' when he located it, we knew we were safe again, and the world and Red Bank Farm were ours again and no one else's. You will have noticed at dinner that out of regard for him his chair of sorrows still stands behind the stove, and if I sit in it now and consider the precocious way I regarded the case of Kienbaum versus Quakatz and would say, Sagamore fashion, to the poor wretch as he came out of his fire-water stupor: Herr Quakatz—oh, good heavens, here she comes again! You don't get a minute's peace from her. Well, Edward, I'll tell you the rest at sundown perhaps."

There she was again and when I looked at her once more, as she approached to join us, laying her hand on her husband's shoulder, I could have gladly done without the "rest." In any case I knew the part that mattered most.

But, without my noticing it, the lovely afternoon had steadily progressed, as is its wont, toward evening. Even our corpulent friend had begun to find it pleasantly cool under the linden tree, and he now indicated that he would like "to stretch his legs a little." He offered his wife his arm and by the light of the departing sun we went around the outermost edge of the old quadrangular rampart of war. Tubby, of course, kept his pipe with him. "You will see that I have trodden myself a path here, like another Prisoner of Chillon, but I have also provided some benches to sit on. Even the most modest soul wants a spot where he can look out upon the world, and if he has an eye to his comfort as well, I can't say I blame him. You will notice, Edward, that here too I have stayed 'under the hedge.' "

And so it was. Each of the four seats at the four corners of Red Bank Farm had shady shrubbery behind it, and it was easy to sit there and dream you were young again and lying happily under the hedge, as he put it. The path was well trodden, but well tended too. "Even in winter I am in the habit of having a look at my world and other people's," said Schaumann.—The view to north and south, east and west, had remained much as it was in our childhood. There far below us was the town, there off to the side the village of Maiholzen, there were the woods, there the open fields, and there the distant blue hills—all as before. Heinrich Schaumann's flora and fauna of all the ages, formations, and changes in the earth's history slept their peaceful sleep on and beneath her bosom, the slumbering giant sloth included. And over it all the late summer afternoon sunlight! Only now a new railway line or two crossed the plain. And the train that had just left the town on one of them, sliding into the distance with its long trail of white clouds of smoke, reminded me again how little hold or contact there was left for me in my native town and in the fields of home.

But instead of drawing my attention to the new means of transportation, all Heinrich Schaumann did, strangely enough, was to draw his wife a little more tenderly toward him and say, "Yes, old girl, it's nice here in winter too, isn't it? Quakatz's castle is a good place to live, and there's little urge to leave it. But, if you look at it right, this can be had everywhere, my dear Edward, and you've earned the right to be called a baron, too, and a South African one into the bargain. Only in every place you have to know how to lay the ghosts that have perpetual haunting rights there, and then you'll be all right. Though I admit a good wife helps too. You try settling down here with a bad one, Edward."

"A sensible husband is necessary too, even if he is half crazy," said Frau Valentina, sighing and smiling at the same time, and Schaumann said very emphatically:

"Of course he is."

And, of course, we had already sat down again—on one of the benches overlooking the town and the village of Maiholzen.

"But a half-sensible person, one who's not at all crazy, mind you, can quickly spoil the comfiest seat and the loveliest view anywhere," Heinrich went on. "Yes, yes, our dear departed father. Do you remember, Tina, how he once chased me round the ramparts, just like that incalculable, stupid, wrathful Achilles chased the only normal, decent character in the whole *Iliad*? And do you remember how differently it turned out from Troy and the *Iliad*? Because I tripped up the man who was unjustly pursuing me, and so he rolled head over heels into Prince Xaver of Saxony's trench, and you, Tina, were able to creep out of your hiding place in the cellar and help me to put the poor devil to bed and leave him there to come to his senses."

"Oh, Father, my poor father. It's true, but, Heinrich, we have never talked like this about him in front of others."

"I think I've already told you, sweetheart, that we aren't dealing today with others, but with one of us. This fellow here showed a certain sympathetic understanding when he was a boy, and was the last to go when the others left me lying under the hedge. And as a young man—well, Edward, you know, don't you, that you are now discretely sharing in the last stages of a development that you lost sight of years ago, when we were no longer innocent children but more or less guilt-laden youths, here or rather over there on the other side of the ditch?"

I nodded my head, not to the fat man, but to his wife, the way you nod when you can't express your most intimate sympathy in words.

Valentina said, "When my husband—or Heinrich, as he was then—was going off to the university and brought you, Edward, to the edge of the field on the last day to say good-bye, a lot of things had changed here by that time, and what was for the better was in large part his doing, as he has already told you in his crazy way. In that respect he has nothing to conceal from anyone about us, Red Bank, and my poor father."

"Yes, it is a charming piece of country in its summer garb, Edward," sighed Schaumann, sweeping the horizon with the tip of his pipe, as if showing me something quite new. "But it was beautiful too that winter's night when I came to Quakatz's castle like the prodigal son and solemnly knocked at the window shutters of the prodigal daughter, eh, Tina Quakatz, little Pussy?"

"Heinrich, Heinrich, it's because of your old friend that you're going into such details. So in deference to him I won't mention all your other tomfooleries, but will just say to him: if I live to be a thousand years old, I could never forget that night. Yes, Edward, it is as he says. And he is a much shrewder and more learned man than he lets on, he only acts the way he does with me because he knows that we've belonged to one another from the start and can't live without one another. But don't you believe all the silly things he says. He's far too cunning in any situation, in the worst or the best moments a person is confronted with. Yes, indeed, he came at the right moment then. Father had had his first stroke and I was twenty-one and mistress of Red Bank Farm. Merciful heaven! what a mistress. What a state the world and the farm were in. Of course Heinrich had to have his jokes. I looked up in his encyclopaedia to see why in the midst of my tears he called me Your Imperial Majesty. He meant the Empress Maria Theresa and he wasn't all that wrong."

"*Moriamur pro rege nostro Maria Theresa,*"[34] growled Schaumann. "She just wants to hear that bit of flattery again in your presence, Edward."

"The doctor had assured me that it wasn't serious this time and Father was soon out of bed again and going round with a cane and me to support him, but the doctor wasn't able to promise me that he would quite get his health of mind back. I had to think of everything for him and find the words for everything that he wanted to say. He was always wanting to talk and had so much to say to me and could never find the right words. He could never hit on anybody's name, no matter how well he knew the person. And then he invented new ones, and nasty ones too, for them all."

"Just listen to her, Edward," cried Schaumann.

"No, don't listen to her, Edward, but let me get this over as quickly as possible. Well now, on that particular afternoon the farmhand had stuck his fist in my face and the kitchen maid had thrown the soup spoon at my feet. I always had at least one of the dogs with me to protect myself if worst came to worst; but on that particular Sunday they had threatened to poison them all. If they had done this before Heinrich came, well, I'd have been completely lost and at their mercy."

There is no describing how calmly the woman related all this.

You had to see her, watch her. Tubby stuffed his pipe from a pig's bladder that he laboriously fished up with a groan out of the pocket of his dressing gown. Valentina went on with her story.

"It was Sunday and there was an all-night dance at Maiholzen; the men and the girls had deserted the place against my wishes and were down in the village at the dance. It had been a stormy winter's day, and it got worse toward evening, turning into a blizzard . . ."

> "Build a wall about us,
> The old dame sang,"

hummed Schaumann; but his wife cried:

"Oh, no, not that night she didn't. She just talked away at her father in his armchair; he had been more restless than ever and more and more confused with murder stories—his own and others—and jurisprudence and executioners. The name of Kienbaum was one he always remembered, and on this evening it was never out of his mouth. Sing, indeed, on an evening like that, Heinrich? With every gust of wind driving the snow against the windows and the house and the trenches of Red Bank: Kienbaum! Kienbaum! Kienbaum! Sing? Not even to keep fear away! But I would have gladly been dead, Edward. Then it came over me like a kind of deliverance, and I said to myself: Yes, what if a gang of them broke in and struck your poor helpless father and you, worthless creature, dead, and helped themselves to everything, and they would be welcome to it, to everything, everything, and set fire to the house over your heads and so made an end of all the misery and the loneliness, the disgrace and the shame, all at once. Sing? Yes, indeed, listen at the window and, between the blasts, watch to see whether it would happen that way, at last, like a gift of God, to see whether something of the sort was stirring outside. But nothing stirred except, as I told you, the wind and the shutters, and now and then a stable door that the man had left open and was banging to and fro. And, on top of that, all sorts of ghostly noises in the house, and an owl calling in the barn gable. Oh, and to sit there with your hands tense between your knees and listen to your father muttering about Kienbaum, rack and gallows, till all the dogs began barking together, as if the whole Seven Years' War was starting up again at Red Bank."

"Philosophy of History, Edward," said Heinrich gruffly. "Even old Fritz had no idea how close he was to the Peace of Hubertusburg, when the Empress Catherine cut his good friend Peter's throat and took her Russians away from him, right under his nose and against his *ordre de bataille*. But Red Bank Farm got its Peace of Hubertusburg,[35] Edward."

"You know, even my father, whom anything like that had ceased to bother, started up out of his chair and trembled and whimpered softly: 'They're coming now.' And I had everything worked out in my imagination for such a contingency—what will you do if it happens in the middle of the night?—so I reached for the hatchet that I always kept under the dresser and held it ready and said to myself as composedly as possible: 'If this is it, one of them at least will get it too.' But it turned out differently, thank God."

"Of course," growled Heinrich.

"The dogs, who had just been barking their heads off, suddenly went dead quiet and I thought of poison again without considering that it would have to be awfully fast-working. I had my ear to the shutter and the hatchet handy with its head resting on the window ledge; and then—Edward, what a start that gave me."

Yes, and me too, Edward, the guest of Red Bank Farm, as my friend Heinrich despite his corpulence began to sing with a fresh and surprisingly youthful voice:

> "What's that coming down the hillside,
>   The hillside, the hillside,
> What's that coming down the hillside,
>   Talley-ho, tan his hide,
> Coming down the hillside."

"Tubby?"

"Yes, Tubby, Edward," said Valentina, smiling. "Would you believe it, Edward, that on such a night the crazy fellow stood there large as life announcing his presence outside the window with that silly song? And, of course, with all the dogs at Red Bank

Farm whining and fawning round him? But after the first yelp everything fell silent as a tomb with amazement, just I did after the first line of his silly song, but it was some time before I had sufficiently recovered from my fright to open the house door to the idiot; I . . ."

"There again you hear how she refers to the lord and master that God sent over and before her, and has done ever since she knew me. Tina, take my advice, and don't bring any unnecessary shame on your sex here in Europe. Remember this chap Edward here is a married man from Africa; no doubt the women there are blacker on the outside than you; but inside . . . "

"Of course, they're much whiter. I know that, or if I don't know it I'm willing to admit it. But please, Heinrich, let me finish. So I opened the door for him, Edward, and in he came. Yes, Edward, and not a minute too soon, as Providence would have it, for right after him the hired man came home drunk and tried to kiss me and then strangle me. And the maid, wearing one of my Sunday kerchiefs, called my father an old murderer in front of me and told him since the public gallows hadn't got him he should go and hang himself from the doornail. They were both very merry and joking and neither of them had any notion who was standing behind the dresser and was hearing and seeing everything that went on. Yes, and he came out from behind the dresser just at the right moment: the head and the master of Red Bank Farm, my . . . "

". . . dear old Tubby, Tubby Schaumann—fair to behold in all his amplitude, and with all his humor and mettle, and the fists appropriate to the occasion as well."

"Yes, and the one who didn't get strangled that night was the farmer's daughter at Red Bank, nor did she have to untie the servant girl's shoelace, either."

"And the fellow who quite simply and cheerfully put down his foot, set things back in order, straightened the pillow for the old man in the armchair, put his arm round the waist of the girl holding the bloodiest of hatchets in her hand, and then gave her the kiss truly intended for her that night, so that the smack of it was louder than the howling of the storm outside, that fellow was me. If you're bored, Edward, just say so. The two of us at Red Bank can stop rattling on about our sillinesses any minute and let you tell us about yours. You needn't pay the slightest attention to my wife in expressing your feelings. I never do myself."

"That remark is beginning to wear thin, Schaumann."

"Very well," said Schaumann, and held the floor now all by himself for a longer spell. I just laid my hand lightly again on Valentina's, as if to say: "Wonderful."

"The story was very simple," said Schaumann, "it was simply this: Being on the outside and studying for a profession that didn't suit me at all. I got unnaturally thin. People would hardly believe me, but it is true, ridiculous as it sounds: even the jolliest side of university life was not for me. A German *alma mater,* you know, is a regular Amazon. She offers you the one breast and you suck or swill. She offers you the other and you are like the proverbial cow in lean pasture. If you want to know what our educated ruling classes are like, just take a peek at a courtroom or lecture platform, a pulpit, a provincial parliament, or, above all, the imperial one. Excuse me, Tina, I'll come back to you in a moment. But when you get talking about your student days with a dear old learned African, you open your heart, as they say. It was a great stroke of fortune for you, Tina, I must say, that, even when we were at school together in that wretched hole down there in the valley, his contribution to my education was not one that led me to the bench or the rostrum, the pulpit or Parliament, but to Red Bank Farm, precisely because he did what the others did, left me lying under the hedge, on account of my weak feet. I was too good-natured for him to have any adequate notion of what I could do with my fists. But it doesn't matter; one thing is sure: all that a man with moderate intellect, feeble feet, and an immoderate propensity to corpulence could do to better himself for Miss Quakatz and Prince Xaver and Red Bank Farm has been done. Isn't that right, Tina Schaumann, Tina Quakatz? It was for you, you poor bedraggled little sparrow, that as the world evolved, I was left lying under the hedge in the sun, or in the shade amid clouds of tobacco smoke in my lodgings. It was in order that I could appreciate you, you angel, at your full worth, that I was given boarding-house meals at the *Universitas literarum* for six semesters. Think what it means, Edward: boarding-house meals for Tubby! The old dame beside you there ascribes the fright she got on that stormy winter night to all sorts of things except the right thing, I mean the bony finger I knocked at her window shutter with. *You* let the man with the scythe knock at your window at midnight in Africa and see if you're not frightened by his fleshless knuckle. Wasn't it the study of my own skeleton in my eighth semester that brought me to my present hobby? Didn't my so-called breadwinning studies give me the most appallingly favorable opportunity to reconstruct the antediluvian giant sloth to the complete satisfaction of science? I could certainly have got my doctorate in the field; but—let's say no more about it, the mere thought of studying is too upsetting for me, even today. . . . When I landed home again, I was trailing a damnable smell of burnt boats, my own I mean. I knew for certain that I should never mount the rostrum or the pulpit or the bench. And what I knew of osteology did not suffice for the practice of medicine. My mother was dead. I had no friends. Even you, the best of my friends, were far away, traveling to and fro all the time, as ship's doctor, if I am not mistaken, between Hamburg and New York and New York and Hamburg. You ask me what my father had to say. Well, I'm naturally tempted to say what I think about it, but I'd rather let it pass. The savage resentment I feel is not unmixed with something resembling pangs of conscience. He was brutally rude and he was entitled to be. When he explained to me that since the world didn't know what to do with me I couldn't expect him to try again for the tenth time, there was nothing I could say. 'Go to your Farmer Quakatz, the villain' was a proposal he didn't exactly have to make, but it was good advice. Whether on that wretched evening when we took stock of our relations with one another he expected me to follow his advice there and then, I don't know, but I doubt it. Yet he didn't call me back, when I growled at him from the doorway: '*Moriturus te salutat.*'[36] The fine old fellow! By his dessicated lights as a petty civil servant, he certainly deserved to have a more ambitious, a less easygoing, a less tubby offspring; but could I help it, that I was his son and not he mine? . . . Thank God, we can smile at it now without pangs of conscience and remorse—oh, Tina, you old sybil. In spite of everything we managed to get on the best of terms again. There under the linden trees behind us my wife has often brought him his coffee of an afternoon. And he even got

interested in my and Tina's bones—the primeval ones, I mean.
You see, after he had retired, he used to like wandering around
Red Bank, more for its own sake than for the scenery, and more
than once I have known him to come back from one of his walks
bringing a calf's skull that had been ploughed up or a ham shank
and wanting to add it to my collection, convinced that he had
made a real find and thinking in this way to make it up to me for
sins of the past. On that particular night—or, rather, afternoon
and evening—we hadn't got that far in mutual kindness, as you
will understand. The old man had made his mind up that I couldn't
be a burden to him any longer and said so, like Father Jobs and
his Hieronymus in Kortum's poem. I'll spare you the many details,
Edward, of my last days and hours at home and my finally leaving
it for good. I suddenly found myself standing out in the street in
the gusts and the driving snow with a very uneasy conscience and
a genuine feeling of sympathy with the old man, and I had ample
grounds for putting a bitter question to the eternal darkness and
the immediate gloom: Who was entitled anyway to set you down
here like this, cretin in both body and spirit that you are, like
this? Fortunately there was a light in the window of the Golden
Arm, and since I couldn't stay standing in the street, I went over
and found the company I needed—no other would have done at
the moment—to help me answer the question I had just raised.
Fortunately it was early yet, so that even the dullest of the philistines had not yet gone to bed. There I found my comfort and took
it, when all the beauty, wisdom, and virtue in the world would
have been no use to me. Hurrah, nothing but good old friends,
who always wished each other the best between one pint and
the next, and wished me it too—on this evening in overflowing
measure. I had come at just the right moment for them. The conversation was flagging, the silence infectious, I was just what they
wanted. All I had to do was listen and they would give me the
answer to every great and burning question. There wasn't one of
them in the whole company who wouldn't have been pleased to
lend me a pencil if I had expressed the wish to write down the
words of wisdom they let fall rather than trust my memory. But
there was no need for that. I am grateful that the gods, who have
denied me so much, have allowed me the gift of knowing how to

take that sort of talk and chatter and to pull the requisite sort of face for it and, if necessary, to give the requisite replies. You fellows didn't nearly appreciate that gift of mine as it deserved, Edward, but I suppose you weren't mature enough. Well, I had money enough on that historic evening to pay for a few pints and in the course of drinking them I heard what I had to hear, thought things over, and came to the right decision. As soon as I stepped into the familiar old corner room the conversation naturally swung round to me. They were kind enough to be pleased to see me: the later the hour, the nicer the people. But it was clear that they knew pretty well how it stood with me at home as was patently clear in every word and every whisper. Although none of them, on his life, would have liked to be in my skin, they were damnably eager to know how I felt in that situation. With the good humor of the despairing, as you might say, I served them up with the plain truth, snatched the noble philistine spear from their hands and let them impale themselves on it—and all according to taproom rules. What better could I have done on that very cheerless evening than to parade my Teutonic sentiments before plunging into the abyss? I conceded that I had left the university for good; but I put the exact circumstances in the proper light. There was no question of compulsion or anything like that; but it had to be brought out, especially on so suitable an occasion and among such intimate and understanding friends, that I had perhaps all too good-naturedly yielded to a sincere request urged upon me in frequent long discussions. Edward, I showed humor that evening. Not Satanic, but the humor of a poor devil whom a disproportion between mind and body had made literally incapable of competing with those who can race through life and prosper. Yes, on that evening I showed them how you can be too far ahead of a desolate world in pursuit of your ideals and the disastrous consequences that can follow if you set too good an example. In my full confession I painted for them the picture of landlords standing in front of empty seats with full barrels behind them, of girls sitting in their bedrooms weeping their hearts out because all my fellow swatters had followed my swatting example too well. All the students in all the professional courses were sitting so close over their books that several times the fire brigade had had to be called out on account of the smoke that went up from their heads. There was nothing else for it: the doctors—the most distinguished physicians—had to intervene, the public health department too. The former went *in corpore,* the latter sent the chairman and two delegates, and they all asked one and the same thing of the vice-chancellor, namely, that I should leave the city as soon as possible. (Look, Edward, at Tina, she looks as cheerful at this point as the mouse peeping out of the oakum.) As if Mother Eruditio,[37] that veiled and Teutonic statue at Sais,[38] could shake a man who weighs as much as I do out of her sleeve as easily as she would a flea. They came to me too. They sent me a deputation, a delegation. Not exactly with the demand, but with the request, 'Go forth of the ark!' Who could have resisted so sincere an appeal, especially since a similar call had come from home? I went forth of their ark, and even at the station there were many who hung sobbing on my neck: 'Brother, at least leave us that part of your knowledge that you have no use for at home.' With one foot in the train, I told them that of course I would, and wasn't lying either. In that respect there was a great deal that I was happy to leave behind with them. I really got going in the Golden Arm, peering comically into the abyss, till suddenly I felt a slap in the face that made my cheek burn, a punch on the nose of my irony that I so richly deserved from both my poor, wretched progenitor and these worthy, these meritorious philistines, these good fellows and citizens.—Says one of them: 'The one thing that comes out of all you have said, Heinrich, is that you've done nothing all these years but study up on that Red Bank Farm of yours, on the departed Kienbaum and your friend Quakatz.' 'What?' I asked.—'Well, it's just as I say, and the others at the table will support me: in the shape you're in now, they might very well have some use for you up there at the moment. They've missed you there long enough.' Oh! how right he was, wasn't he, Valentina Quakatz? 'The voice of the people is the voice of God,' the great proverb says, and he seemed the embodiment of it, sitting there grinning and waiting for what I would say in reply. And I couldn't box his ears, could I, Valentina Quakatz? All I could do was move up closer in my friendliest way to this man who had spoken for thousands, break off my table conversation, and devote a quarter of an hour to him alone, that is to say, amiably put the questions I had to him and the thousands behind. After that I left; but neither before nor since have I felt so firm on my feet as on that evening when I stepped out of the overheated pub with its beer-and-tobacco-laden vapors and into the wintry gale, planting my feeble feet in the deep snow. If you would like to know exactly, Edward, what the right thing to do in this life is, just ask the nearest philistine. He'll tell you. Of course, I don't know how it is with you in Africa, but here in Germany they always talk later on then about intuition, guidance from above, the promptings of the heart, the voice of fate, Providence, and the like—against the wind I could hardly have managed. With the wind I could, and, strangely enough, all the better, the farther I put the streets and gardens behind me. The wind was sweeping toward Red Bank Farm, and from over the ridges it blew the snow off the path and pushed me from behind with a good-natured roar, as if it too wanted to say, 'Where else would you want to go tonight, but to old man Quakatz's, Heinrich?'—The good-natured demon had even filled Prince Xaver's trench and swept the walk clear; but then came a wall of white at the entrance gate and along the hedge through the garden right up to the shuttered window. Well, whether it was snow or rice pudding, the voice of fate, promptings of the heart, guidance from above, and—not to forget him—the man at the Golden Arm down below, it all helped. This is what I was born for, to stick it out till I got to the land of milk and honey and into Mistress Quakatz's soft and open arms."

"Oh, Heinrich," said Frau Valentina Schaumann, blushing.

"Velvet-paws, keep your claws in. We're just telling Edward from Africa about it and he'll not pass it on to his wife and his Kaffirs."

At this Valentina turned to me again and said, "You must have got to know about animals at first hand, so tell me, my friend from Africa, have you ever, I mean when you were young— younger—thought it possible that Heinrich could make eyes like a lion?"

"No," came my curt, abrupt reply. If there was ever a hero whom this rude negative would not offend, it was my friend Heinrich Schaumann.

And, sure enough, he just laughed heartily; but he lost no time in snatching the conversation from his wife, saying, "But I did once, Edward. I rolled my lion's eyes. Not Prince Xaver of Saxony when he came down from Red Bank to receive the capitulation of your wretched town could have rolled bigger. 'Eyes like saucers,' says a poet of those days, but he hadn't seen those with which I took possession of Red Bank Farm as I came up from town. Tina Quakatz, Old Man Quakatz, man, maid, and Kienbaum—the whole murderous bag of tricks. Saucers aren't half big enough. They say he banged the table, that worthy hero of the Seven Years' War, as he sat there opposite the town commandant; but I doubt whether he stuck his tingling fingers in his mouth afterward and sucked away at the pain his excess of zeal caused him the way I did, after I had put the unruly help of Red Bank Farm in their place. Afterwards, of course, I concentrated on this little girl here and triumphed again over all sorts of foolish resistance. Would you believe it, Edward, that she asked me, half-crying, half-laughing, "Heinrich, tell me, is it all right this way? Is it proper for me and for us, when the whole village and the whole town have their eyes and their spectacles on us?' At bottom this was just the appropriate variant on those bashful words, 'Speak to my mother about it.' And I did what the little goose wanted; I didn't rap the table, but rapped the good girl on the shoulder and said with a languishing sigh, 'I don't want to be called Tubby for nothing, young lady; there's your father sitting there, we can ask him about the rest; he surely knows now by experience just what's proper at Red Bank Farm and what isn't. But there was no question of asking him that night. That night you couldn't exchange a sensible word with old Quakatz. His nerves were too jangled by what had just happened. There he sat, struck all of a heap with fright, blubbering like an idiot, but stoutly maintaining as before: 'Murder, murder! But I didn't do it. I didn't, your Honor. I didn't.' Thank God he just managed to recognize me and understood that I wanted to sleep the night at his place, and he pulled his nightcap off and muttered, 'It's the clever fat boy from the town; it's Heinrich. If he has his Latin with him, he can stay. Give him a pear, Tina, and make a bed for him; but let him have the axe. He can knock anybody's head in with it that says I killed Kienbaum.' Tina saw that there was nothing she could do but let me have my way. And things went pretty well. I slept for the first time at Red Bank Farm and the next morning the sun was shining on the snow and—I'm getting poetic today—it looked like a wedding dress laid out the way they did in the days of crinolines. Of course the dear girl had made an extra good pot of coffee that morning and while we were drinking it I had the hired help lined up, and the farmer at Red Bank, in full command of his faculties, introduced me to his realm as *major domus* or, as he put it, the new manager. The courts that had concerned themselves so much with him earlier in his life seemed latterly to have lost all interest in him as Kienbaum's murderer. And that was a boon and blessing for all concerned. As you can judge by what you've seen today, Edward, if you'd be so kind. Emerentia, I believe they're calling you."

"Our poor dear father hadn't yet been put under trustees by the courts," said Frau Schaumann, half-crying. "Heinrich, you really don't need to start dragging characters and events from books in order to say what you have to say. Yes, Edward, so it was. Only they hadn't yet appointed anyone as guardian for my father till Heinrich came, urgent as it often was. But it wasn't so very urgent; because the next morning he understood quite well what was involved both for him and for me, and it was only now that I saw how providential it was that Heinrich and the wretched farmer at Red Bank had got acquainted."

"Even the blindest of the blind could have read those stars. First we pelted dirt at one another, and then fell into one another's arms. And as for the ability to run a farm, well, you know, Edward, from living on the land in Africa, how that's done. You had the knack of it deep down inside you, while I acquired it quickly enough under the hedge and up Tina's pear tree and in the pantry at Red Bank Farm. I had seen Tina loading manure and—such is love!—I took the fork out of her hand and groaningly tried the art myself. You can't do everything in this world with a knife and fork and you don't get a table napkin tied round your neck for every dish that is set on the table. And it isn't necessary. But I did want to send this pretty young miss, this little lady, the lady of Quakatz's castle, back to the kitchen, where she could work with clean hands. After all, cleanliness is next to godliness, Edward. You value it in your Hottentot woman and you take it for granted in your European fiancée. Oh, how grateful she was, my dear old pretty young miss—all clean and tidy as a cat—when I gave her the chance to dive under the water like the Marsh King's daughter and to come up again like Princess Schwanhilde. Tell me yourself, wasn't it so, my lambent elf, mistress of my life?"

"He's no right to tell it that way, not to anyone, not even to his best friend, but it's true, it's true," cried Valentina between laughter and tears. And I felt much as she did in the matter of laughter and tears. But I didn't get to the point of saying anything, because Tubby naturally said with a grin:

"The main thing for me in the whole business was the pleasure I got from how the neighborhood reacted, how the neighbors felt about it. It was only while the deep snow lasted—and it got very deep in the days following my arrival at Quakatz's castle—that I had Tina and her papa and the help all to myself. Never did a god withdraw into a denser cloud of whiteness from a gaping mankind. The world had to wait for the first thaw before it had me again. But after that I was regarded as the most remarkable incident since the Franco-Prussian war; and for weeks the historical event in the Hall of Mirrors at Versailles [39] was nothing to the historical fact: Tubby Schaumann has got the job of foreman at Red Bank Farm. Anyone who wants to can go out and see him treading the clods in the February thaw and hear him tongue-lashing Quakatz's help. And they came out and, arriving at the place, cast a first cautious look at this phenomenon, this portent, from a safe distance on the far side of Prince Xaver's trench. No one had peeped at Tina when she was loading or unloading manure, but they were on the watch for me and, if I ever had fun in this world, it was when I found that I not only liked the job, but was skilled at it, too."

"He tells it all so horridly, but it was just as he says," cried his wife, interrupting again. "He became the best farmhand we ever had, you would have thought he had never been anything else, you'd have thought there never had been a day when my father sent him home to get his Latin dictionary. It came naturally to him as if he had grown up with it, as agriculturist, granger, farmer at Red Bank. Oh, God, how I had to fight back my tears, how I cried with joy and sorrow. Naturally behind the kitchen window where he couldn't see. It was so unnatural, you see."

"Naturally it was unnatural; I mean, that Jacob should serve seven years for Rachel," grinned Tubby. "We made it a bit shorter than that. I took her and she took me much sooner; and now, to be quite brief, O friend of my youth, it was a shame you weren't at the wedding. There you would have appreciated me as I deserve. And if on that occasion you had shouted: 'Oh, what a glutton this Tubby is,' you would have said the right thing in the right place for the first time, both as regards the bride and the bridal feast. Just like the wedding of Comacho, except that I kept the girl for myself. You know, Edward, lying under the hedge, I read all manner of things. But you are learning now for perhaps the first time that there is only one description in world literature that makes me feel poetic myself—always has and always will: the wedding of Comacho. Oh, how hungry Señor Miguel must have felt when he described the preparations for that wonderful feast, so richly larded, glistening with fat on the roasts, and encrusted with sugar, to say nothing of his moderate Southern thirst, smacking of goatskins. I made my mind up when I was young and lying under the hedge that if I was going to make a girl happy it could only be with similar, or rather with the same kettles, frying pans, pots, and spits. Now I had reached that point and could invite the neighborhood to peek over the hedge at the festivities. This was what Tina wanted, but not I, and the bride gave in, saying, though not without a sigh, 'But there isn't one of them that deserves it.' 'That's why,' I said, 'a man is entitled to a joke on his wedding day, so let me enjoy mine. And then you'll see: the joke will be worthwhile and will bring results.' 'You mean, they'll forgive us the suffering they've caused us, and Red Bank Farm will be able to show its face again?'—I said nothing to this ridiculous question; it was excusable, but it showed a lack of experience. Well, as your Cetschwayo would have said, I washed my spears in the bowels of the hostile tribes round me. A free feed was announced for the day as far afield as the rumor of Kienbaum and Kienbaum's murderer had traveled, and I had them all, or nearly all, at Quakatz's farm on the most philanthropic day of my life. They all did us the honor, except for a few, whom I regarded as having trouble with their digestion: the fleshpots called and they came, the whole crowd, and I stood at the gate and received them, greeted them, and invited them to come in, my heart overflowing with the achievements of civilized man down through the centuries. I am convinced that I never looked so fat, so comfortable, so teutonically fat, as on that sunny summer's morning. I had locked up the dogs, but more of that later."

"I can't listen to this any longer," said Valentina. "I really can't, Edward. Oh, and your dear old father, Heinrich?"

"Yes, he came too, over Prince Xaverius's trench for the first time in his life, wearing the dress coat he had been married in, and on this festive day, for the first time in his life, not regretting that he had brought me into the world. Would I have taken you, you creature, if I hadn't known just how nicely, how like a daughter, a daughter-in-law, you would behave to the worthy old chap in his hemorrhoidal affliction? I must have told you, Edward, about how he later went in for paleontology, to please me? But the main attraction that day, Tina, was not my father, but yours."

"Oh, Lord, yes."

"You see, he was very comfortable with us. Even Dr. Oberwasser—you remember in our days you used to call him Longguts in contrast with me, and you may have met him again at the Brummersumm, he's just as fat as I am now—even Dr. Oberwasser came out and assured us that if we looked after him well and humored him in his crazy notions and took care not to cross him any more than was absolutely necessary, we might have the old sinner on our hands for a long time. Well, thank God, we kept him with us for quite a while, and on the day of the party he was a shining psychological example of how a man should live among his fellows. What did I care about our friend Oberwasser? I rubbed my hands in secret at my own psychiatric treatment of old Quakatz. Lord knows, he took it for granted that the whole company of notables that had merrily assembled at Red Bank Farm on my account was an honor, an expression of honor, done to him. And Friend Longguts really didn't need to advise me, or Tina either, that we should let him be with his courtesies and compliments and the agreeable feeling it all gave him. Sitting there in his seat of honor, he was like a regular *Roi des gueux*; [40] because I had also insisted on inviting those who had never given up on him. There was a highly mixed contingent of tramps from the highways and hedges that were not turned away from the trench and rampart of his electoral Saxon and His Royal Polish Highness. The flag with its *Salve hospes*[41] waved for everybody and the dogs were all either on the chain or in the closely fenced pen, relieved for the day, and from henceforth, of their watch at Red Bank. But if anyone really had a high time before food piled high in troughs and mountains of gnawed bones, it was they, the faithful old guard of old Red Bank Farm and of my young wife. As soon as people had drunk the health of the bridal pair I stole away from friends and acquaintances and went to see them in their enclosure behind the henhouse. They all smiled at me—that is to say, they all wagged their tails, except for the one that couldn't, because one of those Maiholzen rascals had chopped off that genial appendix near the root. But the good dog rubbed his nose against my leg with a tender whine and confessed: 'Well, you really know what is best for us at Red Bank Farm.' 'You're the first, are you, to nose that out, after Tina?' I asked, laying my hand on the old veteran's head. Edward, I think we were both right: the one with his remark, the other with his question."

"I'll say no more," said Frau Valentina Schaumann.

"And you're right again," sighed Heinrich, still wiping his brow with his handkerchief in spite of the evening coolness. "But if you have anything more to say, come out with it now and not when Edward has gone tonight or when he is farther on his way back to Africa. Well? Say it."

"No," said Valentina, putting her handkerchief to her eyes.

"Good. That will probably suit Edward best. What is this globetrotter and adventurer going to think of us during his impending journey over the ocean, if we go on much longer like this with our adventures and our way of telling about them?"

Nothing special has happened on board and it doesn't look as if it will. We called at St. Helena. But I was at Longwood once before and didn't take the trouble a second time of going up those awful steps to see the torn and faded wallpaper on which the eye that had seen the Pyramids, Austerlitz, Jena, Leipzig, and Waterloo counted the pattern in the last feverish days and nights of life. I went on deck where the captain had had a shark caught to amuse the children—of the first class, needless to say—but this time, thank

God, they hadn't found anything very horrible in its belly. Contrary to the laws of natural history, the creature hadn't devoured a man, there was no half-digested sailor's leg in it, nor a child's corpse still tied to a board. It just had eaten what natural history said was its proper food. I went back to the saloon and, while the waves ran their smooth course, I let Tubby go on with his tale.

Which is what he did; because the interruption in my log book at this point was not his fault. He reported as follows:

"The morning after the wedding nothing happened but what I had long foreseen. There I was at Red Bank Farm, if not on the chain, penned in at any rate. And my eating bowl ran over—that at least was the first article of faith for all the guests at my banquet on the previous fine day, as with the comfortable feeling of an easy digestion they gazed out upon my future good fortune. Yes, I had now got what I wanted. I was planted down in the midst of my ideal, I was alone with it at Red Bank. The next day I was standing with my rosy-cheeked girl on the ramparts that surrounded our youthful happiness, and as we gazed out on the town and village below and the fair landscape, I quite unnecessarily struck a bargain with her. 'Little girl,' I said, 'there's no question of our going on long journeys. It wasn't for that that I went to such trouble over you. We've more or less restored your papa to humanity. It wasn't exactly pretty to see the way the connection was restored, but what can you do? It must be our care that ties hold. So—let us continue looking after your father the way I've begun. If later at some time you want to see Berlin, Petersburg, Paris, London, and the rest, naturally I'll waddle along with or behind you. But there's no hurry about it. For the present we have quite other things, splendid things, before us.' We certainly had. It was fairly easy to take Red Bank compared with the task of keeping it going and keeping oneself going with it, especially with all the goods and chattels, wife and father-in-law. Tina, it's my best friend that I'm telling all this to and there's nothing he can't hear."

"Oh, but you long ago got me used to hearing you say most anything," sighed Frau Valentina Schaumann.

"Do you think so?" inquired her husband. "This evening I hope to give you proof of the opposite. If it's at all possible, I'll let you hear something tomorrow from someone else that I might be in a position to tell you tonight."

"Oh, God, not about Kienbaum?"

"I was absolutely the heaviest Latin-quoting farmer that the goddess of history ever laid on the agricultural scales, Edward. I worked the fields that gave me my bread, but I also looked into the pertinent documents and papers in my poor, foolish father-in-law's desk. I looked after the money that he had invested in promissory notes on other properties, not all of which were in the immediate neighborhood of Red Bank, but were indeed fruitful in other ways than the paleontological. The voice of the people pronounced me here the cunningest, and indeed most unscrupulous, man that had come out of their midst. You know, my friend, the people need something like that from time to time to restore their moral self-respect. Heaven, the deep money dealings they had with Andreas Quakatz, the man that murdered Kienbaum, in spite of their pretending to have nothing to do with him! The stocks good and bad, the mortgages, the loans, and whatever else goes on in the ups-and-downs of business life that people had slyly talked him into, just man to man, don't you know. The old man had insured Red Bank with three insurance agents because each had told him he was convinced he hadn't killed Kienbaum. There, I'm putting the thread in your hands by which you can feel your way as far as you like down into the dark labyrinth I had to illuminate. Don't ask me to give you all the details. To cut it short, the curse of Adam in respect of the land—the digging, hoeing, ploughing, the potato crop, the hay, the harvest—was a holiday beside the digging, ploughing, and clearing I did at the desk at night. I tell you, Edward, if I hadn't had Tina by me, with her knitting, her knowledge of the world, her suggestions, which often seemed a bit precocious in the evening but not infrequently proved to be mighty shrewd the next morning; Tina with her two callused peasant hands gently drawing my soft cultured ones down from my fevered temples, saying, 'Heinrich, do it to please me, and see if you don't find the missing remainder of Kleynkauer's debt entered against his son-in-law, who has the relay house down in the town, and against the meadow he bought at the back of his house.' Edward, you made a fortune among the Kaffirs: please, don't boast about the efforts it cost you. Look, now, at last the girl is beginning to cry, because she has to leave it to me to tell you in conclusion that we did succeed, she and I, in bringing her father a little of the sunshine he deserved here in the fortifications of the Comte de Lusace, where he sat in the corner by the stove with his wandering mind and swollen knees and numbed feet."

"Yes, yes, Edward," said the heiress of Red Bank Farm, Qua-katz's daughter, with a sob; but Heinrich Schaumann seemed to have less regard than ever for her feelings in this log book of life. He just pulled his eyebrows a little lower and said gruffly (for the first time in his narration you could sense something like a slight growl): "Yes, yes, yes, they had to say 'How do you do?' to me, so they started saying it to him. People are made that way, Edward, and the gray old sinner really enjoyed it; he took the greatest delight in lifting the tip of his cap again to return a friendly greeting to the foolish world. He died completely convinced that he had been reinstated *in integrum* among his fellow men. To what extent his honor was restored up there before the throne of thrones and the Judgment Seat, I'm sorry I can't tell you. And now, Tina, my brave girl, and you, Edward, the most distant friend of my youth—I mean, the most distant in the matter of domicile. I'm now going to do him the final justice he is entitled to. Who knows whether it wasn't solely for this that the great Judge set me down in this neighborhood in all my corpulence and composure? As far as imperturbability goes, he certainly found the right man. So, if you have no objection, I'll come a piece of the way with you later on, on your return journey to Africa."

"Heinrich," cried his wife, clapping her hands together.

"Frau Valentina Schaumann," said her husand, mimicking her note of total surprise.

"Edward," cried his wife, "he has never taken me to Rome, Naples, Berlin, and Paris and such places and I never strongly wanted to go, any more than he did. Not six times since we were married has he set his foot outside the property and the narrow range of his fossil hunting. He never goes into the town unless he's been summoned three times and finally been threatened with imprisonment. He takes my breath away saying a thing like that."

"Just like a woman," sighed Schaumann. "There was nothing

whatsoever to go to Paris, Berlin, and Rome for. But for once we have a piece of business in the town tonight. We, I say, Frau Valentina Schaumann, née Quakatz. Couldn't you trust me to know what is best for our snug life together, tonight as any other time?"

"Oh, Heinrich, I know you do," cried his wife, tremblingly taking him by the arm and looking into his face with anxiety. "But this is something quite out of the ordinary tonight. I know you've been talking all day long in your usual fashion, telling the best and the worst, the silliest things and the most tragic, like unraveling an old stocking. But now it's time you stopped and considered me: the more so if you think I'm just like any other woman. It's my father you're talking about, my dreadful agonies and sufferings when I was a child and growing up. And—Edward, he only pretends to be so foolish because he doesn't want to proclaim from the housetops how much he really did for us. Look me in the eyes, Heinrich, my dear, my husband, and take pity on me. You're going to clear my father finally and completely and that is why you want to go into the town with your friend and you don't want me there. But, man alive, it involves me and you must let me be there. You'll take me with you, won't you?"

"Take you with me," murmured the present undisputed lord of Red Bank Farm, not looking his wife in the eyes for all her touching appeal, but just looking up, doubtfully and thoughtfully. It was some little time before he spoke. "As you will, my girl. Unless the kitchen . . . unless you think . . . I suppose Edward will stay for supper?"

"Man," it was I who shouted, "monster, I've had enough of it. You simply must stop and not go on torturing your wife a moment longer. What do you want to say to her, or to both of us? Can't you tell us here, in your stronghold, where it's so quiet and with the evening light on us?"

"You would rather sup with dread and take your fill of horror outside tonight, Edward? Hm, hm."

And now he tenderly took his wife in his arms and kissed her and stroked her cheeks and smoothed her hair, affectionately, soothingly.

"Sweetheart, my joy, my comfort, it's just a silly stale old mess that I have to stir up again, because there's nothing else for it.

How I wish I could keep the last dismal, dreary odor of it away from our stronghold, as Edward has just so fittingly called it. I can't do that—but, I can tell you about it tonight, after midnight, say, when we both have our nightcaps on. I'll know better what to say when everything is quiet at Quakatz's castle—with 'the stars above, the graves below,' as old Goethe said."

"I'll stay at home and wait for you, Heinrich," the woman said. She was crying and greatly upset, and her fat husband had a way of expressing himself and involving others that no one else could have endured. But she was not only a good woman, she was a happy one too.

"You see, now, that was my opinion too, Tina. Now, this good friend of ours, Edward here, is leaving tomorrow, or the day after, or three weeks from now, by ship. On what's grandiloquently called the high seas. There's generally a fresh breeze there, and he'll see nothing but new faces on his journey, not, like us, the same ones all the time. I want to send the happy fellow off with a nice gust of wind that smells of home and, besides, in a sense he is entitled to it. He's far more deeply involved in all this than he suspects. Yes, go ahead and stare, my boy, with those big eyes you're making. So you really won't stay for supper? Well, just you talk to my wife for a minute while I make myself ready."

He stood up with a deep groan from the seat on Prince Xaverius's rampart and, clutching his cold pipe in his left hand, he took his wife by the chin with his right and said, "Yes, it's better you should stay up here in the sweet air of our farm, sweetheart. It's such a nice evening and so lovely and quiet, with only the late larks in the sky. The sea breeze and perhaps a bit of a shipwreck with an interesting rescue or whatever will take the nasty smell from down below there out of his nostrils. And then, unfortunately, I may never see him again in all my life, after he has gone away, I mean, and so I won't have to soothe and calm him nor help sweep the spooks haunting his fantasy. But with you, between you and me, it's another matter. I have you on my plate once and for all, come good weather and bad, toothache, bellyache, and all the other ills and trials. And I also have the duty to keep my end up amid all toil and trouble and hauntings. Why do you want to stick your old nose in this moldy stew of blood and corruption? See now, I'll put Edward on the road and then—it'll be past midnight—well, Edward, as I said, talk to my wife a bit. I'll be with you in a second."

He tottered ponderously in the direction of the house and from the bench his wife and I watched him over our shoulders, saw him stop once on the way to stroke his tomcat and then disappear through the door with the inscription: Go forth of the ark. Not till then did his wife reach for her handkerchief and exclaim:

"What is there to say to him? Here I sit in the peaceful and friendly evening sunlight, as he calls it. Oh, yes, and you, my friend, can't possibly tell from my behavior just how terribly today's news has upset me. Anyone else who has been through as much as you have would certainly think: this is really too much! And he would be right. But that's the way he is—Heinrich, I mean. He finds out the most important, the most dreadful and disturbing thing there is, and never lets his pipe go out. Never says a word till it suits him. And I, my poor father's daughter, I had such an unfortunate and unsettled life as a child, throwing stones at everyone and scratching their faces, that I'm willing to resign myself to most everything at this stage of my life. I recognize that he knows better, and I never ask any questions, just keep my peace, though it isn't my nature, I wish it were. I'm well aware that we live here at the farm, thank God, so peacefully that there is time for everything. No matter what it is, we can wait till the time comes for having it out, whether noon or night, the worst or the best. And, thank God, I know every fiber in his being and I know that he has no secrets from me. For if he had, we couldn't live the way we do. But there's a limit, a daughter is a daughter and a wife a wife and a woman a woman: he knows who killed Kienbaum. It is possible he could bring him to the scaffold today. He is married to the daughter of the farmer at Red Bank. And he takes it all like sticking your head out of the window and saying, 'It's been pretty close all day, maybe we'll have a bit of thunder.' . . . I ask you, sir, what do you say to it?"

"What I say is that you are the happiest couple that ever found one another and worked out a life together. And I say too that Tub—my good friend Heinrich was perfectly right to go on lying under the hedge and just grin at us young fools and let us go our ways, not having any choice in the matter, or so we thought then."

"Oh, Edward, don't be afraid to call my husband Tubby in front of me. He fully deserves the name," Frau Valentina said, smiling through her tears and excitement. "That is to say," she continued, delicately anticipating any misunderstanding, "you can't maintain that he is greedy or hasty about stuffing himself with life and its good things. Oh, no, he takes his time at meals, and he does the same in all other matters. We're getting a signal example of it at this very moment. But that's the way he is, and I am quite sure that God made him like that for my good, and in more than just a general sense. And in my dearest and most private moments I hope likewise that Providence made me the way I am for his benefit and that he would be lost and wretched in the world if he hadn't found me in it. But without hesitation, I believe anyone who tells me that to the outer world we two at Red Bank Farm must seem an odd, a very odd team, because I often say so to myself. . . . But heavens, has he managed to dress himself, without calling on me thirty times, even if it is only to go out fossil hunting? O God, what more ancient, what grimmer gravedigging expedition is he going on now?"

There he was again. Half parson, half tiller of the soil; but Schaumann the Fat from top to toe.—He now wore a long black coat, a summer waistcoat unbuttoned, a loose tie, and a broad-brimmed hat of brown straw, and he had kept on the same light summer trousers. He had a stout walking stick in his hand and certainly needed it. But for the moment he tucked it under his arm and put the other arm round his wife.

"Kiss me, Andromache, and watch me depart from the walls of Ilium; but for heaven's sake don't worry about me. I should like to see the bright-greaved Achaian from down there who could get Tubby Schaumann to trot or gallop round his castle walls, to honor or avenge the shade of Patroclus. There's another kiss and now let me go. I give you my word for it, I'll come back safe and sound and with having worked up as little sweat as possible, and what I shall bring you may not be pretty, but it will be comforting. Edward will be present when I exorcise the blood, procure satisfaction for the shades of Kienbaum, and, for my part, induce the Furies at last to close the door nicely behind them and leave Red Bank Farm in peace."

I now had to say good-bye to Valentina and, of course, I had to promise that this first visit shouldn't be the last. My friend strode ahead of me across his overgrown embankment without looking around. But I looked around several times and saw Farmer Quakatz's daughter standing on top of Prince Xaver of Saxony's rampart. I felt deeply, but not painfully, moved, and said with all my heart, "A good woman. She certainly deserves a soft pillow. Heinrich, I hope you may live long together under your green trees or by your winter stove, letting the world go by."

"Amen, and then be laid in a grave and play ghost for a generation and torment the respectable neighborhood," said Schaumann.

Soon we began to meet people who first stared at us in amazement and, when we were past, stopped and stared after us and, I am sure, murmured, "Well, . . . I never, . . . that fat fellow Schaumann . . . here."

The surprise we caused increased as we got nearer to town and ran into groups of people or individuals out for an evening walk.

A few times we were stopped and the question whatever could have brought him to town was put to him personally.

"Courtesy, courtesy. My friend Edward is going back home to the Cape of Good Hope and I am just setting him on the way. He had lunch with me today."

More than once I heard someone say, "Would you believe it?"

The day had been fine, but the evening was wonderful. Nature was at peace with herself, and the town lay there tranquil and tidy. It had always been a community that set store by cleanliness and order, green trees on the market-places, and, in the wider streets, playing fountains, and the rest. Even history, that is to say, in this case Prince Xaver of Saxony with his bombardment and then later on several big fires, had contributed to a pleasant and well-preserved town by getting rid of a lot of old lumber. All in all, it was a place you liked to come back to in the evening if you had been out in the country, a place where you could open the window any time and not have to shut it again at once and groan and say, "Pfui, what a stink."

"Delicious, isn't it?" said Tubby, as we came to the trim gardens encircling the town. "It must have felt very nice for you to set foot here again recently. Even the most spoiled of Kaffirs would

have good things to say of our mayor and magistrates and officials, wouldn't he?"

"He certainly would."

"And the nurses with the sweet little children on the benches—
all these fine folk out for an evening stroll. Everything so cosy, so
contented, so—innocent. And now put yourself in my place, walking along beside you, with the authority and even the bounden
duty to see to it tonight that this idyll gets into the next volume
of Pitaval.⁴² Oh, yes, at this point I'm just the fat Schaumann
strolling beside you here through the peaceful town, but when they
look across and up at Red Bank tomorrow, they will picture me
expanding this great belly of mine as if it were swollen with poison, as if I were pregnant with secrets and the demand that sins
be atoned for. Edward, you have no notion really how unpleasant
I find this Kienbaum business and how dreadfully against my nature it goes that the winding-up of it is thrust on me. Me of all
people. Especially when I consider the mob I shall lift to transports of heavenly delight in the name of eternal justice. Picture the
nights I shall spend imagining these people all standing there before me, while I ask myself in each case: 'What? To entertain him?
To please him? To satisfy him?'—God knows, if I hadn't a certain
obligation in this matter to the little girl—my wife, I mean, Edward. She was born a Quakatz and a Quakatz she remains. This
is what always happens in Europe, my dear Edward, when you
marry into disreputable families."

How the citizens of this idyllic town would regard my friend's
physical proportions tomorrow, I didn't know. But for me, even
today, he was growing larger moment by moment. Like that admirable little wife of his I had completely succumbed to him without a word being said one way or the other. I had to let him talk.
I did let him talk, and every time he stopped I waited tensely for
him to begin again, to let himself go and talk on.—

Pleasant as our home town was, we avoided it to begin with.
Tubby took me round the "walls." He didn't say why and I didn't
ask. I had come to the conclusion it was best quietly to let him
have his way with me.

These walls, that Prince Xaverius had once bombarded from
Red Bank Farm, had now been converted into delightful walks.

There were still parts of the old moat left, which had been divided up into charming ponds, fringed with poplars, weeping willows, and garden shrubs. Both main and side streets ran from the middle of the town to these promenades, and one of the side streets also directly behind a row of trees and ornamental shrubbery led to the "poor" quarter, St. Matthew's. In my day people called it the "Last Gasp," and they probably did still.

As we approached the neighborhood, it came over me how well known I used to be there long ago, what good friends I had had there, and how much had happened between my childhood days and now.

"Good God, and Störzer too," I suddenly remembered. "Him too. And you did intend to pay him a visit, didn't you?" What I had failed to do after hearing the news at the Brummersumm I could make good now, and pay my faithful old friend a visit. In the course of his life and duties he had been five times around the globe without leaving home; now that his travels had taken him so very far away, I could at least look in on him and perhaps lay my hand on his weary feet at the lower end of the coffin.

I took my guide's arm.

"Heinrich, I just remembered. It's hardly a hundred yards away. His house . . ."

"Whose house?"

"Yes, you're right. We never get over the egotistical habit of thinking of everything in connection with ourselves. I just remembered that my old friend who has just died, my old friend of the highway, Fritz Störzer, is lying there behind that shrubbery. If it isn't taking you too far out of your way, let us drop in there for a moment. I'd like to pay the old wanderer a visit, now that he has gone to his rest. I don't know yet what you still have to tell me, but, however grim the solution to your riddles, I don't think I can do better than help myself to a little peace and sympathy over yonder."

"If you think so. Why, there's his chimney behind the treetops. Good old Störzer. Well, there'll always be time afterward for what you call my riddles, and it isn't a long way round to the old fellow's place. I am at your service."

So we didn't stay on the wall, but, just as we were leaving it, we ran into a couple who were going around it for an evening walk with their daughters and who knew Schaumann and confronted us with the astonished question: "Lord, what brings you here?"

"It just happened, that's all," said Schaumann amiably. "I don't really know myself how I come to have the pleasure."

It was a blessing that our detour was taking us into the least respectable part of the town: otherwise his friends would have liked to go with us part of the way, they were so interested to see him.

There are so many youngsters in that part of the town, which was by no means as cheerless and forbidding as in larger cities; and, of course, they were all out in the streets and alleys. It quite upset me, when I thought how long ago it was, and yet how recently that I too had dammed up the gutters and blocked the sidewalk, while Störzer looked on. And the mothers still standing in the house doors with their babies on their arms. And it still smelled of pancakes and goat stalls, and they still washed their lettuce. The symbolical companion of the evangelist Matthew is actually a handsome angel; but in St. Matthew's that was not the case. Here it was the pig, the common man's mascot, and here and there you could hear one grunting in its sty. And you could smell it too, but—no one need talk to me in St. Matthew's about eau-de-cologne and such, especially at a time when scarlet runner is in bloom—red, the most beautiful red there is, a miracle of beauty and utility, when it hangs over the fence between the houses of the poor or climbs up behind on its pole. But of course for all these wonders you must be able to smell, to feel, to see them. And whoever can't do that, should go and become an amateur photographer. But he needn't get photographed himself. I have the likes of him in my album in South Africa, and Tubby Schaumann has him in his, too, behind the ramparts at Quakatz's castle.

I have already noted how quiet the evening was out in the country, but not even the most peaceful of landscapes gives anything like the impression of repose to be found in a little street in the evening when work is over in "the poor quarter," as we call it now, or "along the wall," meaning the town wall, as they put it in the Middle Ages. And I once had been a part of it, behind my parents' backs and under the patronage of my friend, Fritz Störzer, and my heart leaped and sank at the thought of how far that lay in the past, of what a hero I was, with what a knapsack full of experiences and achievements, returning here again.

We went around the corner and turned into the little cul-de-sac where stood the house that I knew so well; and today I found something that I had often seen as a child that tickled every nerve of my being with an awesome, but by no means unpleasant, sensation: a house door standing open and a coffin in the hallway.

Everything as it used to be. Only everything shrunk a little: the little square smaller, the houses lower, the windows more cramped, the doors narrower.

And they were all crowding around a house door, the children and the women with babies in their arms, the old women and two or three old men, these latter with pipes in their mouths. There, once again, was a coffin standing in a hallway.

They all had their backs to us, and, although surprised, they made room for us when we tried to look in at the door over their shoulders. But they were still more surprised when we went in the door.

There didn't seem to be anyone at home except old Störzer, and he was asleep, lying quietly in the dark narrow box that stood there on three chairs, with the candles that were to be lit in the morning for the funeral standing beside it on a fourth. It goes without saying that my dear friend, the faithful and weary wanderer, had his flowers and wreaths around him. It cost nothing at that time of year in St. Matthew's, and the neighbors liked to show their sympathy.

There was another chair in the hallway, and there the cat sat, looking gravely at the faces old and young that peeped in at the door.

"Poof," sighed Tubby Schaumann, "I've overestimated my energies. It's hot and sultry." He removed his straw hat from his perspiring brow and mopped his head with his handkerchief. "Excuse me, Edward," he said, lifted the chair by the back, let the cat slip to the floor, and sat down himself. "One moment, Edward, and I'll be completely at your service again."

This or something like it is what he said, while I stood there with nothing to say for the moment, being very much preoccupied with the more or less obscure feelings that gain the upper hand on such occasions.

"Fritz Störzer. Old Störzer" . . . and I did what I had decided to do a little while before: I laid my hand on the coffin over where the feet lay which, as the company at the Brummersumm had calculated, had been five times around the world. Tubby was still fanning himself with his handkerchief.

But you have to say something on such occasions.

"You couldn't help it, Heinrich, you just stayed lying under your hedge," I said. "But I went with him, on the road, and studied his favorite, the excellent Le Vaillant, with him. And if any man can be said to have pushed me off his tracks into my own and despatched me to Africa, it was this fellow here, my good old friend, my oldest friend, Friedrich Störzer. May he rest in peace!"

"Amen," said my friend, Heinrich Schaumann, standing up again. "Yes, I can wish him that—from under my hedge. He wasn't one of the worst. A bit of an idiot, he was, but a good, decent fellow. So—for my part, sleep softly, you gray-haired sinner, you old globe-trotter and creeper by the ways. But now at last let me out of the whole affair, while the three of you settle it over there among yourselves: Kienbaum, Störzer, and Quakatz."

He had clenched his fist; but he laid it as gently on the end of the coffin where the head was as my hand had lain on the feet.

"What?" I said, with a start, and Schaumann said:

"Yes."

The captain says he has never had a man like me (he used the English word and said "gentleman") on board, as long as he has been at sea. He had come down specially on my account to fetch me up and show me the mountains of Angra Pequena on our lee, and I answered, "I'll be there in a moment," and then forgot to go, never even telling the decent old fellow that I had seen those mountains before—I was about to grasp his hand, not the captain's, but Tubby's, when he, Heinrich, gave me a warning nod and pointed to one side with a jerk of his thumb. Then I saw that we were not the only people standing beside the coffin.

A woman had come out of the room, a child in her arms and

another hanging at her apron, and stood there in embarrassed surprise. You could see she had been crying. She said, "I wish you good evening. It's very kind of you. Yes, there Father lies. He was such a help to us. I know you well enough, through your wife, Mr. Schaumann; but this other gentleman, who has come to see us in our trouble—I'm sure we're greatly honored—did he know grandfather too?"

"Of course, Frau Störzer. I realize that it wasn't till later that you married into the family. This gentleman once knew your father-in-law well, though not as well as I did. I suppose that's your boy you have there—the grandson. And the little granddaughter clinging to your skirts."

"Yes, it is, sir. We three are all that's left and we don't know what's going to come of us, left alone like this, now that Grandfather's gone. Who would have thought it could happen so quickly? He was so active. He could easily have gone on working for many a year. People here in St. Matthew's were always astonished at him, and it was a matter of pride to him too, that he was as good on his legs as the youngest of them."

"Well, not everyone can say that at his age, and that's comfort for you; and the rest will work out somehow. A vigorous young woman like you—with just one child in arms and one running about. You'll get along and at a pinch others will help. Was his death hard or easy, Frau Störzer?"

"Not too bad, thank God . . . He didn't suffer a lot, the doctor said. And he deserved not to, because he can't have had much on his conscience. But it is almost like God's hand, Herr Schaumann, that brings you of all people to his last resting place; so kind of you to come. You see, Mr. Schaumann, he was with you or at your farm a great deal in his last days and hours. He kept wanting to go out to Red Bank Farm, said he had something important to do there. He was always talking about it and about a message he had for you or rather for your father-in-law, the late Herr Quakatz, who people said . . . well, you know, sir, and won't take it amiss. It was no use talking to him, he stuck to it that he had to go out to Red Bank; he said he had something to deliver and get a receipt for. But that was the extent of any fancies he had that upset him, and in the end he just dropped off without anyone noticing."

Heinrich shrugged his shoulders, looked at me and looked at the faces of the old men, women, and children who were standing in the doorway gaping at the coffin. He pointed to them and asked, "Well, what do you think, Edward? It won't disturb his sleep if I do it: shall I call the world in to his bedside from the street? Shall I proclaim the secret here myself *ore rotundo*? Or is there a more suitable medium of communication? Or would you yourself like . . ."

I didn't need to answer, even if I had been able. The man from Red Bank Farm took my arm, said a few words of comfort to the daughter-in-law of the departed, bearing on the kitchen garden and the butter and egg trade of Quakatz's castle, patted the grandchildren on the head, and so we stepped out again into the world outside, strode through the gaping crowd, and managed not to send the evening sky tumbling down onto St. Matthew's.

As for myself, it was only in the next street that I awoke from the shock of seeing half a world collapse and asked, "What next? Where shall we go now? Would you like to come with me to my hotel, Heinrich?"

"To your hotel. Hm. A private room again. Hm. Hm. You know, Edward, it's so long since I was out of the ark, it's years since I sat in a real regular pub; I suppose I was too snug with my old girl at home, under the trees, by the stove, behind our ramparts, in short, in the ark. But now I feel a desire to prop my elbows, you know, on one of those tables by the roadside and see life passing through the taproom and on the highway. Come, old fellow, let's sit in the Golden Arm again before you say good-bye and go off on your journey."

I saw everything through a veil: the streets, the people moving with us or coming toward us. Voices, the noise of carriages I heard as in a dream, and suddenly found myself sitting at a table by the window in the Golden Arm, with Tubby Schaumann sitting down beside me. Huffing and puffing and then taking a deep breath he said with a sigh, "There!" and after a while, "Well, well, well, well, who killed Cock Robin?"

At this time of day in a respectable town like ours there was no one yet in the barroom of the Golden Arm except the waitress, the flies, the lindenwood tables polished for the evening, the chairs and benches, yesterday's out-of-town papers, and the day's *Evening News* from the local press. We were so early that the waitress looked up in surprise as we came into the room. But here too it was evident that they knew fat Herr Schaumann from Red Bank Farm very well, even if he didn't often set foot outside his ramparts into the great world.

So the young woman naturally addressed Heinrich by his name, and when she asked us what we would like to drink she also politely asked him how he was.

"Girl, bring us a cool drink first and then we'll have the warm words of affection. But, my sweet, you always used to tap a new barrel for Tubby Schaumann."

"And we just have. Just as if we had known you were coming."

The beer was good. Tubby raised his mug, eyed it like a connoisseur, carefully set it down, gave it back to the girl to fill again, and actually pinched her cheek, as if he spent every night there. And he called her "pet." So the brew must have pleased him.

He exchanged a few jokes with the girl, and then suddenly turned to me again. "And now to business, my dear Edward."

The girl took the hint, went back to the stocking she was knitting in her dark corner behind the bar and only peeped round the corner of the cupboard now and then to see if we wanted anything. We two at the open window, with our elbows on the table in the traditional way, our beer mugs in front of us. And now we had Quakatz's castle, St. Matthew's quarter, the German nation, and the world as a whole here on the spot and all to ourselves for quite a while.

"Doing it this way is really quite enjoyable, and in any case much better than I've often pictured it out when my imagination was running away with me to no purpose," growled my friend. "You may not believe me, Edward, but it is as I say: I've often cudgeled my brains to decide where and when and to whom I could most easily and freely talk . . . well, talk about Cock Robin. Things generally go better, no matter what it is, than you imagine they will when you are worrying about them. The time pleases me immensely, the place is just right, and the girl there behind the bar can only have been put there by the Supreme Being."

"Heinrich?"

"Edward? Now I ask you urgently, Edward, to regard yourself from now on as mere chorus in the tragedy. Off you go tomorrow to your Kaffir land and when you get there sing as many strophes and antistrophes as you wish as an accompaniment to the tale. I don't mind. I'll just say to myself, I've given the good chap a nice souvenir of his dear old home to take with him on the ship."

The only reply I could make was a feeble wave of the hand; Schaumann glanced out into the street again and then behind the bar and said, "Of all the people on earth that have prowled, snooped, and puzzled about this horrid and alarming affair I am by rights the last that ought to be saddled with the pleasure of publicizing it in front of a painted screen to the accompaniment of a barrel organ. Don't you think so, Edward?"

"No, I don't. You are the man of Red Bank Farm, its conqueror, the protector and comforter of poor Valentina, the . . . successor-at-law, I think that is the word, of Farmer Quakatz."

"Nonsense. I'm referring, man, to the criteria of character and physical constitution. By either of these I ought to have nothing to do with it. What had Tubby Schaumann to do with Kienbaum's death and the man who killed him, whether before he was at Red Bank or after? I mean, in respect of the legal solution of the problem? Nothing. Nothing at all. Well, Fate has determined it this way and I can't do anything about it, except to choose and control the formalities myself. If the highest court or whatever government is in charge of this world doesn't find them dramatically effective enough, it's not my fault. If Meta, behind the bar there, doesn't quite understand me yet, a certain poet of Stratford would and he would decide on the spot to dramatize me someday."

"Did you call, Herr Schaumann?" The words came from behind the bar and around the cupboard with the glasses in it. "Is there something you want?"

"No, sweetheart. Not yet, but soon. But stay around: we shall need you again for certain, and I simply can't finish the job without you."

"I'll be right here and my hearing's good."

"Good. You're a good girl. Well, Edward, as we sat there today beneath the trees behind Prince Xaver's rampart, my wife and I told you something about the old gentleman's—old Andy's—last three years, and you will have gathered that we must have done what we could to make him as comfortable as possible. And we succeeded as well as could be expected. This was a task for which Eternal Justice found me more of use, both in view of my physical and mental constitution, and because it suited my taste. I had no objection. It was just as easy to push a pillow under somebody else's head as under my own, especially if it was my wife's father, *vulgo,* my father-in-law. Of course I soon lessened the burden farming brought with it as much as I could. God in his goodness had so arranged things that the best sugar beets in the whole neighborhood grew on our property. So I leased the bulk of the arable land on very good terms to the nearest sugar factory and ploughed only as much of what was left of Tina's estate as would give my farmer's girl the comfort she was used to. You, as an African colonist, Edward, will have noticed that it doesn't look too bad, whether at Red Bank Farm or round about it. I make no concealment of the fact that the farmer Andreas Quakatz was a man of means apart from his property; he had money, no matter where it came from, whether from killing Kienbaum or not."

A woman's head jutted out from around the corner.

"All right, sweetheart, come and fill up. Another for this gentleman too," said Tubby. "Only, Edward, he didn't know what to do with Mammon, Andreas didn't, unless to put it in the pockets of his lawyers. My reaction was to put up a sign with a firebrand on it and the inscription: 'Let the dead bury their dead. In other matters of business apply to Heinrich Schaumann, esquire, interviews by arrangement.' I omitted any reference to the nickname Tubby, because that was something everyone understood for miles around, when it came to me and especially to my present role at Red Bank Farm. Let us stick to the real owner. They had thrown bones enough in his path: I won him over to paleontology. I took him out on my expeditions, took him to my stone quarries and my gravel and marl pits, walking with a stick, or on crutches, or in his wheelchair, and I quite convinced his poor confused brain that this bone-hunting was very closely connected with sugar-refining and so with the ups and downs of our factory shares. If I impressed him as a boy with my Latin, I impressed him now with paleozoology and paleobotany. Tina, who, as a woman, couldn't help finding my hobby ridiculous, respected it from this point of view and wept heartfelt tears, tears of gratitude, for it. When we had discovered our primal sloth and her daddy, chuckling like a child or comfortably grunting, sat there in his armchair rubbing his hands with satisfaction, she said it was lovely, grand, and she cleared out the best closet she had to house the monster suitably. Why should I go on telling you about this, Edward? We helped the old man over his last years as best we could and let him hear as little as possible about Kienbaum, as the doctor advised us. If I may pat myself modestly on the back, I can say that I am proud, rightfully proud, to have put an end to this wearisome ghost story, that I took this specter by its scrawny throat and choked it, that I put my knees on its moldy chest and squashed it, that it was Tubby Schaumann who reduced this skeleton to dust. The other skeleton, our friend with the scythe, I was unable to keep away from Red Bank Farm.

He gobbled up Farmer Quakatz, as he had gobbled up Prince Xaver of Saxony, to say nothing of Kienbaum. And, as far as I am concerned, if I had been able to keep him out, who knows if I would have done it? After all, it was a release, when we laid the last heavy blanket of good loam on the old gentleman. He had probably never pulled a lighter one over his head in all his life, and he is certainly sleeping well beneath it, after all the uneasy dreams bestowed upon him by so-called broad light of day during his term of existence on humanity's tax role. We buried him in Maiholzen on a glorious summer morning, quite early. The village was naturally out at the grave to a man, but there were people from the town there too. For example, there was court bailiff Kahlert, who had turned up on official business at the crack of dawn; there was tailor Busch's boy, who had brought the pastor the new pair of trousers in which, as I will explain in a moment, our spiritual shepherd made my speech. Fräulein Eyweiss was there; she had come out to our village to recuperate and had laid her bottle of Karlsbad mineral water on a nearby gravestone, the better to indulge the pleasant waves of sympathy sweeping over her on this common but always interesting occasion. The country postman, Störzer, who was out there delivering letters, was at the grave too. I saw him. Meta, are you still there? Thou cruel and beautiful one, are you really going to let fat Herr Schaumann of Red Bank Farm die of thirst?"

"Goodness me! Coming, sir! The way you tell all that, a person can't help listening."

"Isn't it the truth, my girl . . . So, Edward, since you are listening too: if there is anyone in the world that I am on good terms with, apart from you, I mean, it is the parson at Maiholzen, my spiritual guardian, parochially speaking. We don't interfere with one another, but we keep a nice, easy, neighborly relation. In this sense we do everything to oblige one another. As one man to another, he appreciates Tubby Schaumann thoroughly and I appreciate him. I don't need to tell you that I had been to see him the day before—before the funeral, that is—and discussed the matter with him. I found him hanging from the gutter of his roof. One of his hives had swarmed and the queen had taken the notion to settle there. I held the ladder for the second fattest man in the district and later, sitting in the arbor, touched up his manuscript. But this last is only a common turn of the phrase since the man speaks ex tempore and—speaks well, when he is in the mood. And a man's mood can owe more than a little to his neighbor, as it did in this case. When we took leave of one another at his garden gate later on—it was a warm evening with heat lightning on the horizon—he said, 'Set your mind at ease, neighbor; I am entirely of your opinion.' And the next day he more or less said what I had to say. I cleared my throat—no, he cleared his and said, 'Look here, Christian brethren, there he lies—dead as a doornail.' "

"Oh, God, Herr Schaumann, the pastor can't have said that," exclaimed a voice from behind the bar.

"I was there, my child.—'He is dead and you are alive. He is as dead as Kienbaum whom the majority of us presume he killed. He stands now before the judge who will speak the last word in this dark matter; ought we not to look a little more closely into our hearts, here in this place, and ask ourselves: have we not possibly thrown too many stumbling blocks in the path of this man who lies here now so quietly? My dear Christian brothers and sisters, have we not perhaps too noisily raised the hue and cry against him? If he were to knock now against that black lid and ask to come out again, if only for a moment, to hand us the decree he has in writing from above, what would we do? Who would stretch out his hand for the paper without a qualm? Oh, my dear brothers and sisters, all of us now here were presumably present at the wedding party of the two chief mourners; but I wish at least a few of you had gone with me to Red Bank Farm the evening before last so as to look on the peaceful face of him who has just fallen asleep. Then, I think, some of you who have seen such faces before would certainly have said: This one must have died an easy death after all.

'Christian brethren, what if he didn't murder Kienbaum? . . . In that case ought he not have been allowed to say his say before the last judge? I believe he was allowed; and, knowing him as I do (and he was not a soft man), I believe he groaned, "Lord, Lord, whatever else I have done amiss they have made me pay for below with their contempt, suspicious looks, pointing fingers, cold-shouldering at the inn, and never once a helping hand in trouble. And if I come to thee now as a soured and embittered man, O Lord of heaven and earth, subtract from my punishment in eternity the daily and nightly penance I did in my mortal life, most merciful God. And forgive them in Maiholzen, and round about, the wrong they have done me in the frailty of our flesh." Dear brothers and sisters, we still don't know to this day, any of us, who really killed Kienbaum. Farmer Andreas Quakatz of Red Bank is dead and has given account of his life; but perhaps—Christian brethren, I say perhaps—perhaps there is another going about among us as a living example of what a man can endure who has blood upon his soul and the consciousness day and night that he has allowed another, an innocent person, to answer for it. If this is the case—if the man who murdered Kienbaum is still alive, then—oh, then, Christian brethren, let us say a silent prayer for him, here, here at this grave, as we prayed for him who is dead and at peace in the coffin before us. To the two chief mourners, and especially to the daughter, I say simply: "The Lord said: Weep not! and he gave him to his mother." But if any one of us, dear brothers and sisters, means to persist in wicked thoughts about Andreas Quakatz at Red Bank Farm and his heirs and descendants, even beyond the grave, let him at least not set his hand to this spade, which I now touch with mine. This grave can be filled without his help. Amen.' "

"Amen, O merciful God," someone whispered behind the bar.

"There came now among the other liturgical formulae the words that never fail of their effect: 'Dust thou art; unto dust thou shalt return,' and the spade went from hand to hand with a nervous haste, a zeal, that I never noticed before on similar occasions. They all threw their three spadefuls of mother earth on the most notorious man in the countryside. All but one.—There was the familiar dull thud and the feelings that attend it, the latter stronger than usual. It seemed as if everyone was trying to take this last opportunity of making his peace with Andreas Quakatz. Perhaps too they wanted to restore the village of Maiholzen a little in the esteem of Red Bank Farm. I, as the one who now stands nearest to the old bulwark of the Prince of Saxony, was naturally the first to be handed the spade by the gravedigger, and I threw my three spadefuls. And here I don't know, my dear Edward, how it came about that when I got to the third I sort of muttered to myself: 'For the man that murdered Kienbaum.' A good evening to you, Herr Müller."

The greeting was addressed to someone passing the window in the street below, who stopped in surprise. "Well, Herr Schaumann, you here again at the good old spot? That's excellent. Save a spot for me. I imagine in half an hour or so the regulars will be back in force."

"I handed the spade to the man standing next to me and found myself looking into a queer face. I might as well have been handing the spade into the void. It fell to the ground and it was left to the next man, the vestry chairman, to pick it up. The man I was trying to be polite to had slipped back among the crowd, that is to say, among the women and children, and probably never noticed—never noticed my act of courtesy, I mean. But it went through me: 'What was that? What can it mean?' and then: 'Are you crazy, Tubby, or does this really point to something?'—None of those standing round the farmer of Red Bank's grave, no one except me—not even my wife—noticed that anything unusual had happened, that someone had refused to throw the three spadefuls for the dead man with the mark of Cain on his brow."

"Herr Schaumann!" came from behind the bar, and for all my

own excitement, I could hear the girl clap her hands together. "And what did you do, what did you do?"

"Me? First I took my wife home. There's no sense in letting these poor creatures, all blinded, stupefied, stultified by their tears, go on standing by open graves, staring down at a coffin with the sod heaped on it. Chiefly I had to say to her some of those grave-yard commonplaces that are all you can say at such a time to someone you love. Maiholzen, by the way, came to my aid as best it could. Everybody wanted to shake hands with us on the narrow walk between the graves, and some of them came up and said, 'Herr Schaumann, if it is all right with you and your wife, we'd like to let bygones be bygones. It's quite right what the pastor says, no man has any right to be too hard on his neighbor. After all, Quakatz had his good sides and many a man could have learned from him.' I answered politely, and then, thank God, Tina and I crossed Count von der Lausitz's trench and found ourselves back in our stronghold again, and the world was left outside, and it was quiet in the house and cool under the trees. And the dogs came and the look in their eyes seemed to reproach me for not taking them to the grave too. And the cat came and rubbed tenderly against Frau Valentina Schaumann, née Quakatz. And Valentina sank into a chair in the half-lit dining room and cried some more. The dim light and cool air were good for her, though, after the bright, hot sunshine at the cemetery."

"But, you, what did you—?"

"Me? What else could I do but let her finish her cry and pat her gently on the back now and then? Then she was called out into the kitchen and so I filled my pipe and thought things over."

"You thought things over . . . ?"

"What else could I do? What else is there for a man to do whom you had all left lying under the hedge? The chief thing is to keep cool, I said to myself. Take your time, Tubby. Pull yourself together. Now just what was that? Did I really see something? Hm? Hm? That old veteran? That old blockhead? The thing is too silly for words. The longer you think about it the sillier you feel. He looks simple and good-natured enough, but that's no guarantee in these cases. My, oh my, Schiller's avenging Cranes of Ibykus flying over the cemetery at the village of Maiholzen? It would be wonderful if the grave's coming up one spadeful short put you in a position now to tell the world: Here he is; he did it. Off with him to the judge.—Yes, but him? Too stupid. Just one of those church-yard ghosts that disappear with the morning sun, nothing more, fat Herr Schaumann . . . But yet, you did see something, and felt something too. What was behind the sudden, numb sensation in the stomach, the buzzing and ringing in the ears, the quick clear leap of the intelligence, saying: There it was, there. And now, and now? Why shouldn't something register under your thick hide? Eh? The thing was at least worth pondering, Edward; fortunately my pipe went out and I had to light it again."

"You had to light it again."

"You see it's a frequent experience with me, that there is noth-ing better you can do when you are in utter confusion and at a loss about something than to light your pipe again when it has gone out. I usually have matches; but it is an old habit with me to go into the kitchen anyway, to my wife, and get a burning splinter from the fire. 'Just you go in, sir,' said the girl at the door of the room, 'she's crying her heart out over the fire.' And so I went and stood beside her and said to her, 'Sweetheart, you've got to stop.' Says she, 'It's just to get relief, Heinrich; I know there's peace and security for me with you at Red Bank Farm; and it doesn't matter in the least who killed Kienbaum and embittered my father's life. Oh, how I wish I might never hear a word of it ever again.'—That was when I saw the light.—She lifted the frying pan from the crackling, spitting, leaping fire and I nodded my head to the flying sparks and the clouds of smoke going up the dark chimney: since she says herself that you've been the right man for her, go on being the right man. Don't spoil her peace and security, let her enjoy the good days that can be hers and—as for the other business: well, ask the old man himself! But, Tubby, if the Lord wasn't in a hurry about it all these long years, a few days more or less won't matter. Get what you can out of the old man as quietly as possible some time when it seems suitable, Tubby. Settle it first with him alone. Keep it for the present all to yourself—under the hedge."—

The waitress came and set down another beer before our portly tormentor, and her hand was shaking. She stared at him with round eyes, but she was no more capable of saying a word than I was.

"To your health, Edward. A few days after the funeral I had my first chance. I got a letter and said, 'Well, Störzer, I wonder what sort of trouble you are bringing into the house this time. Does it call for an answer?' Naturally the old man looked at me in surprise for asking so foolish a question and said, 'How should I know, Herr Schaumann? We're pledged not to meddle with letters and I am the last to want to.'—'Right, my old friend. Yes indeed, we have to deal carefully with other people's secrets. Well, it's a warm morning, you know; have a drink of something cool outside. I'd like to see whether I need to write a reply to this nuisance of a letter for you to take with you on your way back later today.'—'Thank you, but I don't think I care for anything; I'll just sit down on the bench and wait. I'm not in such a hurry.'— 'Don't you feel well, Störzer? What's ailing you?'—'Most everything. You see, Herr Schaumann, you get older with the years.'— 'You're right there, my gray old friend. Well, everybody sooner or later goes to his rest; we saw that again last Wednesday. Even Farmer Quakatz, my father-in-law, finally gave up waiting and turned his face to the wall.' The old fellow swung round, without saying a word, and went outside. I opened the envelope in the hallway and, thank God, to this day I can still get angry just thinking about what was in it. An invitation to the next Paleontological Congress in Berlin and nothing more. Crazy! They'd like that. Me in that hole of a city arm in arm with my mammoth. Nice thing indeed! A fine way to treat me. Ridiculous! Are these people really so stupid or do they know Tubby Schaumann so little? When he excavates a thing he hangs on to it and isn't about to be swindled out of it with fair words and filthy lucre.—So I went out to the old fellow and said to him, 'There is really no answer needed, Störzer. So, happily, there's another letter I'll not have to write.'—'That's all right with me, Herr Schaumann. Where does all that writing and writing get people anyway? So good morning, Herr Schaumann.'—'Goodbye, Störzer, and take care of your old legs. Don't you ever think of retiring at your age?'—The old graybeard shrugged his shoulders; but something also flitted over his stupid, good-natured, weather-beaten face. 'Not yet, Herr Schaumann. You get used to it, the likes of me has more peace of mind out on the highway than sitting behind the stove or on the old geezer's bench in front of the house. If you only have your peace of mind at night in bed, that's enough.'—'Hm, yes, at night in bed! Solomon or Sirach said that when you're lying there and supposed to sleep, the thoughts that you've walked off by day out on the highway by rain or shine come into your head and won't let you sleep. Many's the time I've gone to my father-in-law and said to him: Well, Father? Do let your knees down from between your arms and stretch out—everything is safe and peaceful at Red Bank Farm and all round it. Yes, Störzer, my old friend, you ought to have let my wife give you something to drink to refresh you. What's the matter with you? Tina Quakatz would be glad to give it to you, and with a smile, especially to someone like you that she's known all these years. Really, Störzer, you're pulling a face again like the one you pulled the other day—you know, at Mai-holzen cemetery, when I was handing you the spade at Father's grave. Do you know, Störzer, you remind me vividly of the way Farmer Quakatz would look when people sort of half gave him to understand that they thought he had—killed Kienbaum. Störzer, you ought to think of retiring, really you ought. You are getting too old, too weak in the knees, for the burden that Fate has laid on your shoulders as your share of the world's weight.'—Where-upon he answered, replied—if you can call it an answer or reply—yes, I might be right, he would talk it over again with his children. And then he walked away—if you can call it walking—and I let him go and just watched him from Count von der Lausitz's ram-part till he rounded the bush at the corner on the way to Mai-holzen. There it was. There was nothing I could do about it, how-ever much I wanted. But the relief you get from being absolutely clear about something at last and breathing freely isn't always a relief. 'What next?' is usually the question that a poor tormented wretch has to ask himself in that case. And so it was with me. What answer would you have given to the question if you'd been in my place, Edward?"

It doesn't matter in the least whether I answered or what I an-swered. It is enough that he went on, apparently without waiting for me to speak. "I'm sure you think that what I did was to go back to my wife again first, but you're wrong. This time I went first to the closet where the giant sloth was, took another look at its blessed remains, and said, 'What would it have mattered to you, old chap, if Tubby had discovered you a few weeks later, or a few years?' And after the patient beast had given me a satisfactory answer, I went back to Tina and took another close look at her, from her hairdo to the toes of her shoes; and, as I did so, I thought a bit about myself for once. I stroked my darling's cheeks: it had cost me such unspeakable labor to build this tidy, dainty, delightful Rome of mine—and was it all to be for nothing? And why? Because of whom? What for? To what purpose? For the sake of Kienbaum? For the sake of justice, human or eternal? I looked at my wife, looked at all the people I knew, dealing with each person in turn who lived round about Red Bank. And to prevent any reproach from them en masse later on, I was very thorough with each of them; and I didn't find one among them that I felt it was my immediate personal duty to tell who killed Kienbaum. 'But what about eternal justice?' you will ask, Edward. But you see, my dear friend, in my opinion eternal justice had been free to do what it wanted in the matter for long enough. Since it hadn't done anything, but had let Old Man Quakatz do all the searching, it couldn't expect anything of his son-in-law; I, however, was fully entitled to ask it to spare my wife this ugly business—at least, until there was no help for it—and to leave her in peace and quiet. The only question remaining was: What about yourself? Meaning me, my dear Edward, Heinrich Schaumann, alias Tubby. Now you've got the bug in your ear, Heinrich; do you want to let it stay there quietly, can you stand it, without having to scratch where it tickles? You'd have to be a god to do that, and, highly as I value myself, I hadn't yet risen to that elevation, or, if you like, to that degree of thick-skinnedness. So I said to myself: Well, scratch away, scratch where it tickles and when it tickles. Begin by prosecuting the old sinner yourself. Intercept him somewhere, but all alone. If you've had the thing held under your nose on a platter once, it'll happen again, for sure. Don't let them call you Tubby for nothing. Make a meal of this all by yourself. And, preferably, once more under the hedge, say, under a blackberry bush, with a clear blue sky and a bright sun shining, the crickets of the fields as assessors, and the accused, the rural postman Friedrich Störzer, sitting facing you on the edge of the ditch on the highway . . . But Meta, my dear, let's have another look at you. Come out of your dark corner, girl, and over here to our table."

Our tormentor rapped with his hammer on the thumbscrews—no, he clappered with the lid of his beer mug, and Meta, all pale and breathless and excited, tottered out from behind the bar.

"Oh, heavens, Herr Tub . . . Herr Schaumann, dear Herr Schaumann, I can't help it, but . . ."

"You've been listening. Well, then, make yourself more comfortable, come and sit with us and go on listening. But fill up again first and give the gentleman—no, he doesn't seem to want another, but he's only been listening and letting his pedantic friend do all the talking. There, slide right in here, my dear, and let me tell the tale to you. The usual company will be coming soon, won't they? I can hear the approaching tread of the great fraternity. And, you see, Edward, the thing couldn't have worked out better for me: old Störzer is dead, finished his five-fold march round the earth, and tomorrow Dame Rumor will run out to Tina's for half an hour and sit down with the heiress of Red Bank Farm on the edge of Prince Xaver of Saxony's trench, and that'll make it all the easier for me afterward when I provide the additional commentary. But you've given me short measure, young woman."

"Oh, Lord, you notice something like that? At such a time, Herr Schaumann?" said the young thing with a sob, so upset she was trembling.

"There, sit here, child, and open your ears wide, and your mouth too, if you like, later on: it's all right with me, there's no more harm the mouth can do now in this affair. If Fate wishes to bring people together, it knows how to work it. In this case I did nothing about it: I went my way and let Störzer go his; I'm not the sort of person who would lie in wait for him behind one of my great hedges and then grab him by the collar. Did I say 'my way'? It never took me off my own property, but it did take me across the fields now and then. If you've helped to set up a sugar factory and bought stock in it, you have to see to your own and other people's beets from time to time, even in Africa, however fond you may be of lolling about like a lazy lion, loafing and getting hungry. It was on one of these toilsome expeditions that we had it out. You remember where the Imperial post road coming from the town in the direction of Gleimekendorf runs through that piece of common forest, the Papenbusch. The little trails we used as youngsters still run through it this way and that, though some of them still join with the highway. The trees are taller now, but the ditch that separates it from the main road on either side is just as it was. You have to jump across or climb across, if you want to reach the highway. And this was what I wanted to do. Now, now, don't get fidgety, Marie, or Meta, I mean. I know I'm a bit expansive, even in my way of telling pretty tales. But others are quicker about it, and so, if you take one thing with another, it always balances up. Whether the trees were rustling a lot on the woodland trail as I pushed the boughs aside to make my way through I can't say. Anyway, the man who was sitting there on the edge of the ditch with his back to me was not immediately shaken out of his musings by my arrival and of the Erinyes with me. And on occasion such Furies had been known to appear as the more docile Eumenides. Which was fine with me! If anger and goodwill could be combined in this case, it was all right with me. 'Good morning, old fellow. So this was the place, was it?' He didn't return the 'Good morning' and his answer to the question was to whip round and straighten up with his face so distorted and his stick clutched so tightly in his hand, that I involuntarily lifted mine and shouted, 'Are you crazy, Störzer? Is it your good friend Schaumann's turn now, right here on the spot? I think, now, we'd best leave the tally at one; Kienbaum was enough.' Then something happened that I hadn't foreseen. It was quite in order for the poor chap to drop his stick and lift his two trembling old arms to ward off the angel of judgment that he took me for. But there was no need for him to drop to the ground shouting 'Lord, Jesus, you again' and roll down into the ditch—on his face, his hands over his eyes, like a child, with his hindquarters raised in a posture very tempting for an avenger. Now I had it. I am certain that if ever in my life I had a face like a nutcracker, it was then. What else could I do but follow him down into the ditch with a groan, seize the poor devil by the shoulder, shake him and say, 'Just calm yourself, Störzer. Things have gone pretty well with you all these years; so just sit up a bit and let me look at you. I give you my solemn word for it, old man, that I'll talk with you about it in a quiet and sensible way.' Yes, you try talking quietly and sensibly to someone in such a situation, my dear Edward. It was some little time before his shoulders began to heave and jerk in the way we all know so well, telling me along with certain other signs and noises that he understood, the sorry old sinner, what his brother in this life's hurly-burly was trying to tell him. After that, however, we did indeed have a long confidential talk, in which a good deal was said, while we sat side by side on the edge of the ditch. The old fellow had the thickest skin in the territory, the envy of his neighbors, but it would have been a bit too much, I must say, if he had still not wanted to let something of his secret to seep through the pores. Don't you agree, Edward?"

I neither agreed nor disagreed. I could hear the man from Red Bank Farm, the successor and inheritor of the wicked farmer Quakatz, telling me all this in the Golden Arm, but at the same time I was sitting at the side of the ditch in the Papenbusch with my friend Friedrich Störzer, listening to him talking about Africa and how beautiful it must be and how nice it was to read about how peaceable it was there, and about all the adventures one could have, in that beautiful book of Herr Levallyang's.

Tubby laid his hand on the lid of his mug.

"Not yet, my dear. Perhaps a last one later on with our visitor to cap off the evening. Yes, yes, Edward, the things that can happen between life's beginning and its end. And how neat and clear the order and patterns are when you stop to ponder how it is all possible. I'm not talking about you, whom your friend Störzer with his Monsieur Le Vaillant sent off to the land of the Kaffirs. I'm talking of Störzer himself and Quakatz, the farmer, and his little Tina, and, incidentally, a little bit about myself. And then Störzer said to me, 'Yes, it was me that did it, and I've borne it all these years, knowing that they were looking for me and couldn't find me.'—'Hm, and is that all you thought about—whether they would find you?'—'O Lord, O Lord.'—'For instance, you never gave a thought to my poor father-in-law?'—'Oh, I did, I did, sir, but then again not really, sir. I know I was sorry, very sorry, about him spoiling his life all shut off like that through no fault of his own, all for nothing, nothing at all; but there wasn't anything I

could do about it. And he was a man of means anyway and had
a good living, and money put aside too. That was a comfort, and
they could never get much on him at the courts. But don't think
it wasn't asking something of me to have to be going to Red Bank
Farm all the time with letters. And whenever I could I sent someone else with the letters and the newspaper. Oh, Herr Schaumann,
Herr Schaumann, every day, every day, every day on my rounds I
had to go past the place where—I did it. Nobody helped me in my
misery, and I couldn't help Andy at Red Bank Farm out of the
trials I was causing him.'—'Couldn't help, Störzer?'—'No, sir,
sorry, it was against nature. Oh, merciful God, if I could tell you
how utterly it was against my nature.'—'A nice sort of nature,
Störzer!'—'How often, sir, have I said that very thing to myself,
here, where we are sitting now, down on my knees when I had
the woods and the road to myself.'—'Here?'—'Yes, here in the
Papenbusch on the spot where I paid him out for all the wrong he
had done me from the time I was a child. If it went beyond what
was right, I have borne the heavy burden of the crime and the
suspense all these long, long years, God in his mercy knows. It
wasn't any comfort to me at all knowing what sort of a man Kienbaum was and especially what he'd done to me. But I didn't find
out till the next day what it was I had done. If I had seen him
lying right here in front of me, then the farmer at Red Bank, your
father-in-law, would hardly have had to suffer for what I did. They
would certainly have found me beside the body, and they could
have taken me straight before the judge. That one night between
the evening and the morning was what eased my conscience and
gave me some measure of peace, but it also meant that your father
got the heavy, heavy burden laid on him for life.'—'Hm, hm, Störzer, it makes sense, what you say there, but that conscience of
yours is a bit easygoing, isn't it, or, shall we say, very accommo-
dating. Your letter bag might be said to have the same feelings as
you for what's in the letters it carries.'—'I don't rightly understand what you mean, Herr Schaumann, and I don't know how it
is with others in such dreadful cases, but one thing I do know—
it's out now and people will be able to put their minds at rest,
because of your kind intervention in the matter. And as for God
above, it comforts me in my bitter remorse to think that he knew

Kienbaum, and that he knew me when I was young, and knows better than anyone else how it happened.'—'Yes, but now I want to know better too.'—'It's entirely up to you what they do with me now. It doesn't matter to me any more. But my children and grandchildren will have to deal with the bad smell I leave behind me. There was only a year or two more and the law wouldn't be able to touch me. I thought I could hold out till then, but it hasn't turned out that way at all. So, if only for your father-in-law's sake, do what you feel you must, Herr Schaumann, do what you feel is right.'—'We'll deal with that later. Tell me now how it was, how it happened.'—'Ah, that's just it, there's not much to tell, though it ended so badly. There wasn't even a quarrel between us about a girl or about money, the way it usually is. It was just that the devil put his hand to it, and that's how it had to be. We were the same age, Kienbaum and I, our two cradles lay, you might say, on two sides of the same wall; we grew up together and knew one another through and through. There wasn't much to him, and it did comfort me a little now and then in all those long years to hear other folks say so.'—'A nice comfort, you poor unfortunate man.'—'Poor unfortunate man, indeed. You're right there. All the more reason for finding what solace you can on the hard road, notwithstanding. Oh, sir, you don't know how hard he made it for me from the time we were little, from our schooldays to here on the Imperial highway. It was him that started calling me Mutton Chop in the classroom and he hung the nickname on me for life. It was him more than anybody else from schooldays on that made me feel the difference between poverty and riches, and between slow thinking and fast and a nasty loud mouth to go with it. Sir, I know his blood is on me and I'm ready today to wash it off with mine, if it can come of itself without me doing anything about it: but, sir—he must answer, Kienbaum, for his share, for all the fear and anger and fury and vexation he churned up in me almost every day we lived from the time we could walk. For the Lord ordained it for him to be a prosperous cattle-dealer who was forever on the road. I tell you, sir, that if a highwayman of the olden days had been lying in wait for me and my letters at every turn of the road, it couldn't have been worse than having to say to myself eternally: "Kienbaum will be driving up any minute and giving you the time of day in his usual fashion." Herr Schaumann, you're known hereabouts to be a good quiet man, and I've been a quiet man all my life and have gone my ways and interfered with no one, even delivered him his letters at his house in Gleimekendorf year after year and endured his vileness and mockery as part of my duties, until the dreadful moment came, here in the Papenbusch, and his fate and mine, and your poor father-in-law's miserable fate, too, was loaded on me. But, sir, as I live, I only half did it, it was all an accident. The great Judge knows it was an accident and that must be why he has allowed me to come to be as old as I am in some sort of peace; and this has been my second source of comfort on the highway, in thunder and hail and snow and heat, day in day out, alone with myself and my thoughts. Yes, Herr Schaumann, everybody works it out in his own way, doesn't he? You'll work it out in yours about your duty to me and your wife and old Quakatz and Kienbaum?'—'I must say, I wish the Lord had chosen someone else for the job, Störzer.'—'Oh, don't let it worry you: I'm ready, now that it's all come out this way. Today—tomorrow—the day after. And no judge on earth who cross-examines me will be able to accuse me of lying. I swear that to you now by all that's holy.'—'Just imagine Tubby Schaumann and Mutton Chop sitting in the confessional together as priest and penitent, my dear Edward.—'What are you supposed to do,' said the latter, the penitent, 'if you've been born absolutely defenseless against whatever rascal you have to grow up with? Oh, God, it was murder for sure, what I did to Kienbaum, but everything he ever did to me is part of it, both when he was a boy and a lad and a grown man, all those little things and all mean and crude ones, too. There's nothing Kienbaum didn't do to me, nothing that one lad would be willing to put up with from another. If all the punches and pinches he gave me at old Schoolmaster Fuhrhans's had left their mark, there wouldn't be a white spot left on me, but everything blue, green, and yellow. And if the angry tears that I fought down when he'd finally leave me were to come now, there'd be three buckets full. I think I just told you that there wasn't a girl in it, but there was one at one time. During our military service. We were both in the army together—seems like the Lord wanted to nail the two of us together. I wanted nothing of her, but I saved her, her and her baby, from drowning, all in my second dress uniform, and it would have been better if I'd left her in the water, the pair of them, poor creatures. He dodged paying for their support later, and the child died neglected and she ended up in jail. But I'll say no more about that, it really only affected me the same way as anyone might feel. But his money! I told you before that the trouble between us didn't come over money or anything, and that was true. I owed him nothing and he owed me nothing. The bad thing was that his business and his prosperity meant he had to travel about a lot. No doubt cattle trading was the right thing for him, if not always for those he bought from and sold to. But why couldn't the Lord have let him make his money another way, why did he have to throw him across my path every, every, every day, with his contempt and his mockery and his scorn? He had bought the farm at Gleimekendorf, right in the middle of my route, and so he was always passing me on the road, high and mighty on horseback or driving—and me footing it along. It's a long time now since the young men at the post office started calculating every so often how many times I've been round the world. At that point by my calculation I'd been round it about once, but that was enough, if I had to meet a scoundrel like him daily—a man who tries to come at you from behind and give you a flick with his whip and then gallops off, taunting you with: "Baa, baa, black sheep, Mutton Chop, run your legs off, bring me the dollars and get your pennies; the name is Kienbaum." Herr Schaumann, the time comes when you can't stand it any more. And it did come, and there'd be nothing much to it, if it hadn't been so dreadful. Oh, merciful, merciful heavens, what is it that gives a man his life's peace and his clear conscience or else makes him wreck them for himself or someone else, like your father-in-law, Herr Schaumann? It was just such a fine evening as now. But sultrier, felt more like a thunderstorm coming up. And I'd had a heavy day, a full bag and half a dozen money orders, which I always found hardest because of the responsibility and having to enter them correctly and settle later at the office. I was worn out and felt it in every bone in my body and was just crawling along, and I came this way into the Papenbusch just as twilight was settling into the thickets. "You're not the Wandering Jew,

Störzer," I said to myself. "There's time for five minutes," and then the devil took hold of me, or the Lord willed it so, and I sat down for five minutes here at the side of the ditch; it would have been better if heaven instead had driven a hay wagon with four runaway horses over my body five minutes before. And then— would you believe it?—I said, "It'll be the finishing touch if Kienbaum comes along and finds you like this, all tuckered out." And at that very moment I had to prick my ears, for there round the corner came a wagon or something, and a long way off I could hear someone lashing his horses and shouting, "Get up, damn you." Then it went through me with a stab: "Well, there you have it," and I knew that I was to be spared nothing that day. I resigned myself to whatever might happen, but the air was heavy with the approaching storm and I also reached for my stick, and said to myself, "Störzer, if it comes to the worst, be a man and stand up to the sneering fully." But, as usual in such cases, it turned out differently. When Kienbaum saw me sitting there, he drew the reins and stopped with his empty cattle wagon. Says I to myself, "Well, he's in good form today," and he was. For once he had met a man smarter than himself. Your father-in-law, as it turned out afterward, the farmer at Red Bank, Herr Schaumann. The cattle trade they did that morning was made a lot of later on in court as evidence against Farmer Quakatz of Red Bank. The second piece of evidence against him, as you know, Herr Schaumann, was that he was seen late in the evening on the same day on the way to Gleimekendorf. There were lots of people in the town, at the Blue Angel, who had heard them hurling curses at one another around noon—calling each other a damned scoundrel, rogue, knave, and whatnot. But when Kienbaum's had the worst of a deal, who better could he take it out on than on somebody like me? Your father-in-law and he didn't meet up again that day in the Papenbusch, but Kienbaum met up with me, his Mutton Chop ran into me right here on this very spot just at the moment when he needed someone to take it out on. He stops his wagon, and I was up and had my bag in place and my stick ready. I see that nasty twisted look come over his face in the twilight, and then he shouts at me, "Mutton Chop, sure. Well, there he sits hatching other people's eggs. Have you been running your legs off again for five groschens, you clown? Don't be offended, now. Weren't we at school together and in the army, and always chums? There now—hold out your hand, my friend." And saying this, he slashes at me with his whip, thinking, as was his way, that this was a good joke, and the switch curls round my arm and gives me a nasty weal across the hand. He didn't mean it as badly as that, I don't think; but what came now was what had to come. I drop my stick and in my pain snatch for it on the ground, but instead, oh, merciful God, I put my hand on the nearest stone. I threw it, not thinking, not aiming, but it hit him—with God's will and the devil's. He totters sideways, I can see it, and gives the reins a shake. The horses start up and the wagon goes past me into the dusk. "Take that home with you, and put a cold knife blade on it, you skunk," I shout after him. I don't know whether he heard or not. I came to the conclusion afterward, in many an anguished night, that he didn't. It seemed to me queer, in spite of the rage I was in, that he didn't keep straight on the highway to Gleimekendorf, but turned off to the right into the lumber road through the wood that leads to Red Bank Farm. I was so mad, though, I didn't think further about it, but went home sucking my sore wrist all the way like a whipped child. The rest of the story came out afterward, you know it as well as I do, Herr Schaumann. You know that on the lumber road the horses must have dropped into a trot and probably stood still for hours before they found their way by the road across the fields to the farmyard at Gleimekendorf about midnight, ending up at the stable door. People came running with lanterns and looked in the wagon and found Kienbaum in the straw, and the doctors decided that it must have been a blow or a stone on his left temple that did it. It's all there in the proceedings, in detail, all but me. I'm just mentioned in passing, as one of those Kienbaum might have met on the road and talked to. Oh, God, Herr Schaumann, why did the Lord make me the way he did, if he was going to bring this horror on me? You can't blame people or the lawyers if they went after Quakatz for it and not Störzer, the postman. It was in his nature and in the way he felt about Kienbaum for him to murder him. It wasn't in my nature. God be praised and thanked, they at least didn't call me up as a witness against him, your father-in-law. Then I might have made a clean breast of things right there at the bar. But to give myself up of my own accord after those awful nights and solitary rounds—I tried to do it, but I couldn't—I wanted to do it, but I put off and put off and the years went by and, in spite of his trouble, things went better all the time with the farmer at Red Bank. Oh, that silent fear, that silent fear, for a generation, Herr Schaumann. I ought to have delivered my confession with every letter I brought to Red Bank Farm, passing by it every day, for a generation, but I couldn't do it. I couldn't give myself up as the man who did the deed, the man that murdered Kienbaum. Oh, sir, it's too late now in a way, but I shall do nothing to stop you; you won't need to pack me by the shoulder: I'll follow you, willingly, if you want to take me into the town, now, tonight and tell the first man you meet at the gate: "He did it, he's just told me himself." ' " . . .

"What's the matter here? No light yet?" said the first of the guests. "It's getting so we'll have to bring a light with us. Hey, Meta, where are you anyway?"

"Here, sir. Oh, it's the public prosecutor. I'll be right there," cried the girl with a trembling voice. Even the match she had struck trembled in her hand and she had to try several times before she could light up the separate room at the Golden Arm where important guests sat.

"Well, what do you know," said the solicitor, "you here, Schaumann, and leaving just as we're coming. Come, Tubby, my portly old friend, and you, Edward, do stay now that you're here. It'll be like the good old days. What is left of the old crowd in this vale of tears will never forgive me if I let you go now; the one back to his Red Bank Farm, the other to darkest Africa. Meta, bring these two gentlemen another round. Boys, this is grand. We finally have the chance for another jolly evening like in the old days. You'll stay, won't you?"

"I'd love to, if it were possible and my doctor hadn't forbidden it," laughed Schaumann. "Oh, if you had any idea, Schellbaum, how emphatically that man Oberwasser has forbidden me intellectual stimulus of any kind, you would leave me lying under my hedge as in other and better days."

We took our hats. The room was filling up, but fortunately with visitors who knew nothing of Joseph and only knew Tubby Schaumann from hearsay or at a distance. And so we managed finally to get outside the front door, and poor Meta came running after us, trembling with excitement:

"Goodness, Herr Schaumann, I heard everything you said. Is it possible? And the gentlemen inside? Can anybody know? Can I tell them everything tonight?"

"Everything, my dear."

The captain is getting more and more puzzled. He has just said to me, "Well, sir, it used to happen often enough that we ran out of drinking water, it might even happen nowadays, and it's quite an inconvenience; but what would you say if I were to tell you with deepest regret, Sir, we've come to the last drop of ink? It's a good thing, isn't it, that from tomorrow we shall be looking out for Table Mountain?"

"It is indeed."

And the old salt went back on deck shaking his head and muttering to himself that, thank God, this damned scribbling didn't happen all the time on board ship. I firmly believe that in a crisis he would have taken me for the bird of ill omen on his vessel and, without a qualm, have pushed me overboard into the raging sea to save the rest of his cargo by means of expiatory sacrifice.

But we were standing, Tubby Schaumann and I, out in front of the Golden Arm again, under that warm, dark, restful, summer-evening sky, and I was as busy mopping my brow quite as much as my fat and astonishing friend. He hadn't merely told the story of Kienbaum's murder in his endless droning way; he had sweated it out, let it seep through his pores. Was it for this, I asked myself, that I had been through so much by land and sea—to stand face to face with Tubby and Mutton Chop in the quiet nook that was my home and to say to myself that neither I nor anyone else had ever seen the like before?

Which of the two, I asked myself, was the greater enigma, the greater mystery now? Oh, this fellow Störzer. And oh, this fellow Schaumann. To think that my old friend, my oldest really, the man I played with as a child, was the man that murdered Kienbaum. The man who with his Le Vaillant had in fact sent me off to sea and into the desert—and it was thanks to him and him alone and his long talks as we wandered around the world along highways and byways that I had become the owner of my estate at the Cape of Good Hope. I couldn't take it in—at least, I could say no more about it for the present.

Schaumann accompanied me to my hotel, and at the door I ventured one last question.

"Won't you come up for a minute?"

"I'd rather not," said Heinrich. "My wife hasn't had to worry about me for years. At this time of day I'm always at home. Well, I admit today was a legitimate exception. What doesn't one do for a dear old friend that one has been out of touch with, to make him feel snug and at home again in the old place. We'll see you again, old fellow, before you go, won't we? You'll have to see the face the old girl makes once she has found out from other folks— and I'm sure that's the best way, just as I'm sure everyone will be talking about it tomorrow—what I ought to have told her long ago myself. Good night then, Edward, for now. Thanks for coming out to see us. That really was not just what you might call an ordinary day for Red Bank."

"Good night, Heinrich," I said, there being at the moment nothing else I was able to say, and he seemed to take this for granted, because he waddled off through the pleasant evening air toward his lifelong stronghold, his "mighty fortress," leaving me alone in my hotel with thoughts of him, his wife, his departed father-in-law, Störzer, and Kienbaum. If in years gone by I had ever left him lying, as he put it, under his hedge with his thoughts, his feelings, his moods, making him and him alone his own private court of appeal, he was paying me back today a hundredfold, and I watched him go off into the night as few can ever have watched.

And now I was under *my* hedge, alone in my rented room in my home town, and I had the night before me in which to think over what had happened during the day. But when the morning sun came in at my window and fell on the bed and I took stock of my waking and dreaming, I found that I had, strangely enough, occupied myself strictly only with Frau Valentina Schaumann, née Quakatz, and relatively very little with Kienbaum, Störzer, old man Quakatz, and Tubby.

The dear, the poor dear woman!

And could one blame Tubby, if when he thought of her peace and contentment at Red Bank Farm he came to regard earthly justice as less important, as secondary? By about midnight I had put myself completely in the fat man's place, I had put myself right inside his skin, or, better, found myself put there. My body had swelled to the size of his, and I had risen to the heights of his serene disdain for the world, and I said: "We'll show this parched African, this Edward, something of what we can do at home in the old place, we'll prove to him that we know at Red Bank Farm how to stamp our heels on the heads of the philistines. We'll let him see how time and eternity shape themselves for a man who was left lying under the hedge when he was a boy, and who stays there and, for the good of his soul, goes in search of Tina Quakatz, and to keep himself from going thin, gets possession of Red Bank and in his spare time digs up yesterday as if it were a mammoth's bone that had been buried for tens of centuries."

And then, this night, before I went to bed and in bed too, I went over the day that had just become yesterday for me, hour by hour, word by word. And more and more I realized the truth of the principle of sufficient reason: *Nihil est sine ratione our potius sit, quam non sit,* as old Wolff[43] has it; and as the Buddha of Frankfurt[44] translates it: "Nothing *is* without a reason for its being so." Just as Le Vaillant, translated by Johann Reinhold Forster—in the library of Störzer, the country postman—had taken me to the Boers in Pretoria, so the stone thrown by Störzer's hand at Kienbaum's head had brought my friend to Tina Quakatz and made him master of Red Bank. And thus, if Kienbaum had not been Kienbaum, Störzer Störzer, Tubby Tubby, and Tina Tina, I wouldn't have been myself and, thinking over this murder story, wouldn't have fallen toward morning into the deepest of sleeps and wakened with comfortable thoughts of my place out in Africa and my wife and children at home, saying: "Well, the whole affair didn't turn out too badly."

But I wasn't finished with this affair just yet. I could read that much on the waiter's face as he came in answer to my ring and stared with youthful eyes for the longest time before grasping that it was fresh water and warm water I wanted. And there was friend

Sichert, the landlord himself, behind him, staring at me likewise, saying, "Sir, is it possible? You must please forgive me, but you are the first person in the town who has heard all the details from Herr Schaumann. And there have been some of your good friends in the dining room below and they were asking whether you were up yet and whether it really was like that with Kienbaum and Störzer?"

"Why yes, Herr Sichert, it seems it was."

"You don't say. I ought to tell you that part of the town heard about it last evening, last night, as the news spread from the Golden Arm, and they were all terribly excited about it. But, unfortunately, you had already retired, when the exciting news reached me, why I didn't want . . ."

"To wake me and ask me for the whole story at once. It was very kind of you . . ."

"But, forgive me, my dear sir. This is your home town, too. You're one of us, so to speak, and when folks have been stewing about such a difficult and interesting matter for years now—and then you get this queer light suddenly thrown on it. And old Störzer. Nobody thought he was anything but a good-natured, harmless old man, an old sheep. And tomorrow they'll bury him and the arm of earthly justice can't touch him at all. And our good Herr Schaumann of Red Bank, who could have done so much long ago to clear it up, could have . . ."

"Given us a last uncanny thrill of pleasure, you mean. No, my dear Sichert, he was too fat for that, too clumsy, too ponderous, or whatever you like to call it. Perhaps a little too good-natured as well, too easygoing. And then—well, it was an old, old story, so far in the past, nobody's business any longer, unless perhaps his wife's a little bit—Herr Schaumann's wife, who was a Quakatz herself. Yes, and why should the two of them, especially now that they're dug in at their farm, start bothering the high courts about dear old Störzer, and by putting them on the right track actually end up putting them to shame? Just think that over."

"I can't take it in," sighed my landlord and went off, shaking his head, not at all satisfied. But I clapped my hand to my brow: heavens, how right Schaumann was. Even that little bit I saw was in store for me now was enough for me to understand completely his position in the days that followed that fine summer morning when at his father-in-law's funeral he had suddenly noticed something. But then I immediately reflected: "And now you will have to pay the price, or some of it, for what he has kept from the world so long and so disdainfully, pulling up his drawbridge behind him. And the monster is capable even now of strengthening his fortifications around himself and his wife and calling up the ghosts of all those mastiffs, bulldogs, sheepdogs, and vicious Pomeranians, in short, all those savage guardians of his father-in-law's, out of their graves and of leaving it to you alone to settle the case of Störzer-Kienbaum with the rest of humanity."

I didn't believe that he was looking for a second visit from me notwithstanding his invitation. And I've said it already: Red Bank Farm was the last place at home that I owed a visit to. I had no business left to do. I had revived and refreshed all my memories, pleasant and unpleasant, and could take them back with me to Kaffraria. If I now made a bolt of it to escape the shades of Kienbaum, I would hardly leave a regret behind me, at most brief surprise at my sudden departure. There was no one here of either sex who would have torn at my coat in an effort to keep me "just a few days longer."

How would it be, Edward, if you pulled your head out of the noose and took your share of the business on shipboard with you?

No sooner had I said the words, or thought them, than I was no longer standing on the solid ground of the Fatherland, I was on my sea legs again, on those unstable boards riding the ocean waves, and a very refreshing sea wind was blowing in my face.

"I'll go," I said, and—I did. I didn't let silent reproaches disturb me and, should there be any loud ones, I was to be found in Africa and ready to give anyone an account of myself, that is to say, ready to send him this travel diary of mine to read.

But I must say it cost me some toil and cunning just to get away from the Three Wise Men unnoticed. It was only by means of something very near to bribery that I was able to obtain my bill at once behind the landlord's back. It cost me money, but I found a helpful soul who enabled me to dispense with the hotel coach and secretly took my baggage to the station for me in a wheelbarrow. I didn't disguise myself by pulling my theater cloak up around my ears and my slouch hat down over my nose; but I didn't depart by the most direct public way, either. I slipped out by the back door and through the garden of the Three Wise Men. I got out of the garden by another little door into a narrow lane that was known to me as a child and that was still there, thank God, leading past gardens, stables, and other back premises. If I had killed Kienbaum myself and had the Myrmidons of the law on my heels, I couldn't have made a stealthier getaway; I rejoiced that the town had changed so little since I was here before and that I was able to find my way even in the less familiar streets with the help of my sense of direction and feeling for the place.

It was getting close to nine when I reached the station, not exactly going through the town, but around it behind the gardens. In my desire to avoid the main streets I had overlooked the fact that the way I was choosing took me through St. Matthew's, and, careful as I had been to keep out of people's way for the time being, I had no reason to be surprised at the crowd I ran into here.

It would be an exaggeration to say that half the town was on its feet to attend the funeral of Störzer, the country postman, but a good part of the population was gathered in the streets and lanes round about his house—among them Fräulein Eyweiss with her bottle of mineral water and several friends from the Brummer-summ also.

Nobody claimed that he was standing there waiting for the procession so as to give the old man an honorable escort to his grave. But everyone had the right to steal a few moments from his morning duties, or neglect of duties, to take a look, before it was too late, at the black coffin that housed the man who was for the moment the most remarkable personage in the town or, for that matter, in the whole neighborhood for far around. They all wanted to see his coffin, if they couldn't see him, the kindly, simple old fellow, old Störzer, who had been five times around the globe with his burdened conscience in the course of his fifty-four thousand one hundred and sixty-four walking work-hours and who had let the whole town from top to bottom go on talking all these years without ever saying a word—Störzer, the man who killed Kienbaum.

And then I felt a friendly slap on the shoulder.

"Well, Edward. It needed you to come home from the Cape of Good Hope to help provide us with this surprise. We went over it all pretty well at the Golden Arm last night, how you—you and Schaumann—unburdened yourselves yesterday out at Red Bank Farm. It was really excellent of you to get that fat man into a communicative mood at last and make him talk. Oh, yes, Tubby. Yes, he was always like that. Yes indeed, you had to come, for it to take this turn. But for you, Edward, we might have waited a long time to find out who really killed Kienbaum. And this old Störzer: you don't quite know whether he makes the story more gruesome than before or whether he makes it, you might say, all nice and friendly. But as I said, above all what can you say about our Tubby? Isn't he priceless? Just the same as ever, isn't he?"

"Just. We don't change as easily as that. But excuse me, is your watch right?"

My friend looked to see. "To a minute. Nine-twenty exactly."

"Then I haven't a moment to spare. The Hamburg train goes in twenty minutes."

"Are you going to Hamburg?"

"A little farther. I'm going to Africa. Glad to have run into you this way. Good-bye for now and good luck!"

"But, Edward? You're joking, Edward. Why so suddenly, why all at once?"

Fortunately the wretched little funeral procession came around the corner at this moment and I didn't have to answer. The death-dealer, who had escaped his earthly penance in so droll a way, was of even greater interest to my friend than my sudden departure. The spectacle so drew his attention that I was able to slip away at once, after throwing one last brief glance at the coffin of my oldest friend in the town.

The poor coffin—followed now by a procession consisting of a woman with one baby in her arms and another clinging to her apron! . . .

They had all refused to go, those that would normally have gone. Even the Imperial Post Office had decided that it wasn't fitting to send their minor employees to walk behind the old globe-trotter, the faithful servant—the very cunning murderer; and they weren't wrong, no, they were perfectly right.

"Well, he promised both himself and the poor woman only last night that he would do something for the children and grandchildren," I said, as I came to the station. There was an early excursion train passing through on its way south, and it was alive with merry holiday-makers, with green sprays in their hats, songbooks in their pockets, hampers of provisions and baskets and whatever else belongs to the encumbrances of such a flight from the daily round. I couldn't have got into a hubbub that better suited my mood. There was the world for you!

I had some difficulty reaching the northbound train, but it was not an unpleasant sort of difficulty. I didn't run a child down nor in my haste elbow a woman and make her shout: "Oh, my God." But as I sat down in the compartment—a corner seat, mercifully— I sighed, "Well, Tubby . . ." and after a while I added, "Yes, at bottom it all amounts to the same thing, whether you stay lying under the hedge and let adventure find you out or whether you let your good friend Fritz Störzer and his old Le Vaillant and Johann Reinhold Forster send you abroad to find it on the high seas or in the desert."

A shrill whistle, a hissing sound, a snuffing and snorting, a breathing and groaning that got faster and faster, and my home town with all its permanent inventory, physical and spiritual, living and dead, father and mother, uncle and aunt, friends, schoolmasters, good drinking partners and bad, church and marketplace, lay behind me again. And the Brummersumm, the Golden Arm, the Three Wise Men—and Tubby Schaumann too.

No, not Tubby Schaumann. Since the day before, my whole visit home had revolved too closely around his corpulent person for that. Even there at home, without moving out from under their hedges, people had their adventures and dealt with them with a wonderful lightness and ease. Mankind might be calm, tranquil, fat perhaps, but it could muster the power to hold its own with the brawniest, leanest, most reckless of adventures. Heinrich Schaumann, alias Tubby, had taught me this lesson very thoroughly. And I certainly did not rush by in my express train without gazing at his stronghold.

The train passes below Red Bank Farm within a minute and a half of leaving the station and for a brief space you have a clear view of that military molehill of His Highness, Count von der Lausitz, Prince Xaver of Saxony. The walls, the trees, the house roof stood out sharp and clear against the blue sky that summer morning, and I waited with keenest attentiveness, at once both strangely melancholy and pleasant, for the train to rush by, for the farewell I would take as it did.

And just as I had hoped, I could see it all. They were no more than two bright dots, but they were there, in the sun-drenched, golden-green landscape of my home. He stood on his rampart in his summer dressing gown and had his Tina beside him—just as I was certain he had his long philistine's pipe. And I was certain, too, that his wife had linked her arm in his, and if now at last she also knew who had slain Kienbaum, she could, with fullest trust in her Heinrich, wait for the tide of consequences that would wash in upon them this lovely morning from the world outside that had also learned the facts last evening. And now they were two, both of them left lying once by the world beneath the hedge, who would go on lying peacefully there now, no matter what the world, the world outside, might say about their incomprehensible indolence.

"Oh, that Tubby Schaumann!"—

If he had had any notion that his "good friend Edward" was riding by him down there, he most certainly would have lifted his pipe in the air and waved his nightcap. And then his wife Valentina, née Quakatz, but now Mrs. Tubby, would have let her handkerchief billow in the breeze. But perhaps she would also have remarked, "I must say, I don't understand his doing that at all!"

What my fat friend Heinrich Schaumann might have replied to that other than "hmm," I cannot say.

And on past Red Bank Farm! Still, it was a joy to know that it went on being where it was and what it was; and that I could remember it that way: a sunny spot at home in the green countryside.

The person seated opposite me lost no time in asking me please to shut the window as this was the drafty side and the window opposite was open. Seeing that the sun was coming in too, spending its warmth, I gladly complied with the lady's wishes. I pulled up the widowpane and drew the blue curtains and I must admit that the blue dimness was welcome after peering out for that brief strained moment into the sharp morning light with its dazzling greens and yellows at the two tiny figures on the ramparts of Red Bank—my last peep at my fat friend and his dear wife, Valentina Schaumann, in my old homeland. A bit of coal dust or something from the engine had got into my right eye besides.

And I might as well admit this too: that the blue light, or the light-blue twilight, in which I closed my eyes as I was leaving home to rest them awhile, stayed with me notwithstanding till Hamburg, till I was on board, till this very moment. No doubt sensible people will say: "What won't a man turn his hand to to pass the time when the weather is good and the sea is calm? Well, it's a matter of taste what shifts you snatch at when you are bored."

The captain has just been down and said something similar: "Do you know, sir, you are the only novelty we've had on the whole voyage. We always get a touch of bad weather, but this time not a trace; one can hardly count the squall we had the other day. On deck we're beginning to look out for Table Mountain, but, damn me, what I'd really like to see is what you've been writing there, for a whole month, aboard my ship."

"It wouldn't interest you, captain. Just a private matter," I said, closing my manuscript.

When I went on deck afterward to join the others and watch Table Mountain rise out of the sea, and when a little blue cloud on the horizon was pronounced by the crew to be that famous mount, I had to put my hand to my brow and ask, "Edward, how has it happened? Are you back here again?"

It was a day and a half before we were able to land, and meanwhile I wandered many a time on the high road at home with Störzer, the country postman, and heard him tell his tales of Le Vaillant and the South African hinterland, not without curious side-glances at Red Bank Farm; and all the time I had the certain knowledge, filling me with joyful impatience, that I should soon have my wife in my arms again and my young Dutch-German brood clinging to my coattails saying: "*Vader, wat hebt gij uns mitgebracht uit het Vaderland?*"

Notes

Notes to HORACKER

1. The scene of *Horacker* is a wooded region called the Solling, whose hills are an extension of the Teutoburger Forest on the eastern side of the valley cut by the Weser River.
2. Haparanda, Hernösand—towns with weather stations in the north of Sweden.
3. A union of German states north of the Main River, formed in 1867 under Prussian hegemony following the Prussian victory over Austria in the Seven Weeks' War of 1866.
4. Decisive Prussian victory of July 1866.
5. Prussian victory over Hanover, which was allied with Austria, in June 1866.
6. Austrian victory over Italy, June 1866.
7. Maximilian was executed at Benito Juárez's order on June 19, 1867.
8. Raabe is mistaken here. Antonio Lopez de Santa Anna did not die until 1876.
9. This line of a German noble family had ruled this and other principalities in Thuringia since the 12th century. It's capital was Gera.
10. The son of Ludwig I of Bavaria, Otto was placed on the Greek throne in 1832 by the European powers but with little national support on the part of the Greeks. He was ousted from the throne in 1862.
11. The postal franchise enjoyed by this German noble family was terminated by Prussia in 1867.
12. Ottoman sultan, 1861–1876.
13. Latin: in the midst of things, traditionally the starting point for any epic narration.
14. Literally, "goose corner."
15. English ivy.
16. Latin: as a body, as a whole.
17. It was at Mark Antony's instigation that Cicero was murdered in 43 B.C.

18. Latin: formally.

19. Roman essayist and grammarian, 130–180 A.D.

20. Latin: By Pollux!

21. Latin: By Hercules!

22. Latin: By Castor!

23. Cornelia, the mother of the tribunes Tiberius and Gaius Cracchus, was considered the embodiment of Roman maternal virtues.

24. This was a classical metrical foot of four short syllables. Its origin appears to have been in rowing songs of Greek galleys, and the term literally means "serving to incite or animate."

25. Latin: domestic rhythm.

26. Latin: farewell.

27. *Blätter für literarische Unterhaltung,* a leading literary journal published from 1826 to 1898.

28. Very popular in his day, this eighteenth-century German poet and novelist was best known for his "Fables and Tales," verses of a didactic and moralizing character, and for his religious poetry. By the middle of the nineteenth century, his reputation was considerably in eclipse.

29. A nickname, a variation of Christian taken from the Slavic languages.

30. A rephrasing of a verse from Johann Heinrich Voss's pastoral idyll *Luise* (1795), Book I, 1.38.

31. One of the principal ecclesiastical issues of nineteenth-century Germany was the reform that allowed clergy to be paid through the central church office rather than through traditional parochial contributions. The quarter-money at issue here is a remnant of the older system.

32. Johann Bückler, called Schinderhannes (1777–1803), was a famous brigand. Bavarian Hiesl was the nickname of Matthias Klostermeier (1738–1771), another such figure, as was Hundssattler, also of the same period.

33. These collections of crime stories were published by Julius Hitzig and Georg Häring (pseud. Willibald Alexis) regularly from 1842 on. Their model was a similar work by François-Gayot de Pitival (1673–1743), which was translated into German by Schiller.

34. Basses Verlag published a "library of interesting criminal cases" in 1859.

35. Latin: hurrah (lit.: may he live); may they live forever and ever!

36. Greek: By Apollo!

37. A Roman historian (100–25 B.C.) whose texts were used for first-year Latin instruction.

38. Latin: come, breeze! Taken from Ovid's "Metamorphoses" (7, 836), it is spoken by Cephalos to his wife Procris, who in her jealousy assumes Aura to be another woman.

39. Latin: *The Art of Love,* also by Ovid.

40. Roman historian of the fourth century A.D.

41. Ovid's full name.

42. From Goethe's sonnet "Nature and Art" ("*In der Beschränkung zeigt sich erst der Meister*").

43. The tomcat in Goethe's "Reineke Fuchs" (1794).

44. The mountain from which Moses gazed over into the Promised Land before his death.

45. The common European cuckoo.

46. Karl Friedrich von Steinmetz (1797–1877) was the Prussian general in command of the army that took the Bohemian town of Schweinschädel (lit.: pig skull) in 1866.

47. Latin: let us refresh ourselves.

48. Latin: now.

49. Helmut Graf von Moltke (1800–1891), Prussian Field Marshal, commanded the victorious troops at Königgrätz in 1866.

50. Following the Seven Weeks' War of 1866, it became fashionable to claim that the battle of Königgrätz had been won by the German schoolmasters in that they were responsible for the discipline shown by the German troops.

51. Latin: to your health, colleague. To Jupiter the Liberator! The second phrase, according to Tacitus in his "Annals," was spoken by the dying Seneca.

52. Latin: the mountains will be in labor. This is the first part of a line from Horace's "Ars poetica," and continues "nascetur ridiculus mus"—a ridiculous little mouse will be born (1.139).

53. Latin: hail, goddess of the wood!

54. Dutch painter (1605–1638) famous for his realistic portraits of common people.

55. Perhaps a reference to a drama of the same name (*Sohn der Wildnis*, 1843) by the Austrian poet Friedrich Halm.

56. An aria from Auber's opera *Fra Diavolo* (1830).

57. A verse from the novel *Rinaldo Rinaldini* (1797–1800) by Christian August Vulpius.

58. These are the nominative, genitive, and dative forms of the Latin *lepus*, rabbit, a word that is termed epicene because it is both masculine and feminine in gender.

59. A famous highwayman executed in 1715 and featured in Gellert's fable "The Dog" ("Der Hund").

60. From Gellert's fable "The Suit" ("Der Prozess"), 11.5–10.

61. The great standard translation by Johann Heinrich Voss of the *Odyssey* (1781) and the *Iliad* (1793).

62. See note 30.

63. From the *Neues Braunschweigisches Gesangbuch* (*New Braunschweig Hymnal*) of 1857, hymn 262, verse 3.

64. In *Nathan the Wise* (1779), I, 3.

65. Lessing's "Briefe antiquarischen Inhalts" were a series of controversial essays written by Lessing in 1768 against C. A. Klotz in defense of his own "Laokoon." The statement about spiders occurs in letter 56.

66. Goethe deals with this mystic of the Counter Reformation (1515–1595) in both his "Italian Journey" (May 26, 1787) and in his essay, "Philipp Neri, the Humorous Saint."

67. The name of the dog in Goethe's "Reineke Fuchs" (1794), itself a recasting of the Low German medieval satire "Reinke de Vos" (1498).

68. See note 31.

69. An allusion to Schiller's poem "Der Spaziergang" ("The Walk"), 1.200.

70. The dispute between France and Prussia in 1867 over the status of Luxembourg almost led to war.

71. One of the major reforms of Gregory VII's papacy (1073–1085) was the insistence on clerical celibacy.

72. A couple who entertained Zeus and Apollo when all others refused them hospitality. As a reward they were granted the wish to die at the same time. In old age Philemon was changed into an oak and Baucis into a linden tree. The tale is told in Ovid's "Metamorphoses" 8, 620 ff., and was also used by Goethe in *Faust* II, Act 5.

73. Latin: the like with the like. This adage is the basis of homeopathic medicine and means that the elements of the cure should be similar to the symptoms of the disease.

74. This is a pseudobiblical quotation combining Proverbs 31:10 ("Who can find a virtuous woman?") and Psalm 1:3 ("he shall be like a tree planted by the rivers of water").

75. Latin: by this sign you will conquer. Constantine the Great fashioned this motto from the Greek monogram of the name of Jesus, IHS.

76. 1.49 of Schiller's poem "Die Schlacht" ("The Battle").

77. There is no known source for these lines, but they are most probably by Raabe himself, since he notes them in his diary in July 1875.

78. Authors of standard Latin textbooks used in German gymnasiums.

79. A text used in the final two years of Latin instruction.

80. Latin: By Fidius! (the god of faithfulness).

81. The Roman name for the goddess of rumor.

82. The Greek name for the goddess of rumor. This account of her birth is taken from Vergil's *Aeneid* IV, 178 ff.

83. A village near Königgrätz.

84. Homeric epithet for Apollo.

85. A town northwest of Königgrätz. Outside of Germany, the battle of Königgrätz was most commonly called the battle of Sadowa.

86. Horace, Epode XVII, "The Poet and the Witch," 11.27 ff. The Sabines and Marsi were ancient tribes of Italy.

87. Title of the head of the Lutheran church in Prussia, comparable to a bishop.

88. Decimus Iunius Juvenal (55–120 A.D.), Roman satirist.

89. Heine lived in France after 1831, and Dr. Neubauer therefore thinks of him as "Monsieur" Heine.

90. A Roman witch referred to by Horace in his "Satires," II, 1, 48.

91. Gellert's poem "Der Kampf der Tugend" ("The Struggle of Virtue").

92. See note 50.

93. German folk saying.

94. In 1817 the Wartburg, a hill above Eisenach, was the scene of a nationalist demonstration by German students. This led to repressive measures by the reactionary governments of various German states.

95. Spoken by Emperor Charles V of Spain, these same words are placed by Schiller in the mouth of Philip II in his *Don Carlos,* I, 6.

96. The allusion is a bit unclear, but presumably Raabe is continuing his reference to the Spanish Empire, which stretched from the West Indies in the Caribbean to the Philippines and the East Indies.

97. From Schiller's *The Robbers* II, 1.

98. Latin: alone.

99. Latin: pastor of the place, a humorous allusion to the more common *genius loci,* the guardian spirit of the place.

100. The standard listing of Latin verbs of feeling that demand a particular grammatical construction. They mean: I rejoice, I take delight in, I admire, I glory in, I congratulate, I thank.

101. Latin: next, please!

102. Latin: that, because.

103. Latin construction analogous to English: I hear him sing.

104. A quotation from Seneca's "Epistulae" 71, 2. (The translation follows.)

105. The names of the three fates. Lachesis means "getting-by-lot," Atropos means "irresistible."

106. French: little by little.

107. Exodus 8:12.

108. An allusion to *Hamlet,* II, 2, 585.

109. This is a student's verse to help recall a point of Latin grammar. The verbs mean: grieves, embarrasses, is sorry, disgusts, and moves to pity. They demand that the person who is afflicted stand in the accusative case.

110. French: let us go.

111. *Richard III,* V, 4, 7.

112. Johann Wilhelm Ludwig Gleim (1719–1803), a minor German Enlightenment poet, a praiser of wine, women, and song.

113. A newspaper published by the poet Matthias Claudius (1740–1815), which served as an organ for his pious and somewhat sentimental view of the world.

114. The proverbial traitor, object of Cicero's famous orations, which foiled his conspiracy.

115. Greek she-demon or witch.

116. Latin: mixer of poisons.

117. A debased citation of the beginning of Cicero's first oration against

Cataline: "Quousque tandem abutere, Catilina, patientia nostra?" ("How long, Cataline, do you intend to abuse our patience?")

118. Horace's description in the "Satires," II, 7, 86, of the perfectly wise man.

119. The Latin word *vates* was used for the divinely inspired poet, cf. Vergil "Ecologues" 7/28.

120. Latin: before an audience, in public.

121. Even into the nineteenth century it was popularly believed that Kashmir was the location of the Garden of Eden.

122. Latin: runaway, fugitive.

123. An allusion to Goethe's essay "Shakespeare und kein Ende" (1813) ("Shakespeare and Still No End").

124. Latin: hostess, mistress of the inn.

Notes to TUBBY SCHAUMANN

1. August Graf von Platen-Hallermuende, German poet, 1796–1835.

2. "We have changed all that," from Molière.

3. In 1850 Prussia had put its army on alert in preparation for conflict with Austria, Bavaria, and Württemberg, which then was resolved peaceably.

4. *Levallyang:* Francois Le Vaillant, French explorer who wrote two books (1790 and 1795) describing his travels into Central Africa.

5. Lines on a map connecting points on the earth's surface that have the same mean summer temperature.

6. German geographer, 1779–1859.

7. German naturalist, 1729–1798.

8. Campe, author of "The Discovery of America," 1780.

9. Franz August Xaver von Sachsen (1730–1806); as a general in French services during the Seven Years' War, 1756–1763, he led a contingent of Saxon soldiers against the Prussians.

10. Count von der Lausitz, name of Prince Xaver while serving in the French army.

11. Edward's ship; also the name of the protagonist in Raabe's novel *Abu Telfan* (1868).

12. Battle during the Danish-Prussian War, 1864: 1866; Prussian-Austrian War; 1870: Prussian-French War.

13. Prussian general and chief strategist.

14. University.

15. "Long live all virgins."

16. Virgin.

17. Mannish women, shrew.

18. Senate and people, i.e., authority.

19. Karl Spitzweg, popular German painter, 1808–1885.

20. Character in Puss 'n Boots, in the French version of the fairy tale by Charles Perrault, 1628–1703.

21. French writer, 1777–1849.

22. French writer, 1766–1817.

23. Wife of a German writer, famous for her literary salon in Berlin, 1771–1833.

24. Empress of Austria, 1717–1780.

25. Empress of Russia, 1709–1762.

26. Marquise de Pompadour, mistress of Louis XV of France, 1721–1764.

27. Roman historian, 95–28 A.D.

28. Gotthilf Heinrich von Schubert, natural scientist and philosopher, 1780–1860.

29. German code of civil law.

30. With rounded mouth; i.e., hopeful expectation.

31. German poet, 1810–1876.

32. Johann Karl August Musäus, 1782–1786, collected fairy tales.

33. Arthur Schopenhauer, 1788–1860.

34. "We are ready to die for our king, Maria Theresa."

35. End of the Seven Years' War, 1763. Tsar Peter III had made peace with Prussia. After his assassination, his wife, Catherine II (the Great), resumed hostilities.

36. "He who is about to die, greets you."

37. Here: university.

38. In Schiller's poem the veil covers truth.

39. Site of the proclamation of the second German empire, at the end of the Franco-Prussian War, 1871.

40. King of the beggars.

41. Welcome, guest.

42. Collection of criminal cases, after the French jurist F. G. de Pitaval, 1673–1743.

43. Christian Wolff, German philosopher, 1679–1754.

44. Schopenhauer.